# SCHOOL CULTURE

# School Culture

*edited by*

Jon Prosser

Paul Chapman
Publishing Ltd

Paul Chapman Publishing Ltd
A SAGE Publications Company
6 Bonhill Street
London EC2A 4PU

SAGE Publications Inc.
2455 Teller Road
Thousand Oaks, California 91320

SAGE Publications India Pvt Ltd
32, M-Block Market
Greater Kailash-I
New Delhi 110 048

**British Library Cataloguing in Publication Data**
A catalogue record for this book is available from the British Library

ISBN 1 85396 433 6
ISBN 1 85396 377 1 (pbk)

**Library of Congress catalog card number available**

Typeset by Dorwyn Ltd, Rowlands Castle
Printed in Great Britain by Athenaeum Press, Gateshead

A  B  C  D  E  F    4  3  2  1  0  9

# Contents

# General Editor's Preface

This is an important book for the field of Educational Management, unmasking the phantom who infuses the operas of school and college life. In exploring different aspects of what might be understood by culture in educational organisations, it makes readers keenly aware that this entity is shaped and formed from many levels and sites inside and outside schools. As this book argues, pupils are among the actors within a school who help to shape its culture. They are not merely passive baskets to be filled with bread neatly wrapped in National Curriculum packages.

Part of this debate is about how external values and attitudes, from levels of public policy to levels of popular mythology, infiltrate and influence the internal cultures of schools and colleges. It brings to readers' awareness the importance of the ephemeral and non-rational influences which permeate the social construction of what are claimed to be rational and even 'objective' organisational structures and management processes.

To understand these influences, managers and school leaders need to be able to know where and how to look for the evidence of them and to interpret them, as this book suggests. Although the evidence is often visible, it is so taken for granted in the ordinaries of everyday life and work in organisations that it is frequently overlooked. In order to manage educational institutions more effectively, this book encourages educational leaders to become more consciously aware of the multiple dimensions and frameworks of organisational culture.

Hugh Busher
March 1999

# Notes on Contributors

*Dena Attar* taught Gender and Education at the Open University and was a researcher on the Fact and Fiction Project. She is now researching gender and new electronic texts at the University of Sussex. Her previous books include *Wasting Girls' Time* (1990, Virago) and *Disputes from Babylon* (forthcoming).

*Jenny Corbett* is a senior lecturer at the University of London Institute of Education where she teaches and researches in the area of special education. Her particular interest is post-compulsory education, terminology and the influence of cultural contexts upon definitions of special need. Her most recent book is *Special Educational Needs in the Twentieth Century: a cultural analysis* (1998, Cassell).

*David Hargreaves* is Professor of Education in the University of Cambridge and a Fellow of Wolfson College. Over the last thirty years he has written on a wide range of educational topics and is currently working on the creation of professional knowledge by teachers. He is a member of David Blunkett's Standards Task Force.

*Máirtín Mac an Ghaill* teaches in the Faculty of Social Sciences at Sheffield University. He is the author of *The Making of Men: Masculinities, Sexualities and Schooling*. He has just completed a book on *Contemporary Racisms and Ethnicities: Social and Cultural Transformations*.

*Claudia Mitchell* is Associate Professor in the Faculty of Education of McGill University, where she teaches literacy, gender studies and qualitative research methodology. She has collaborated with Sandra Weber on major research projects in teacher education for many years.

*Gemma Moss* is a lecturer in Education with special reference to Literacy, at the University of Southampton. She is currently directing the Fact and Fiction Research Project, funded by the ESRC. Previous research has concentrated on young people's use of a range of different media; gender, literacy and the romance genre; and the secondary English curriculum. She is co-authoring a book on the gendering of literacy in the 7–8 age-group, with Dena Attar.

*Pamela Munn* is Professor of Curriculum Research in the Moray House Faculty of Education, University of Edinburgh. She has recently, with others, completed a major study of school exclusion in Scotland and is currently researching the relationships between schools and their local communities. Her most recent publication in 1997 is a co-edited collection with Margaret M. Clark, *Education in Scotland: Policy and Practice from Pre-School to Secondary* (Routledge).

*Jennifer Nias* holds a part-time post as Rolle Professor of Education at the University of Plymouth. Her research into primary teachers' work and lives has led her recently to explore teachers' moral responsibilities and values, particularly as these contribute to occupational tension and stress. Her publications include *Primary Teachers Talking*, 1989; *Staff Relations in the Primary School*, 1989, with G. Southworth and R. Yeomans; and *Whole-School Curriculum Development in Primary Schools*, 1992, with G. Southworth and P. Campbell.

*Sally Power* is a senior lecturer in Policy Studies, Institude of Education, University of London. Teaching and research interests include all aspects of education policy and particularly those relating to state and private education and the secondary school curriculum. She is the author of *The Pastoral and the Academic: Conflict and Contradiction in the Curriculum* (1996, Cassell) and co-author of *Devolution and Choice in Education: the School, the State and the Market* (1988, Open University Press).

*Jon Prosser* is a member of the research and graduate School of Education at the University of Southampton. He teaches qualitative methodology, management and institutional culture, and is course director of the Doctorate in Education programme. His research interests include school effectiveness and improvement, and the visual representation of institutional culture. His most recent publication is *Image-based Research: A Sourcebook for Qualitative Researchers* (Falmer).

*Louise Stoll* is Professor of Education at the University of Bath. She is involved in partnership improvement projects with schools and LEAs and set up the School Improvement Network. Current and recent research includes a study of new LEAs, the Improving School Effectiveness Project for the Scottish Office Education and Industry Department, and the Capacity for Change project for the European Commission. Her publications include *School Matters* (1988) with Peter Mortimore and colleagues; *Changing our Schools* (1996 – with Dean Fink) and *No Quick Fixes: Perspectives on Schools in Difficulty* (1998 – edited with Kate Myers). She has presented and consulted in many countries.

*Terry Warburton* is a lecturer in Research Methods for the Education subject group in the Faculty of Arts, Science and Education at Bolton Institute. His research interests are the professional cultures of teaching; images of teachers and teaching, particularly political cartoons; and education and the media.

*Sandra Weber* is Professor of Early Childhood Education at Concordia University in Montreal, where she teaches curriculum theory, qualitative research methodology, children's popular culture and second language acquisition. She has collaborated with Claudia Mitchell on major research projects in teacher education for many years, resulting in a series of co-authored articles and two recent books, *That's Funny, You Don't Look Like a Teacher! Interrogating Images and Teacher Identity in Popular Culture* (1995, Falmer) and *Beyond Nostalgia: Reinventing Ourselves as Teachers* (1998, Falmer).

*Geoff Whitty* is Karl Mannheim Professor of Sociology of Education and Dean of Research at the Institute of Education, University of London. He has written and lectured extensively on the sociology of the school curriculum and education policy. His latest book (with Sally Power and David Halpin) is *Devolution and Choice in Education: The School, the State and the Market* (1998, Open University Press).

# Introduction

The details of my schooldays are mostly a distant memory. Nevertheless, as a pupil in an inner city school with a 'reputation', certain details are engraved in my mind. There were special places such as smokers' corner, the bike sheds, and the Head's office, that still make me wince, chuckle or send shivers down my spine. There were 'characterful' teachers like Mr Hall (a failed actor), Mr Frogatt (an ex-wrestler who helped me after school with maths), Mr Black (who was violent), and Mr Taylor (nicknamed 'splash' because he splashed when he spoke), who in turn I admired, appreciated, hated or whose eccentricity was distracting. The memory of school dinners, assemblies, changing rooms, corridors, and arts rooms are evoked even now by certain films, books, noises, smells, or tastes.

Other memories of school are less distant. I can distinctly remember the first day of my first post as a maths teacher in a secondary modern school in Blackpool. I wore a white shirt, nondescript tie, hairy sports jacket, grey flannels and plain black shoes. I carried a cheap briefcase from Woolworths that contained detailed lesson notes for the day, sandwiches, and a new coffee mug. The first year was a struggle: I followed the usual wisdoms ('don't smile before Easter'); avoided sitting in the someone else's chair in the staffroom; tried to demonstrate my professional competence by keeping my classes quiet; feigned camaraderie and playing for the staff cricket team; and most importantly kept on the right side of the caretaker. I mimicked other teachers' behaviour and dress code because I desperately wanted to look like a teacher, act like a teacher, be accepted as a teacher.

More recently, as a parent, I see schools in a different light. The 'Open Days', 'Christmas Plays', 'Speech Days', and 'Parents' Evenings', are all part of me trying my best for my children by involvement in their school. Through them I revisit distant memories of my school days and it is as though life is turning full circle and that schools have not changed to any significant degree. Of course the experiences I'm relating are repeated millions of times in a myriad of subtly different ways by each passing generation of pupils, teachers and parents. They are manifestations of *school culture* and the central focus of this book. It aims to provide both understanding and insight into school culture that will be of interest to practitioners, policy makers and theoreticians. It is concerned with everyday perspectives, realities, systems and patterns of school life and prominence is given to theoretical frameworks (sometimes necessarily complex), behaviours and meanings (of those who create, manage and maintain school culture) because they underpin our understanding and inform practice.

Culture is a useful if intricate and elusive notion. In its broadest sense it is a way of constructing reality and different cultures are simply alternative constructions of reality. In the past metaphors such as 'climate', 'ethos', 'tone', 'atmosphere', and 'character' have been used to orientate our thinking about schools. However, they are limiting since, by their nature, they incline and confine our understanding to very particular aspects of schooling while neglecting significant others. The cultural perspective is a more beneficial way of viewing schools because it provides encompassing methodological and theoretical frameworks that are less limiting than other metaphors. This does not exclude acceptance that problems arise when using a single framework to understand the immense complexity of schools; nor does it preclude the advantages, for example, in 'overlaying' a cultural framework with a historical, political or managerial perspective that may produce a hybrid orientation that is 'concept rich'.

In practice, the operational definition of culture is seen as a system of related subsystems, which in turn organise the relationships among cultural patterns. Classical sub-systems used by social scientists include *organising communication, resource allocation, social interaction, reproduction* and *ideology*. In this book, whilst drawing on such extensive sub-systems, emphasis is placed on *values* and *beliefs, norms of behaviour, social structures, social systems, social groups, status, roles, control systems, rituals* and *traditions*. School culture is not only the particular patterns of perception and related to behaviour, but also the system of relationships between those relationships. In practice, school culture is often viewed as either a totality and therefore a summation of behaviours *or* as a system of dynamically related sub-cultures. Hence, because this book is intended to cover diverse positions on 'school culture', the book naturally forms two parts: authors of Chapters 1–6 perceive school culture as essentially a holistic concept, whereas authors of Chapters 7–11 adopt the stance that school culture comprises significant sub-cultures. Each of the eleven authors offers an interpretation of school culture and collectively they represent a diverse range of disciplines, theories, and research methodologies.

## Chapter 1 – The Evolution of School Culture Research

'School Culture' is a term widely used and abused by practitioners, policy makers and academics. Only in the last decade have we come to terms with the paucity of our knowledge and begun to explore what constitutes school culture, how it is identified or changed, and how it impacts on the quality of educational provision. Chapter 1 examines the evolution of school culture research in the UK and is a good starting point for those new to the topic. It traces how the notion of school culture has evolved over the last thirty years and in particular how it was shaped by: trends in educational practice; the differing terms and meanings attributed to it; trends in research methodology; and political influences. The chapter concludes by examining three contemporary issues: the meaning of school culture; evolving theoretical frameworks; and the relationship between school culture and improving practice.

## Chapter 2 – Market Forces and School Culture

Whereas Chapter 1 covers considerable ground, albeit superficially, Chapter 2 is an in-depth discussion of the influence of market forces on school culture. It takes the position that whilst schools may have an 'institutional culture', that culture does not exist in a vacuum but is part of and related to regional, national and international cultures. More importantly, Sally Power and Geoff Whitty point out that marketisation of education is a global phenomenon and link political agenda (essentially new right) with the influx of new subjects and curricula. There is an awareness of important global features of schooling and that certain features (such as what is to be taught) are political and implicit in that they constitute an international form of 'hidden curriculum'.

## Chapter 3 – School Culture: Black Hole or Fertile Garden for School Improvement?

Chapter 2 conceives of school culture as holistic and universal and suggests that changes in school culture are formed by an agenda external to schools. However, Chapter 3 perceives school culture as a set of context related normative parameters within which improvement may take place. Two important questions of school culture are posed: how is it changed and what are the practical implications for schooling? Each question in itself is difficult to answer but those who seek to improve the effectiveness of schooling must wrestle with these and other questions simultaneously. Louise Stoll argues that if improvement is to take place then significant across-the-board transformations need to take place. Without a refined understanding of the dynamic relationship between school culture and change management, and indeed making this combination integral to a school's culture (i.e. 'reculturing'), school improvement is destined to sink into a 'black hole' rather than flourish in a 'fertile garden'. There is a clear message here for practitioners: whatever theory, framework or synthesis you bring to school culture, school improvement comes about from within, when changes in taken-for-granted practices are made. As with Chapter 1, this chapter draws on a wide range of literature and would be a good starting point for those new to both school culture and school improvement.

## Chapter 4 – Helping Practitioners Explore Their School's Culture

School culture is viewed by some as a topic that is obscure, opaque, and impenetrable. Chapter 4, more than any other chapter in this book, goes some way to overcoming such views. The chapter is directed at practitioners, particularly senior members of staff who are engaged in improving the effectiveness of their school. Three important tasks that are related to school culture are considered: the diagnostic task (identifying a school's culture); the directional task (deciding which way a school's culture should move); and the managerial task (after decided where a school's culture is going it is necessary to arrange and implement a plan to get it there). In this carefully constructed chapter David Hargreaves combines substantive theory, thought provoking questioning and pragmatism, enabling practitioners to confront important issues which, if engaged in and followed, act as a 'springboard' for action.

## Chapter 5 – Primary Teaching as a Culture of Care

School culture may be considered as a system of sub-cultures of which teacher culture is just one – but one which pervades the whole institution. Cultural systems pass from generation to generation through the process of learning. At the centre the learning process for teachers is the ongoing absorption of generic values and beliefs about the teaching profession. Jennifer Nias considers such values and beliefs in a primary school context and examines how they combine to form a 'culture of care'. A number for theoretical frameworks are used to explore the origins of the 'culture of care', especially how values in action interact with personal identity to produce contemporary everyday practice. This is a thought provoking chapter which leads us to ponder what other deeply held values and beliefs that are rooted in the past remain part of everyday professional practice.

## Chapter 6 – Visual Sociology and School Culture

Past studies of school culture have in common the application of a qualitative methodology that is ethnographic in orientation. This approach normally entails participant observation and emphasises participants' interpretation of cultural elements of schooling. Chapter 6, whilst also drawing on ethnography and anthropology, offers an alternative mode of investigation in that it is more concerned with the visual world than the written or spoken word. There are very sound reasons for this. Schools are rich in visual culture, usually of a symbolic nature embedded in gestures, ceremonies, rituals, or artefacts, situated in both constructed and natural settings. It is argued that the visual representation of school culture offer data sets that are important to practitioners and academics because they provide an insight into the values, beliefs, and priorities of those who shape that culture.

## Chapter 7 – Schooling, Masculine Identities and Culture

We know that school culture is influential in determining pupils' academic achievements and behaviour. Only relatively recently has there been an interest in pupil culture. Perhaps the lack of interest was because it was thought that pupils were merely the recipients of school culture and not influential in shaping it. Alternatively the new impetus could be a result of concern when, following the monitoring of national examination results, it was recognised that during the secondary school years girls were outperforming boys and that many boys were underachieving. Explanations for this are varied and weak and expose the paucity and limitations of our knowledge of pupil culture. Máirtín Mac an Ghaill exposes the complexity of (Anglo) ethnicities and (hetero) sexualities among male pupils. He draws on contemporary theory and his own data to suggest that pupils are not simply recipients of schooling nor do they reproduce the normative ethnic/gender as expressed by wider society or at home. He implies that there is a dynamic relationship between pupil culture and school culture, the outcome of which is that pupils create their own identities whose subtleties and influence of which we are only now beginning to understand. Only by increased awareness of pupil culture, can we go on to answer the questions many headteachers are asking themselves – why are those groups of pupils underachieving or achieving beyond expectations?

## Chapter 8 – The 'Darker Side' of Pupil Culture: Discipline and Bullying in Schools

One way of looking at the culture of schools is to view it as a reflection of societal values. Different sectors of society will prioritise different values for schooling – some groups emphasise academic outcomes whilst others stress citizenship and interpersonal relationships. Those who emphasise the former recognise and acknowledge the 'hidden curriculum' although they view it as a by-product of teaching and learning rather than being central to the educative process. Nevertheless, what is undeniable is that pupils are influenced by the overarching culture of their school. The nature of that influence is subterranean and hidden within the everyday milieu that is schooling. In this chapter Pamela Munn reflects on discipline and bullying – both important elements that are part of pupil culture – which, although managed by the institution explicitly by regulation, in practice reflects individual and group perception of acceptable or normative behaviour. She goes on to describe a range of strategies which schools can take up to promote good relationships among pupils and between pupils and teachers. Although the chapter is concerned with the 'darker side' of pupil culture it proposes a positive stance and proffers enlightened remedies.

## Chapter 9 – Inclusivity and School Culture: the Case of Special Education

This chapter is also concerned with bullying but of a particular sort. With successive government emphases on the effectiveness of schools come comparisons of academic standards and market forces that ultimately may shape a school's intake. Government policy on assessment and evaluation juxtaposes interestingly with its policy on inclusivity and special educational needs. Jenny Corbett points out that incorporating special needs pupils into mainstream schools is likely to have damaging repercussions. She argues that mainstream schools seeking to improve their academic standing will not encourage special needs pupils and that those remaining special needs schools will become 'sink' schools. For true inclusivity to take place institutional orders and structures will be insufficient. There will need to be a shift in the 'deep culture' of mainstream pupils if special needs children are not to suffer rejection by their new school peers. This chapter is also instructive on another level in that it provides an insight into the dynamic relationship between sub-cultures. If we believe that school culture is the summative effect of its sub-cultures which can only be understood by exploring the significance of their dynamic relationship, then this chapter provides an awareness of the resultant interplay between dominant and less dominant sub-cultures. Moreover, if we accept that a measure of a civilisation is the way in which it treats its most vulnerable individuals, then the case of inclusivity will provide a gauge of the quality of our culture.

## Chapter 10 – Boys and Literacy: Gendering the Reading Curriculum

In recent years there has been a shift in emphasis from school-wide factors of school effectiveness to looking at what happens in classrooms. One way to improve teaching and learning is to understand how pupils learn and adopt appropriate teaching strategies. We are only now coming to question taken-for-granted classroom culture: what is the appropriate age to start formal learning; should we begin education by teaching the three 'Rs' or teach pupils social and behavioural skills that underpin the effective teaching and learning? Only by putting together the micro-cultural 'jigsaw' of the classroom will we begin to establish effective teaching and learning. Chapter 10 is a good example of this important work. Gemma Moss and Dena Attar draw on a recent findings which indicate that boys do less well at reading than girls and in their ESRC funded study ask how 'boys and girls gender reading for themselves in the classroom and in the context of their own leisure time; and how reading is gendered for them through their interactions with adults at home and in school'. The chapter focuses on the school and examines the structuring of the reading curriculum, particularly how such structures lead to different forms of activity. The findings of the study provide an insight into boy's evasive strategies and provides us with substantive theory on how texts 'construct' child readers.

## Chapter 11 – Teacher Identity in Popular Culture

The culture of organisations and institutions is most often perceived in terms of managerial theory and examined by orthodox qualitative research methodology. What makes the final chapter quite different from this approach (and therefore different from the majority of chapters in this book) is its emphasis on 'popular culture', post-modern tenets, and the importance of narrative to enable practitioners to resonate with the topic of teacher identity. It is refreshing in its embrace of a cultural studies methodology and because it opens up the possibility of additional and alternative approaches to conducting research and the exploration topics that lie outside of anthropological or managerial perspectives. The chapter briefly considers the significance of teacher images to teachers' work and identity before examining in more detail how cultural images outside of school impinge on teacher identity and indirectly on school culture.

The chapters in this book provide a blend of insights into school culture and represent the continuum that exists between the *'holistic'* and the *'summation of sub-cultures'* perspectives. They also deliver a combination of practical and theoretical observations and mixture of culture as anthropological or culture as popular. The potential for future school culture research is considerable. However, schools are complex systems and clearly there is a need to rethink and refine our theories and methodologies in order to reflect that complexity. As we strive to classify phenomena and build a systematic understanding of schooling the cultural framework is well placed to provide a serviceable platform for exploration. Nonetheless there is a need to remember that school culture is in a continuous state of flux and not easy to identify or examine for 'Education can be said to be a process which redefines culture in the act of handing it on' (Chitty, 1997, p. 60). Future studies should take account of the dynamic properties of school sub-cultures and assimilate theory emanating from disparate disciplines, methodologies and frameworks. Most importantly school culture studies are obligated to ask questions that will help practitioners improve educational provision.

Jon Prosser

# 1

## The Evolution of School Culture Research

### JON PROSSER

Organisational culture is: 'the interweaving of the individual into a community and the collective programming of the mind that distinguishes members of one known group from another. It is the values, norms, beliefs and customs that an individual holds in common with members of the social unit or group'.

(Ogbonna, 1993, p. 42)

And is about: 'how organisations work when no one is looking'.

(Morgan, 1997, p. 145)

## INTRODUCTION

The term 'school culture' is popular and frequently used but despite over thirty years of research it remains enigmatic and much abused. The aim of this chapter is to provide a brief overview of the evolution of studies in school culture in the UK. The task is not an easy one. School culture research in the UK (and throughout the world) does not form a homogeneous body of literature and hence plotting its progress is a tenuous exercise. Also it is not appropriate to proffer a single definition, interpretation, application, or even assume that the term itself 'school culture' is appropriate. Indeed, this chapter rests on the dangerous assumption that the notion of 'school culture' used here reflects practitioners' and the research community's diverse and implicitly agreed parameters of meaning and application of that term. Nonetheless, the exercise is a worthwhile one. It provides one interpretation of how school culture and related terms have been used in the past, identifies how disparate epistemological and methodological stances have been applied to aid understanding, maps a range of theoretical orientations taken, and examines how school culture has been employed to improve schooling.

The chapter is in two parts: 'The Shaping of School Culture Research' which considers school culture as a holistic entity, covers the period from the 1960s until around 1990; and 'Contemporary School Culture Research' which briefly reflects on significant themes from the late 1980s until the present day.

# PART 1 – THE SHAPING OF SCHOOL CULTURE RESEARCH

As with any topic research varies from country to country due to differing trends in educational theory, differences in definition and interpretation, the application of diverse methodologies, and changes to schooling as a result of political vicissitude and subsequent shifts in educational policy. Each of these factors, always in combination but often one assuming a pivotal role at different periods, contributed to determining the UK's evolutionary 'map' of school culture research. Over the last thirty years four key factors shaped the adoption and application of school culture research in the UK:

- trends in educational theory and practice;
- a profusion of meanings of school culture;
- trends in research methodology;
- political trends and their influence on educational policy.

These factors interacted with each other to give UK school culture research a distinctive character. The remainder of this section will consider these factors in more detail (with the exception of 'political trends and their influence on educational policy' which will be discussed in Part 2) recognising that in discussing them separately, whilst aiding clarification and enabling discussion of central issues, implies boundaries where none existed and a static relationship where there was a dynamic one.

## Trends in educational theory and practice

During the mid-1960s and early 1970s several large nationally funded studies on both sides of the Atlantic, for example, Coleman *et al.* (1966), Plowden (1967), and Averch (1971), were proposing that students' social background was more significant than schooling as a determinant of their academic outcome. These findings appeared to support and reinforce the educational theories of Bernstein (1970) that schools cannot compensate for the inequities of society. In addition a fundamental change to schooling took place in the UK in the mid-1960s when the separation of pupils at the age of eleven on the basis of academic ability was replaced by a 'comprehensive' system. The combination of the findings of large-scale surveys and the emphasis on exploring the consequences of restructuring schools diminished substantive holistic school-wide research (such as school culture) in the UK until the late 1970s. Instead educational research focused more narrowly on issues central to comprehensivisation, for example, 'curriculum evaluation', 'mixed ability teaching', 'pastoral care', and the impact of raising the school leaving age. However, in the 1970s there were moves by a minority of researchers to understand comprehensive schools in holistic rather than partial terms. They drew their inspiration for school culture studies from the USA such as Halpin and Crofts' (1963) 'Organisational Climate Description Questionnaire' (OCDQ). Clearly it and similar instruments fulfilled a perceived need in determining the 'climate' of educational organisations. Finlayson (1970, 1973) for example, adapted the OCDQ to form the SCI (School Climate Index) as part of the 'Comprehensive Schools Feasibility Study' which sought to apply a number of instruments of a cognitive, affective and social nature, to be used in studies of the newly formed comprehensive schools.

Once again the winds of educational change blew and as before the source was North America. The school effectiveness studies of Brookover et al. (1978) and Edmonds (1979) suggested that whilst schools cannot compensate for society they do constitute a major influence and one which was susceptible to change and improvement. The school effectiveness movement gained favour with researchers in the UK but it was a study by Rutter et al. (1979) that placed school culture (they used the term ethos) high on the agenda of researchers throughout Europe. Rutter et al. not only highlighted school effectiveness research in the UK but most importantly linked the notion of school culture with the effectiveness of secondary schools, thereby refocusing researchers' concern for holistic features of schooling and school culture in particular. Mortimore (1980, p. 68), a member of the Rutter team, explained the relationship between factors which contribute to school effectiveness and the 'ethos' of a school in the following way:

> Because schools are complex institutions, in which pupils influence teachers as well as the reverse, there are likely to be many determinants of behaviour. Further, different pupils may be influenced by quite different teacher actions. Because, however, of the stability of the performance measures, it is likely that an influence more powerful than that of any particular teacher, school policies or indeed behaviour of dominant pupils, is at work. This overall atmosphere which pervades the actions of the participants we call ethos.

As a result of the Rutter et al. study there was a shift away from 'mixed ability teaching', 'curriculum evaluation', 'pastoral care', 'teaching style' etc., and a refocusing on school culture. By the early 1980s the terms school ethos, climate, culture, atmosphere and tone were ubiquitous. They were the education 'buzzwords' of the decade to be found in anything from academic journals to glossy magazines and the popular press. Other school effectiveness studies followed including Mortimore et al. (1988)[1] who focused on primary schools and used the term 'school climate' rather than 'school ethos', and Smith and Tomlinson (1989) who focused on secondary schools and reverted to the use of 'ethos'. Ultimately school effectiveness research did little to explain how school ethos was constituted or refine the role of ethos/climate in determining a school's academic proficiency. Later notions of ethos and climate took on a prescriptive mantle, i.e. 'orderly', 'safe', or 'positive'.

During the 1980s a second major movement, which focused on school improvement, gathered momentum. Fullan (1982) produced 'The Meaning of Educational Change', highlighting the importance of school culture and in particular a school's guiding value system in enabling change and enhancing educational provision. Deal and Kennedy (1983, p. 15) were aware that a guiding value system (values and beliefs are believed to underpin school culture) was not the norm in schools:

> in many schools, teachers and students do not know what is expected of them nor do they understand how their actions are related to school-wide efforts. Parents, teachers, students, administrators, and support staff often form sub-cultures around immediate, parochial interests that pull the school in several directions. Under such conditions it is not hard to see what happens to beliefs, standards, motivation, effort, consistency, and other ingredients essential to teaching and learning.

Those involved in the school improvement movement recognised the significance of school culture. They were aware that school culture was instrumental in bringing about improvement; of the need to assess a school's potential to accept change; of the complexity of changing a school's culture; of the worthwhileness of identifying and agreeing the direction of change; and of the significance of leadership in change and therefore managing culture.

During the 1980s there was a resurgence of interest in management and organisation theory again mainly derived from American studies. Organisational culture and leadership and the relationship between them became a focal point for writings on school culture. A wide range of organisational theories were adopted, some of which gained popular acclaim (Peters and Waterman, 1982), some focused on organisational culture (Schein, 1985), some carrying the 'effective management' label (Torrington, Weightman, and Johns, 1989), some educationally based (Weick, 1988; Nias et al., 1989), and some exploring the relationship between school culture and change (Sarason, 1971, revised and reprinted 1985). Formal organisational theory did not account for the dark 'underworld' of school culture or the 'street realities' of headship. This subterranean aspect of school culture was considered by Hoyle (1982), Ball (1987), and Blase (1991) and referred to as the 'micro-politics' of school organisation. The micro-political perspective recognised that formal powers, rules, regulations, traditions and rituals were capable of being subverted by individuals, groups or affiliations in schools and took account of the summative dynamic influence of friendships, cliques, gender, individual rivalry, historical emnity etc.

## A profusion of meanings of school culture

Although trends in educational theory and practice were central to the initial adoption of school culture as a worthwhile enterprise, its take-up and development were confused by a proliferation of meanings. There are many underlying reasons for this confusion. We base our assumptions and expectations of schools on personal ideology and collective assumptions of the local and wider community. In addition our beliefs and perceptions of schooling are shaped by the roles we play in society – as pupils, parents, teachers, industrialists or academics. It is not surprising that a wide range of vocabulary is used to describe overarching themes of schooling. Equally, it is not surprising that there is no agreement on the definition or meanings of the terms school culture, climate, ethos, atmosphere, character and tone, used to evoke what is too often assumed to be a common phenomenon that needs little explanation.

The evolution (and a significant weakness of school culture research) can, in part, be traced by the use of particular terms. Why one term is used in preference to another and the boundaries of their use is rarely explained in texts. Early studies of human relationships and interpersonal dynamics in organisations, for example, Lewin *et al.* (1939), Cornell (1955) and Argyris (1958) perceived the term 'organisational climate' as self-explanatory and unproblematic. Equally, when Halpin and Croft (1963) applied 'organisational climate' to educational settings, they transported the term and borrowed concepts from studies of complex organisations without taking account of the dangers or limitations this incurred (see Meek, 1988). To rest on the assumption that climate (or culture) is something 'felt', as many did, is a wilful lack of precision that limits our understanding and neglects its full constituency. All subsequent users of organisational climate, school climate and school culture assimilated these weaknesses. Widely used contextual exemplars of organisational climate such as:

> As any teacher or school executive moves from one school to another he is inexorably struck by the difference he encounters in organisational climate. He voices his reaction with such remarks as: 'You don't have to be in a school very long before you feel the atmosphere of a place.'
>
> (Halpin and Croft, 1963, p. 4)

or analogies, such as 'Personality is to the individual what climate is to the organisation' (Halpin and Croft, 1963, p. 1), proliferated in the literature, undermining the potential of an important theme in educational research. Clearly, 'climate', and similarly 'ethos', 'atmosphere', 'character', 'culture' and 'tone' were meaningful to researchers but their meanings varied considerably. The adoption of a particular term does not follow a pattern although in the UK, generally speaking, 'climate' is used by school effectiveness researchers, 'culture' by school improvement researchers and qualitative sociologists, and 'ethos', 'atmosphere' and 'tone' used to describe ethereal qualities of schools. To add to this confusion terms used are influenced by geographical location – in the USA 'school climate' is preferred whilst in Scotland 'ethos' is used.

It is clear that terms are often used in a loose, uncritical way that lack clarity. Too often researchers have assumed that their choice and definition of a term is a 'given' and their interpretation of the chosen term has agreed terms of reference when they do not. They fail to disclose what influenced their definition/choice, or discuss the parameters and framework within which the term is set. Such ad hoc meanings and assumptions have undermined critical reflection and impeded school culture research. These weaknesses span the evolutionary period from 1960 to the present.

## Trends in research methodology

Researchers and practitioners use a range of terms to describe a loose set of assumptions that constitute a collectively agreed phenomenon I have termed 'school culture'. An agreed phenomenon appears to be a holistic and overarching feature of schools whose dimensions are objective or subjective depending on one's methodological stance (an alternative contemporary view is culture as a combination of sub-cultures and is not dealt with here). Generally speaking, school 'climate' is the preferred term of quantitative researchers whereas qualitative workers prefer to use 'culture', 'ethos', 'atmosphere' or 'tone'. Methodologies applied to the study of school culture are disappointingly impoverished and have in the past been sited at opposite ends of the positivist-interpretative continuum. Very little research, with occasional exceptions (for example latterly the 'Improving School Effectiveness' study), attempted to combine strategies.

In the 1960s the emphasis was on the measurement of school climate. Climate was the in-vogue term at this time possibly because it had overtones of measurability and had 'currency' because of its association with 'organisational climate' and therefore managerial theory. The work of Halpin and Croft (1963) and Stern (1963) are fairly typical of this period. Stern's Organisational Climate Index (OCI) was complex (over 300 items), difficult to apply and mainly concerned with intellectual climate. Halpin and Croft's Organisation Climate Description Questionnaire (OCDQ), on the other hand, was easier to use (only 64 items) and gained favour with researchers throughout the world. Anderson (1982, p. 372) who examined various forms of statistical instruments used in school climate research summed up early failings as 'a result of poor models, inadequate measures, and too few variables'. In the 1970s the quantitative/qualitative divide was at its greatest and their respective ontological and epistemological virtues most hotly debated – a period referred to as 'the British sociology's war of religion' (Dey, 1993). Following the work of Rutter *et al.* (1979) there was a burgeoning interest in school ethos/climate and an expanding enthusiasm for school effectiveness studies. Since school effectiveness research is dominated by a quantitative approach there followed a resurgence of interest in statistical methods. Scheerens (1990, p. 67) for example, suggested that school climate could be 'operationalised in terms of relatively uncomplicated scales or questionnaire items'. However, by the mid-1980s the enthusiasm for quantitative studies had began to wane. Finlayson, once a protagonist of the quantitative approach, encapsulated the views of many interested in school culture research at this time and argued against Anderson's quantitative position:

> She (Anderson) suggests that researchers like herself, who hoped that improved statistical designs will be the means of trapping the climate beast, are hunting a phoenix, born of the ashes of past school effects research . . . The difficulties of measurement, variable selection and control, and statistical analysis are such that (they) have given up the search for school climate as a holistic entity
>
> (Finlayson, 1987, p. 167)

Finlayson's belief that statistical researchers measuring school climate were 'like blind people fumbling about the elephant that they call "organisational climate" and dutifully reporting the warts, the trunk, the knees and the tail, each of them confidently asserting that they have discovered the true nature of the beast' Perrow (1974, p. 43). Striven (1985), likewise, concluded his review of school climate by stating that researchers should employ 'the skills of the ethnographer in exploring the elusive nature of a school's atmosphere'. He reasoned that school participants have choices and freedoms, that there are unintended outcomes, plural values, conflicts and emotional conflicts in schools, all of which contribute to climate and therefore require 'qualitative' consideration.

Contemporary research continues to be shaped and influenced by trends in educational theory and practice, meanings attributed to 'school culture', and trends in research methodology. As will be seen in Part 2, current research, although coming to terms with past deficiencies, rarely focuses per se on school culture but more often in association with, or as a framework for, studies of 'effectiveness', 'improvement', or 'change'.

## PART 2 – CONTEMPORARY RESEARCH

In the late 1980s school culture research entered an absorbing and fruitful period. Significant changes were afoot. Contrary to trends in America and mainland Europe a qualitative approach to the study of school culture became standard practice. Also around this time 'culture' became the predominant term to describe the overall 'character' of a school but, as with other holistic concepts, its meaning remained problematic. The 1990s is a period rich in ideas but also one of fragmented and diverse interests as more stress is given to school sub-cultures, change and improvement. The remainder of this chapter will focus on issues that are representative of this period: 'Meanings of school culture', 'evolving theoretical frameworks', and 'school culture and practice'.

### Meanings of school culture

The increased use of 'culture' was probably due to 'the concept's [culture] analytic power in understanding school life' (Hargreaves D., 1995, p. 25), and because it offered, via ethnography, an accepted methodological framework. Nevertheless, despite culture becoming the predominant term there are few signs of conformity in terms of agreed meaning and application. As with previous favoured terms, its meaning is mostly dependent on an author's discipline. Indeed writers rarely explicitly address the issue of meaning, instead relying on definitions to implicitly convey meanings. Below are my interpretations of some frequently used but rarely stated meanings drawn from the literature. The emergent broad categories I have termed 'wider culture', 'generic culture', 'unique culture', and 'perceived culture':

- Schools do not exist in a vacuum and national and local cultures are impregnated into and are part of all schools. Culture used in this way not only reflects universal human experience and its local or regional manifestations, but also a vast array of socio-cultural systems such as ethnic, professional, sexual, political, artistic and communicative systems. Studies that draw on the 'wider culture' emphasise the relationship between a nation's culture and the culture of its schools and recognise that it is a myth to consider schools as enclaves operating a separate reality to that outside of their walls. A good example of researchers emphasising the wider culture is provided in Chapter 2 where Sally Power and Geoff Whitty discuss how free market advocates influence the restructuring of public education in the UK.

- Hospitals, prisons, banks and schools are institutions separated by their differing organisational cultures yet recognised as belonging to a particular institutional group by unspoken norms. The very nature of the taken-for-grantedness means that the 'generic culture' of such institutions is difficult to identify since 'It is in the nature of culture to be unperceived by those who share it and difficult to penetrate by those who do not' (Anthony, 1994, p. 52). Generic culture of schools reflects their similarities in terms of norms, structures, rituals and traditions, common values and actions, and it is this shared vision that underpins school culture. Generic culture is also used in the literature to differentiate between sets of schools, for example, private, secondary and primary schools (see Cooper, 1988). Although generic culture is holistic in nature and occasionally reported in the literature as such it is more often reported partially as a sub-culture of schooling. Jennifer Nias gives an example of a dimension of generic culture of primary schools in Chapter 5. The second section of this book is concerned with sub-cultures of schools' generic culture often in relation to wider culture.

- Because school participants possess a degree of freedom of choice and the capacity to interpret and reinterpret the generic culture of schools they create their own particular and therefore 'unique culture'. Predominant values embraced by an organisation that determine the guiding policies and provide insiders with distinctive in-house rules for 'getting on and getting by' are the basis of a school's unique culture. The difference between generic and unique culture is recognised by practitioners and is reflected in teacher folklore – 'all schools are the same but different'. Halpin and Crofts (1963) 'Organisational Climate Description Questionnaire' (although essentially a measure of the 'atmosphere' of a school), Rutter *et al.*'s (1979) 'school ethos', Mortimore *et al.*'s (1988) 'school climate' are examples of studies of dimensions of the unique culture of schools.

- In addition to above main categories it may be useful to apply an additional term – that of 'perceived culture'. This is reported in the literature in two forms: 'on-site perceived culture' which describes staff and casual visitors' views of a school which reflects elements of its unique culture; and 'off-site perceived culture' which describes outsiders' view of a school. Here parents and the local community base their interpretation of unique culture on a battery of indicators – a school's prospectus, newsletters, gossip, pupils' behaviour outside school, the uniform, or the amount and type of graffiti seen on buildings as they drive past. Perceived culture reflects culture 'given off' by a school and, rather like meeting someone at a party, first impressions may or may not be a reflection of their character. Perceived school culture, often referred to in terms of 'atmosphere', 'character', 'ethos' and 'tone', is at best a manifestation of cultural values and beliefs in action and not necessarily commensurate with a school's unique culture.

It is clear that there is no singly agreed meaning of 'school culture' and that meanings are assumed but rarely articulated. Equally, there are no studies that draw on a combination of the above categories to provide a holistic analysis of school culture. It is common to read studies that unwittingly emphasise one category or combine two categories. Researchers' choice of combinations and therefore the meaning they attribute to school culture is often determined by their own field of study and their own field of interest. A further examination of the appropriateness of culture is given by Hoy (1990), its meaning by Nias (1989), and the strengths and limitations of the culture metaphor by Morgan (1993).

Disentangling what authors' mean when they use 'school culture' and what combinations of perspectives of school culture are being applied is made difficult by academic writing convention. It is expected that authors provide definitions of key terms in a paper and many follow this practice. Since definitions of school culture are so general and all encompassing they are of limited worth and convey little in terms of the meanings attributed. Future studies of school culture would be better served by avoiding reliance on definitions and by placing greater emphasis on clarifying its meaning within the context of use.

## Evolving theoretical frameworks

Despite the issue of the meaning of school culture remaining problematic, there have been advances in substantive theory. There is only space here to identify a narrow range of developments that have contributed to our understanding of school culture since the late 1980s.

### Political trends and their influence on educational policy

An important contribution to school culture research is being made by critical observers of national educational policy. School culture, especially in its generic form, is very difficult to change because it is shaped by values that are communally agreed, deeply embedded and taken-for-granted. Curriculum innovations of the 1960s and 1970s failed because little thought was given to the context of their placement and because teachers possessed the capacity to accept or reject them and consequently content and practice remained unchanged. Data collected prior to the Education Reform Act (ERA, 1988) suggest that schools were impervious to outside influence:

> Whatever the pressures upon them from the outside, primary schools have the capacity to become the kinds of organisations that the adults who work in them choose

that they will. Cultures lie within the control of those who participate in them;
leaders and the members together make their own school.

> (Webb and Vulliamy 1996, p. 456, quoting Nias)

This statement remains true of schools' unique culture but is less valid with
regards to schools' generic culture. Central government policy makers now
know which 'buttons' to push to change elements of school culture. Recent
history has demonstrated that generic culture of schools is changed by ensuring
schools adopt a specific curriculum, be accountable for educational outcomes
(what is measured becomes what is taught), by introducing market forces, and
by the exertion of external financial controls. Numerous Education Acts during the 1980s and especially the ERA of 1988 have led to a change in some
core values of schooling. The impact of government legislation on the culture
of schools is the focus of a number of studies. Woods (1992; 1993; 1994)
reporting on the PASCI study (Parental and School Choice Interaction) described significant changes in parental choice and secondary schools' response
to 'local competitive arenas' and market forces in general; Deem et al. (1994)
considered governors' reactions; and David et al. (1994) parents reactions.
Gerwitz et al. (1995), however, drew on data from parental choice, school
response and the distribution of educational resources to illustrate how market
forces have impinged on key features such as such as leadership and organisational structures, thereby creating fundamental changes to school culture.
Meaningful changes to generic school culture are rare and difficult to achieve
and consequently monitoring shifts in educational policy constitute an important element of contemporary school culture research.

## Organisational culture

Issues arising from marketisation are only the tip of the school culture 'iceberg'. Change, leadership, management, and staff professional culture are also
the foci of contemporary educational theory which explicitly or implicitly
draw on the notion of school culture. During the last twenty-five years management theory in the form of 'organisational culture' has provided a useful
resource for reflecting on the management of schools. But schools are not
companies producing an objective product, where consensus on outcomes is
agreed, or where there is acceptance that financial success is all important.
Schools are not (yet) directly related to organisations operating an enterprise
ideology and no studies have made a case for ecological validity justifying
transferability of either mid-range or grand theory between them. Nonetheless,
'organisational culture', despite having conceptual weaknesses, is an important
source of 'parallel reading', provides a variety of stimulating ideas and frameworks, and is often quoted in the literature.

Organisational culture is a concept that has its roots in anthropology and
like school culture has 'an embarrassment of definitional riches' (Brown, 1997,
p. 5). It is often referred to in terms of a 'social glue' that holds organisations
together (Seihl, 1985) or as an umbrella term for inter-related
sub-cultures (Martin, 1985). Some writers assume that organisational culture

is plastic and can be shaped, constitutes a unifying force, and link it to organisational effectiveness. However, Meek (1988, p. 453) does not share this view and suggests that 'The problem with some studies of organizational culture is that they appear to presume that there exists in a real and tangible sense a collective organizational culture that can be created, measured and manipulated in order to enhance organizational effectiveness.' Schein (1985) in his seminal work 'Organisational Culture and Leadership' takes a different stance seeing organisational culture as a product of the experience of social groups (see also Schein, 1997). He emphasises the influence of homogeneous and stable groups within an organisation which he considers as pivotal in determining strong or weak cultures and the 'character' of that culture. Abercrombie *et al.* (1994, p. 297) sum up Schein's perspective as follows:

> Culture forms and changes slowly, particularly at the level of taken-for-granted assumptions. New members of a group have to be socialised into its culture. This analysis has significant implications. (1) Organisations may contain various sub-cultures based on different groups, rather than a single organisational culture. Organisation theory shows how emergent behaviour in groups differs from formal organisational role prescriptions, and group cultures may similarly differ from those propounded by top management and be resistant to manipulation. (2) Group cultures may be forces of organisational disunity; e.g. when a labour force unites around a set of assumptions and beliefs that oppose top management. (3) Creating an organisational culture is likely to be a difficult and slow business and, if it contradicts existing group cultures, is unlikely to succeed however long organisational leaders persevere.

Organisational culture, then, is a way of looking at and thinking about behaviour of and in organisations, and offers a useful perspective for understanding what is occurring in schools. When used in this sense, organisational culture refers to a collection of theories that attempt to explain and predict how organisations and the people in them act in different circumstances. Louise Stoll gives a further explanation of Schein's work in Chapter 3.

## School sub-cultures and their dynamics

There is a belief that a school's unique culture is the aggregation of its sub-cultures. During the 1990s there has been a move away from research grappling with holistic notions of school culture and a growing interest in sub-cultures and their dynamic relationship. This development may be due to theoretical advances, personal research interests, or government policy which places stress on specific aspects of education such as leadership, the curriculum, the teaching-learning process, school improvement, and academic outcomes. These topics can claim to be important dimensions of school culture.

The sub-cultural perspective resonates in the work of many distinguished writers of the past including Waller (1932), Jackson (1968) and Wolcott (1973). Most studies of sub-cultures focus on teachers, for example by Andy Hargreaves (1994) and Acker (1990), on pupils (Rudduck *et al.*, 1996), or on common themes such as racism in schools (Gillborn, 1995) or discipline

(Johnstone and Munn, 1992), or less frequently on such structures as geo-political space, pastoral or phase groupings, or subject departments. These topics, inherently interesting, are given an extra dynamic dimension when their properties are related to a broader cultural theme (for example Chapter 9 by Jenny Corbett, who considers special educational needs in the light of contem-porary changes in wider and generic school culture). Similar studies on sub-culture dynamics are reported by, for example, Nias *et al.* (1989) who sug-gested that headteachers are cultural leaders, supporting Schein's (1985) view that leaders' primary task is to 'create and manage culture'. An alternative approach to sub-cultures is one which focuses not on collective or interperso-nal dynamics but emphasises their relationship to cultural patterns, organisa-tional structures, and subsystems that include communication, resource allocation, reproduction and ideology, cultural artefacts, the built environment, the nature of time and space, that are part and parcel of the milieu that is school culture.

## School culture and practice

For the past two decades schools have experienced innovation overload and 'successful' schools have learnt to manage change. There are many ways of managing change but here we will briefly consider two practice orientated research movements. The first, school improvement, is concerned with the management of innovation that accomplishes targeted educational goals (see Chapter 3); and the second, the study of effective schools which has two basic aims – to identify differences between schools' outcomes, and distinguish fac-tors that are characteristic of effective schools (see Chapter 4). Both move-ments draw on school culture studies to help schools to 'thrive on chaos'.

A very interesting study that applies notions of school culture and draws on knowledge gained by both movements is the basis of a collaboration between the University of London and the University of Strathclyde. The study, 'Im-proving School Effectiveness', combines quantitative and qualitative meth-odologies, and emphasises 'school ethos' as a key feature of change and improvement. It is a longitudinal study which involves primary and secondary schools and is designed to develop a value added framework for the investiga-tion of pupil progress and an understanding of how change in educational practice is best achieved (see MacBeath and Mortimore, 1993). Potentially findings from the 'Improving School Effectiveness' study provide an insight into the role of school culture in creating academically effective schools and explaining the role culture plays in the management of change in schools.

Other approaches, rather than developing theory from observing practice, emphasise theory into practice. It is generally accepted that an important stage in the management of any innovation or improvement programme is to under-stand the context of change and also the culture of the school. One aid to identifying a school's culture is to use pre-determined conceptual frameworks such as those devised by Handy (1985), and Beare *et al.* (1989) or applying one of the many organisation survey instruments available (for example Walters, 1994). There are problems with this approach since they may not account for the rhetoric-reality gap, failing to reflect the full range of values, beliefs and objectives of participants. An alternative is offered by a Cambridge University group (Ainscow *et al.*, 1994) who help practitioners debate the unique culture of their own institution. The underlying theoretical model is provided by David Hargreaves (1995) in his paper 'School Culture, School Effectiveness and School Improvement'. Using the Hargreaves model, via a user friendly manual of adapted research techniques, schools are in a better position to identify their own culture and underlying structure to map the process of change. The belief is that schools who map their own culture are in a good position to understand, maintain, and alter that culture.

However, perhaps the most 'practice' orientated of programmes that pursue school improvement strategies was inaugurated by the International School Effectiveness and Improvement Centre (ISEIC) at the University of London's Institute of Education. Stoll *et al.* (1995) for example, report on the collaboration between expert 'critical friends', Local Educational Authorities and schools, that encourages schools to move forward on a broad front by shifting key elements of their culture (see Chapter 3). Not only is this 'hands-on' approach beneficial to schools but also there is potential for theoretical development here since they utilise school culture within defined parameters and apply it within a specific context and are thus able to observe both processes and outcomes.

Finally, there are studies which adopt a 'theory in practice' approach that are both observations of school culture in practice and consideration of the practical implications of theory. Wallace (1996) for example, reflects on changes in the unique culture of a school by charting a transition in staff professional cultures when three primary schools merge. The resultant study provides a useful insight into dynamic relationships, sub-cultures, intended and unexpected outcomes of cultural combinations. Bell (1989) offers similar insights in his study of secondary school amalgamation. More importantly, these studies illustrate how, by adopting a 'theory in practice' approach, theory is refined and issues identified that have important implications for policy makers who oversee cultural fusions in the shape of school reorganisations.

### Concluding remarks

School culture is a complex and important topic. It has its roots in anthropology and sociological traditions such as those advocated by Durkheim. This chapter has traced one interpretation of the evolution of school culture research in the UK. Four key factors were identified as having shaped early school culture research in the UK: trends in educational theory and practice; different meanings attributed to 'school culture'; differences between and shifts in research methodology; and political trends and their influence on educational policy.

One way of thinking about school culture is to see it as a holistic entity that pervades and influences everyone within a school. This perspective is favoured by managerialists who equate a distinct homogeneous culture with effectiveness and success, and believe that organisational culture can be manipulated to achieve agreed educational objectives. This view implies that organisational culture pervades the very fabric of the institution affecting all participants similarly. An alternative view is that school culture is the result of multiple interaction: multiple in that individuals and groups who form sub-cultures are influential, and in the sense that there is two-way interaction between school culture and sub-cultures. Here there is an attempt to understand the relationship between co-existing sub-cultures to identify values and beliefs by which they are created and maintained and are in conflict or harmony with each other. School culture is an unseen and unobservable force behind school activities, a unifying theme that provides meaning, direction, and mobilisation for school members. It has both concrete representation in the form of artefacts and behavioural norms, and sustained implicitly jargon, metaphors and rites.

Whether school culture is viewed as a holistic entity resulting from a synthesis of group aims that is summed up as 'the way we do things around here', or is perceived as the consequence of sub-cultural fragmentation there is an agreement on the need in the future for:

> a clearer definition of the term; greater attention to the beliefs and values at the heart of all cultures; detailed studies of particular school cultures and the creation of appropriate typologies; empirical and conceptual accounts of school cultures which allow for micro-political activity and internally initiated change; and detailed explorations of the links between particular cultures and macro-societal forces.
>
> (Nias, 1989, p. 143)

School culture research of the future will continue to pursue these elements with the intention of understanding how they influence schooling and how that understanding can be applied to improve the quality of educational provision.

## NOTE

1. Mortimore et al. (1988), a member of the Fifteen Thousand Hours team, with the benefit of further methodological refinements, conducted a similar study to that of Rutter et al. but with primary rather than secondary schools. However, Mortimore et al. used mostly the term 'climate' where Rutter et al. generally used 'ethos'.

# 2

# Market Forces and School Cultures[1]

## SALLY POWER AND GEOFF WHITTY

### INTRODUCTION

Speaking at the Institute of Economic Affairs, London, in 1988, Bob Dunn, then Under-Secretary of State at the Department of Education and Science (DES), speculated whether 'a study in the life and teachings of Adam Smith should be compulsory in all schools' (*Education*, 8 July 1988).

There is little doubt that throughout the 1980s and early 1990s the ideas of free market advocates were highly influential in restructuring public education in the UK and other countries. While the Conservative government never went so far as to write the life and teachings of Adam Smith into the school timetable, we should not assume that the lessons of neoliberalism are not being learnt. This chapter looks at the hidden curriculum of marketisation and explores the extent to which schools are teaching new subjects – or even 'new right' subjects.

### THE MARKETISATION OF EDUCATION – A GLOBAL PHENOMENON?

Public education systems are in the process of rapid and far-reaching change. In many countries, various policies have been introduced that attempt to reformulate the relationship between government, schools and parents through the application of market forces. Our own research concentrates on recent education reform in England, Australia, New Zealand and the USA, but countries with quite different histories, such as Chile, Sweden, Poland and South Africa, are seeing the introduction of similar policies. Although, as Green (1996) illustrates, not all countries are extolling the virtues of the education market place, the almost simultaneous emergence of comparable reforms across different continents has led some to suggest that the marketisation of education needs to be understood as a global phenomenon. Indeed, it has been argued that this trend is related to a broader economic, political and cultural process of globalisation.

The precise features and significance of 'globalisation' are contested, but are generally considered to be connected with a shift in the nature of economic production and cultural consumption. For some writers, this shift marks a fundamental break with the past and the arrival of qualitatively different conditions that have been variously described as, amongst other things, postmodernity (Baudrillard, 1988) and post-traditionalism (Giddens, 1994). For others, it marks a phase within capitalism, from Fordism to post-Fordism (Murray, 1989) or neo-Fordism (Allen, 1992), from organised to late (Jameson, 1991) or disorganised (Lash and Urry, 1987) capitalism.

Whatever the ultimate significance of these transformations, there is general agreement that the role of the nation state is in a process of change. It is frequently claimed that it is becoming less important on economic (Reich, 1991), political (Held, 1989) and cultural (Robertson, 1991) grounds. As capital becomes more mobile, nations lose control over economic activity. New international regulative bodies limit national sovereignty. Technological innovations render geographic boundaries less significant, and the penetration of commercialisation into all spheres of public life is deemed to reduce cultural differences between nations. Within advanced capitalist countries, the demise of industry has led to a fragmentation of past collectivities and communities. As the old power blocs break down, archetypical modernist projects of social engineering are abandoned and national systems of welfare provision dismantled. With reference to schooling, education ceases to be a publicly prescribed and distributed entitlement and becomes a commodity available for private consumption. Usher and Edwards (1994, p. 175) contend that, in this situation:

> the state plays less and less of a role as the information available for circulation in the social formation comes from a wide range of sources. The control of learning through state-sponsored institutions is replaced by networks of information, in which to be 'educated' is to have consumed the information necessary for the optimising of performance.

However, we suggest that such a scenario is some way off. Indeed, in some instances, recent developments would seem to have strengthened rather than diminished the role of the state.

## RESTRUCTURING PUBLIC SYSTEMS OF EDUCATION

Dale (1994) reminds us that a whole set of political-economic variables will affect the ways in which different education systems respond to processes of globalisation. Nevertheless, the disaggregation and diversification of public systems of education is evident, to different degrees, in all of the countries we have researched.

In England, prior to the 1980s, the vast majority of children were educated in schools maintained by democratically elected local education authorities (LEAs) which exercised political and bureaucratic control over them. After the

Conservative victory at the 1979 election, the Thatcher and Major governments set about trying to break the local government monopoly of public
schooling through the provisions of a series of Education Acts passed in the
1980s and early 1990s. The Local Management of Schools (LMS) policy has
given schools control over their own budgets (including that for teachers'
salaries) which they receive according to a formula determined directly by the
number and ages of pupils. Only a very small proportion of their funds (at
most 15 per cent) are retained centrally by the LEA. Schools were also given
the opportunity to 'opt out' of their LEAs entirely. After conducting a parental
ballot schools could run themselves as grant maintained (GM) schools with
direct funding from central government. Open Enrolment allows popular state
schools to attract as many students as possible, at least up to their physical
capacity, instead of being kept to lower limits or strict catchment areas in order
that other schools could remain open. This was seen as the necessary corollary
of per capita funding in creating a quasi-market in education. Although the
new Labour government will modify some aspects of these reforms, it would
seem that the overall emphasis on devolution and choice looks set to continue.

In New Zealand, the initial reforms were introduced by a Labour government in October 1989 following the Picot Report 'Tomorrow's Schools' and
taken further by the National Party administration that succeeded it in 1990.
They led to a shift in the responsibility for budget allocation, staff employment
and educational outcomes from central government and regional educational
boards to individual schools. Schools were given boards of trustees originally
composed of parents (but extended in 1991 to encourage the inclusion of
business people) who had to negotiate goals with the local community and
agree a charter with central government. Because these boards were given
effective control over their enrolment schemes, the New Zealand reforms have
ushered in a much more thorough-going experiment in free parental choice in
the public sector than was introduced in England.

Australia's federal constitution makes it difficult to talk of a national system
of education with any precision. Nevertheless, as Angus (1995, p. 8) comments, the drive towards decentralisation has 'spread like an epidemic across
systems and state boundaries'. The importance of parents as 'consumers' is less
evident in Australian policy discourse than in our other three countries, with
the reforms stressing the benefits of economic rationalism in a drive towards
enhancing standards and efficiency. Common features of Australian state-led
reforms include the requirement that schools produce corporate plans and the
allocation of budgets to individual institutions which are controlled by local
decision-making groups, typically including community representatives. Some
states have gone further than others down the road to decentralisation.
Victoria and New South Wales have introduced a version of 'opting out' which
grants schools even more autonomy and is likely to break up the single state-
wide system of public schooling.

In America the past decade has seen federal pronouncements on education
policy, such as America 2000, which advocate the marketisation of public

schools, but most policies are made at state and district level. Although the range of programmes is wide, parental choice and greater school autonomy are among the most popular restructuring reforms (Newmann, 1993). Marketisation schemes include controlled choice in Cambridge, Massachusetts and Montclair, New Jersey, the East Harlem 'choice' experiment in New York, and the Milwaukee private school 'voucher' experiment. The USA has also seen some of the clearest examples of the commercialisation of education. Since the late 1980s several companies, from Federal Express to Burger King, have made plans to set up schools. Among the most ambitious plans were those of Whittle Inc whose Edison Project was designed to create a nationwide system of profit-making private schools (Molnar, 1996).

The implications of these changes for the provision of education are likely to be profound. Much research has focused on the impact which the restructuring of public education will have on efficiency, effectiveness and equity, but it is also likely to influence the nature of educational transmissions. The link between corporate involvement in schools, changes in the structure and governance of schools and the form and content of the messages they transmit to their students will not be straightforward, but its significance should not be underestimated. Indeed, the delegitimation of national education systems could be considered to herald the end of a key element of economic and cultural reproduction. As Green (1996, p. 5) argues:

> Through national education systems states fashioned disciplined workers and loyal recruits; created and celebrated national languages and literatures; popularized national histories and myths of origin, disseminated national laws, customs and social mores, and generally explained the ways of the state to the people and the duties of the people to the state . . . National education was a massive engine of integration, assimilated the local to the national and the particular to the general. In short it created, or tried to create, the civic identity and national consciousness which would bind each to the state and reconcile each to the other . . .

Green argues that the marketisation of education and concomitant reduction in state intervention will lead to a lack of social cohesion which may weaken economic development. Others, however, suggest that education systems are teaching new forms of identity that are more appropriate to these new times. Nations no longer need disciplined workers and loyal recruits; the old order is swept away with the advent of the transnational economy. From this viewpoint, Marquand's (1995) comments (cited in Avis et al., 1996, p. 11) on the economic vision upheld by the Thatcher and Major governments in the 1980s and 1990s in the UK might apply to any of our countries:

> The global market-place which the new-style Tories celebrate is cold and hard; in a profound sense it is also subversive. It uproots communities, disrupts families, mocks faiths and erodes the ties of place and history. It has created a demotic global culture, contemptuous of tradition, hostile to established hierarchies and relativist in morality. Above all, it has made a nonsense of national sovereignty, at any rate in the economic sphere.

## THE CORPORATE CURRICULUM?

One indicator of the alleged ascendancy of the global market-place over tradition and culture might be the increasing presence of corporate interests in the classroom. Whereas the school curriculum has traditionally transcended – indeed actively distanced itself from – the world of commerce (Wiener, 1981), the marketisation of education is forging a new intimacy between these two domains.

Commercial penetration of the curriculum is evident in all four countries discussed here. In America, for instance, commercial satellite network 'Channel One' offers schools free monitors on condition that 90 per cent of students watch its news and adverts almost every day. The proposed 'free' provision of email facilities to British pupils will also enable companies to promote their products in the classroom. Molnar (1996) cites a wide range of examples where businesses are using schools as advertising sites. In each of these countries there are schemes whereby equipment can be purchased with vouchers from supermarket chains, the take-up of which is enhanced as a result of budget constraints and the removal of public control (Roberts, 1994). Harris' (1996) research on the Australian Coles programme reveals not only the vast amount of time teachers can spend tallying dockets (589 hours in one school over 6 months), but also the promotional space occupied by visible tallies and scoreboards as well as the advertising on the computer equipment eventually acquired. In Britain, there has been such a proliferation of commercially sponsored curriculum materials that an independent organisation (National Consumer Council, 1996) designed to protect consumer interests has seen fit to publish a good practice guide for parents, teachers and governors.

Sometimes the objective of this commercial penetration seems to be product familiarisation, but curriculum materials can also be used to portray a partial, and inaccurate, account of business interests and impact. Molnar (1996) quotes a study guide on banking which defines 'free enterprise' as the symbol of 'a nation which is healthy and treats its citizens fairly'. Harty's (1994, p. 97) international survey of corporate products in the classroom found that 'the biggest polluters of the environment – the chemical, steel, and paper industries – were the biggest producers of environmental education material'.

Critics fear that the commercialisation of education will not only lead children to adopt an uncritical approach to corporate activities, it will also damage the cultural work of the school. In common with many critiques of what is sometimes called 'McDonaldisation', commercialisation is seen to impoverish cultural heritage. Harty (1994, pp. 98–9) believes that schools will develop 'an anti-intellectual emphasis' and 'a consumptionist drive to purchase status goods'. Indeed, she alleges that the permeation of multinationals 'contributes to a standardised global culture of material gratification . . . [which will] impinge on the cultural integrity of whole nations'. In this scenario, far from encouraging students to appreciate the particularities of their regional or national inheritance, schooling is about the training of desires, rendering subjects open to the seduction of ever changing consumption patterns and the politics of lifestyling.

One of the concerns about allowing businesses to run their own schools is that commercial interests will prevail over more genuinely educational activities. However, while corporate interests *are* penetrating the educational domain to a greater extent than hitherto, there is no evidence of a business takeover. In the USA, an attempt by Educational Alternatives Inc to demonstrate that private firms could run inner city schools in Baltimore more successfully than the local school district and make a profit at the same time ended in abject failure (Molnar, 1996). The Edison Project, mentioned earlier, reduced its plans for a nationwide chain of schools to four after it managed to raise only $12 million of the $2.5 billion originally envisaged. In Britain, the City Technology College initiative of the mid-1980s – held up as auguring a new partnership between business and education – was supposed to be funded primarily by private companies. However, central government found it extremely difficult to secure sponsorship, which at best amounted to 20 per cent of capital expenditure with public funds making up the shortfall (Whitty *et al.*, 1993). Only some 15 such colleges opened under this scheme in the end.

## THE STATE-CONTROLLED CURRICULUM

Claims that the content of the curriculum is being infiltrated by corporate control overlook the extent to which recent government policies have sought increasingly to regulate what counts as appropriate school knowledge and how it is to be assessed. Despite incentives to business and industry from governments in all four countries, there is little to suggest that they are prepared to relinquish control of the curriculum. Usher and Edwards' (1994, p. 175) claim, quoted earlier, that in these new times 'the state plays less and less of a role' is not borne out by evidence – at least in the compulsory phase of schooling. In Britain successive central governments in the 1980s and 1990s have clearly consolidated their position through the centralising measures of the National Curriculum and its associated assessment procedures. McKenzie (1993) argues that they have 'actually increased their claims to knowledge and authority over the education system whilst promoting a theoretical and superficial movement towards consumer sovereignty'. Although other countries have not been as prescriptive as Britain, many governments at state or national level have tightened their control over the curriculum in terms of what is taught and/or how this is to be assessed.

Central regulation of the curriculum is not only geared towards standardising performance criteria in order to facilitate professional accountability and consumer choice within the education market-place, it is also about creating, or recreating, forms of national identities. In the UK, the formulation of the National Curriculum has been underlain by a consistent requirement that schools concentrate on British history, British geography and 'classic' English literature. During the development of this curriculum, the influential Hillgate

Group (1987) expressed concern about pressure for a multicultural curriculum and argued for 'the traditional values of western societies' underlying British culture which 'must not be sacrificed for the sake of a misguided relativism, or out of a misplaced concern for those who might not yet be aware of its strengths and weaknesses' (p. 4).

This privileging of one narrow and partial version of national culture is less visible in Australia and New Zealand – although the importance of 'knowledge of Australia's history' is a key element in ministerial pronouncements on the objectives of the nation's schools (Slattery, 1989) and in both countries there have been attempts to generate a distinctive national identity (Fiske *et al.*, 1987).

The issue of a national curriculum has attracted considerable controversy within the United States, but individual states can legislate on curricula and for many years have controlled the selection of school textbooks. Texas, for instance, has a policy of excluding publications which do not promote 'traditional' life-styles and values (Delfattore, 1992). The general shift rightwards and the influence of powerful fundamentalist and conservative lobbyists is likely to ensure that any legislated curriculum, whether at state or national level, will draw on a partial and narrow selection of American culture (Apple, 1996).

McLean (1992) argues that international comparison is generally concerned with examining the interaction between global change and national resistance. At the same time as there has been a move toward the interpenetration of cultures characteristic of globalisation, there have been counter movements and responses. These curriculum reforms, pronouncements and proposals appear to represent a conscious attempt to reposition subjects in ways which hark backwards to some imagined past, rather than forwards into new globalised times. The global market-place may be, as Marquand (1995) claims, 'contemptuous of tradition, hostile to established hierarchies and relativist in morality' – but the visions of little England or small town America conjured up by new right curricula certainly are not.

Commercial messages emanating from the corporate production of curriculum materials may conflict with those which are underscored by new right governments highlighting the inalienable rights to national sovereignty, the inviolability of 'our' cultural heritage and the absolutism of traditional (often nineteenth century) morality. However, while the overt content of the curriculum may reassert the values of liberal humanism and a reinvigorated traditionalism, these are embedded in an increasingly marketised system. It may be more subtle shifts in the form and governance of schooling as much as changes in the content of the curriculum which are interpolation subjects within the market-place.

## LEARNING FROM MARKETISED RELATIONS

The marketisation of education has changed relations between and within schools in a number of ways which can be seen to reflect and reorient students tacitly within new phases of consumption and production. Ball (1994, p. 146) claims that 'insofar as students are influenced and affected by their institutional environment then the system of morality "taught" by schools is increasingly well accommodated to the values complex of the enterprise culture'. Old values of community, co-operation, individual need and equal worth, which Ball claims underlay public systems of comprehensive education, are being replaced by market-place values that celebrate individualism, competition, performativity and differentiation. These values and dispositions are not made visible and explicit, but emanate from the changing social context and permeate the education system in myriad ways. Just as there are tensions within the overt curriculum between the cultural elitism of 'nationalist' curricula and various forms of globalised commercial sponsorship, so too there are tensions both within and between elements of the hidden curriculum. Diversification sits uneasily alongside homogenisation and hierarchy. The new era of consumer empowerment becomes articulated with a reinvigorated traditionalism.

One facet of the changed institutional environment arising from the fragmentation of national and state systems of common schooling is the desire to encourage diversity on the supply side. In Britain, the Thatcher and Major governments made a number of provisions for specialist schools. CTCs were intended to be new secondary schools for the inner city, with a curriculum emphasis on science and technology. GM schools, which had 'opted out' of their LEAs, were permitted to change their character by varying their enrolment schemes and encouraged to emphasise specialised curriculum provision, for instance, in music or languages. In the USA, applications for charter schools status have been made for schools such as the Global Renaissance Academy of Distinguished Education, EduPreneurship, the Global Academy for International Athletics (Molnar, 1996) – in addition to the many magnet school initiatives. Diversity has been less dominant in the early rhetoric surrounding the Australian and New Zealand reforms – but in both countries market mechanisms have been put in place which seek to fracture existing systems of unified public provision.

The breakdown of these 'mass' systems of education and the drive towards diversity of provision have been seen by some to correspond with changes in the economic context. In particular, the alleged shift from Fordism to post- or neo-Fordism, from organised to disorganised capitalism, may have altered the range and nature of subjectivities which schools produce. Education systems may no longer be required to produce a stratified labour force, but rather one which is differentiated and specialised. Here the context and mode of learning may be more significant than the content of the lessons.

In the US, the planned Edison Project incorporated a high tech image of the school of the future 'where each student will have a computerised learning station, without textbooks or classrooms, and each teacher will have an office, just like real people – with phones' (*Tennessee Education Association News*, cited in Molnar, 1996, p. 159). In England, CTCs appear to be in the 'vanguard' of such a transformation with their 'shopping mall' or 'business park' architecture designed to emulate the world of finance (Whitty *et al.*, 1993).

Gewirtz *et al.* (1995) provide a semiological analysis of the impact of market reforms and comment on the 'glossification' of school imagery. Many of their case study schools had revamped reception areas to enhance the 'corporate' image of the school, installing fittings that would previously have been associated with banking and commerce. Principals were concerned to promote the 'corporate colours' of the school – even, as in one case, extending to the colour of the gas taps in the new science laboratories. Although it is difficult to evaluate the significance of messages transmitted through the organisation and presentation of the physical environment, they are unlikely to be as superficial as phrases such as 'glossification' imply.

While it is hard to envisage the disestablishment of schooling in the near future, it is often considered that technological innovations are beginning to transform the social relations of education. Kenway *et al.* (1996) talk of a new pedagogy which can be characterised by 'infinite lateral connectedness' and 'vertical porousness'. Old hierarchies and boundaries will be swept aside as schools develop less directional modes of learning. Corresponding to alleged changes in the workplace (Mumby and Stohl, 1991), relationships between staff and between staff and students will move towards a 'flatter' structure. Perhaps in correspondence with the rise of 'homeworking', Usher and Edwards (1994) speak of a 'reconfiguration' of the regulation of students who will no longer be required to attend educational institutions at all (see also Smith and Curtin, 1997). The boundary between home and school will also be eroded through the development of cross-site learning based on computer technologies. The high status conventionally accorded to print-based culture will be reduced as more high tech modes of knowledge production and transmission come 'on line'.

There is little evidence to indicate that schools are experiencing such sweeping transformations. Attempts to diversify provision have been a good deal less innovative than promised and have tended to reinforce, rather than diminish, hierarchies between schools (Whitty *et al.*, 1998). Moreover, certainly within the UK, as was argued earlier, it is important to note that these 'new' kinds of school have been Government, rather than market-led, initiatives. There is no indication that recent reforms have modified the distinctions which are commonly made between 'bad', 'good' and 'better' schools. And far from introducing horizontal forms of differentiation, the evidence thus far suggests that marketisation of education leads to an increase in vertical differentiation – exaggerating linear hierarchies through traditional rather than alternative criteria.

Social relations within schools do not appear much changed, either. Blackmore's (1995) observations of staff involvement in self-managing schools point to 'strong modernist tendencies for a top-down, executive mode of decision-making . . . [alongside its] 'weaker' post-modern claims to decentralise and encourage diversity, community ownership, local discretion, professional autonomy and flexible decision-making' (p. 45). Evidence of the arrival of a 'new' pedagogy is even harder to find. Although at one level schools are becoming more 'business-like' in approach and appearance, many are placing a renewed emphasis on pupil dress and authoritarian modes of discipline. In our research on GM schools (Halpin *et al.*, 1997), we found a reinvigorated traditionalism in which relationships between staff and students were more, rather than less, formal and hierarchical. Some research also shows that it leads to greater tracking within schools. Gewirtz *et al.* (1995) found increasing segregation of 'able' children and a move from mixed ability grouping towards setting. It is true that new technologies are rapidly finding their way into schools, but there is little evidence that they are contributing to a shift from teaching to a culture which emphasises pupil-directed learning. Even in those centres of innovation – the CTCs – lessons tend to be conducted along conventional lines with few instances of new technologies being used outside IT lessons (Whitty *et al.*, 1993) – an aspect noted by Kenway *et al.* (1996) in their own research. Far from seeing new technologies as the start of a new and different epoch of learning, Apple (1986) has argued that we should recognise them as part of an intensifying process of proletarianisation and deskilling.

The connection between performance and accountability within marketised education systems has tended to lead to the fragmentation and delineation of curriculum content and the reduction in teacher and learner autonomy. In parallel with criticisms of other centralised curricula, Robertson and Soucek's research within a Western Australian secondary school found that the new curriculum 'was at the same time both highly tailored and modularized into consumable packages and excessively assessed' (Robertson, 1993, p. 129). They claim '[t]hese features worked to compartmentalize school learning and teaching, as well as to develop an intense sense of alienation between the student and the teachers . . . exaggerating the reductive, technocratic and fragmented nature of much school knowledge' (pp. 129–30).

What is striking here is how reminiscent these words are of Bowles and Gintis (1976). Writing over twenty years ago, at about the time when economic production could be characterised as 'organized capitalism' (Lash and Urry, 1987), albeit in its final phases, they claimed structural correspondence between the social relations of the educational system and those of production in which:

> relationships between administrators and teachers, teachers and students, students and students, and students and their work – replicate the hierarchical division of labour. Hierarchical relations are reflected in the vertical authority lines from administrators to teachers to students. Alienated labour is reflected in the student's lack of control over his or her education, the alienation of the student from curriculum content, and the motivation of school work through a system of grades and other external rewards . . . Fragmentation in work is reflected in the institutionalized and often destructive competition among students through continual and ostensible meritocratic ranking and evaluation.
>
> (Bowles and Gintis, 1976, p. 131)

## THE COMMODIFIED CURRICULUM – A NEW CORRESPONDENCE?

The apparent continuities and discontinuities between past and current practices reveal tensions in claims concerning the extent of wider social change and whether and how such change affects education systems. The similarity between Bowles and Gintis' analysis and more recent accounts, such as that of Robertson and Soucek, raises the issue of whether schools are engaged in the production of 'old' rather than 'new' subjectivities. More specifically, are marketised education systems simply a new way of producing 'old' subjects? Such a position would presumably be supported by those (e.g. Weiss, 1993) who argue that the marketisation of public education is a state-initiated response to the recurrent problem of legitimating the mode of production, and the state's role within it, at a time of crisis in capital accumulation.

If so, this would suggest that the case for claiming 'new times' is less than convincing. Hirst and Thompson (1996) certainly claim that there is nothing particularly new about the current degree or rate of international interaction which has always been, and still is, patchy and sporadic rather than the more universal and inexorable process implied by globalisation theorists. Even if we concede that there has been, within our four countries, a reduction in the profile of the nation state as an international entity, there is nothing to suggest that it is weakening its grip on areas of internal regulation. Nor is the evidence of a global culture overwhelming. Transnational acculturisation is hardly reciprocal and can be seen as little more than the hegemonic influence of the West. Abu Lughod (1991) analyses critical cultural moments, such as the crisis over Rushdie's Satanic Verses, to reveal how *un*globalised culture has become.

The problem with arguments about the scope and pace of change is that they are to a large extent irresolvable. Even if recent changes are less ground-breaking than some social theorists suggest, this does not mean that the picture is only one of continuity.

Marketised education systems provide evidence of both changes and continuities which appear to both match and contradict other social trends. This lack of correspondence between education systems and the wider social and economic context may result from delayed response or complete structural disarticulation. For example, at the level of further and higher education, in particular, it is possible to see a commodification of learning packages, a drive towards 'pick and mix' courses which have been described as a 'cafeteria curriculum' and a degree of de-institutionalisation with the growth of distance learning through new technologies.

On the other hand, it could be argued that these changes are only evident at the margins rather than in the core of the education system, and that the central structure and function of the compulsory phases remain unchanged. However, any claims for the distinctiveness of the compulsory dimension of public education may be increasingly difficult to sustain. There has been some debate among neo-liberals (e.g. Tooley, 1995) on the merits of disestablishing schools. But even if schools retain their institutional location, it is perhaps only a matter of time before they experience the changes which are taking place in the later phases of formal education.

Nor would acknowledging such correspondence necessarily mean making a wholesale commitment to the kind of correspondence expounded by Bowles and

Gintis. As Bailey (1995, p. 482) points out, 'it may be that correspondence does not have universal applicability, but nevertheless is an insightful idea to apply to certain places and at certain times'. Indeed, Hickox and Moore (1992) argue that stronger claims can be made for correspondence under post-Fordism than the system of mass production analysed by Bowles and Gintis. Similarly, Bernstein (1990) holds that within the market-oriented visible pedagogy, the specialisation of curricula 'allows for an almost perfect reproduction of the hierarchy of the economy within the school, or between the schools (as in the case of 'magnet' schools), through the grading of curricula . . .' (p. 86).

If this is so, then we may be at the beginning of a process of change which will have profound significance not just for the organisation of schools but for the nature of educational transmissions. But, whether these changes are anticipated with optimism or concern, we should be cautious in presuming that schools will successfully mould the future citizens and consumers required for the 'new times'. Formerly, the publicly-controlled national education systems may have produced disciplined workers and local recruits, but they also produced other sorts of dispositions that appeared less than functional to the needs of capital. As Bernstein pointed out in 1977: 'Consider various forms of industrial action over the last hundred years. The school in this respect is highly inefficient in creating a docile, deferential and subservient work force. The school today has difficulty in disciplining its pupils' (pp. 187–8).

It might be argued that if education systems had problems fulfilling the relatively simple tasks of Fordist modes of production, how much more difficult to create the kind of flexible postmodern subjects apparently required within the global marketplace. Or, it could be claimed that the erosion of the collectivities characteristic of systems of mass production will facilitate the interpellation of subjects within the new order. Viewed in this way, the indiscipline to which Bernstein refers becomes not merely evidence of inadequate socialisation into the labour force, but a manifestation of resistance. If the solidarity of the factory floor provided Willis' (1977) lads with the cultural resources for opposition, will the demise of mass production remove the basis of similar counter-hegemonic strategies?

It is not just working class solidarity which is threatened. Hall (1991, p. 44) argues there has 'been a fragmentation of the great collective social identities of class, of race, of nation, and of the West'. Identities, it is claimed, are no longer fixed, but fluid and adaptable. As Featherstone (1995, p. 110) puts it:

It is the capacity to shift the frame, and move between varying range of foci, the capacity to handle a range of symbolic material out of which various identities can be formed and reformed in different situations, which is relevant in the contemporary global situation.

## IMPLICATIONS?

It could be argued that if opposition arises out of collective action and awareness, as has traditionally been held by theorists on the left, then the atomised and flexible consumers of marketised education will be unable to counteract the penetrating individualisation of global markets. On the other hand, we should be careful not to misrepresent the nature and impact of earlier modes of collective engagement. Past solidarities were often more imagined than real. As Featherstone (1995) demonstrates, accounts of working class life, both in sociology and popular culture, typically overplay its homogeneity and capacity for communal bonding. They also frequently overlook the sexual and racial basis of exclusion and inclusion within such 'solidarities'. Theoretically, conceptions of the decentred subject and radical pluralism also undermine the notion of 'fixed' identities and enduring allegiances.

We also need to be careful not to overestimate the influence of globalised consumerism. Despite the intrusion of commercial interests in schools, teachers may be able to do much to help students question the relationship between business and education. The ethics of encouraging children to shop at particular supermarkets have no doubt already been widely debated by students and teachers. It is hard to envisage health educators *not* pointing out the ironies of fast food manufacturers promoting good health guides. Similarly, curriculum materials designed by multinationals can be used to highlight omissions and distortions and expose the vested interests of their producers.

This does not mean we should be complacent about the commercialisation of the curriculum. As Harty (1994) points out, many teachers do not discuss the commercial origins and implications of the materials, an aspect which is likely to increase as teachers cope with all the other pressures of devolution and marketisation. Nevertheless, the process of inculcating these new values and desires is unlikely to be straightforward. There is evidence of increased involvement of business and industry within marketised education systems than in the earlier system based on public control, but the messages promoted by commercial sponsorship tend to be highly visible. This visibility makes them more accessible to interrogation and, therefore, potentially less insidious than other aspects of marketisation.

It is perhaps those less visible aspects of marketisation that may be the more influential. While at the level of direct transmissions, students are to be taught the values of the cultural restorationists (Ball, 1990), the context in which they are taught may undermine their canons. While the content of the lessons emphasises heritage and tradition, the form of their transmission is becoming increasingly commodified within the new education market-place.

The need to address the tension between the overt and hidden curriculum is apparent in discussions about alternatives to current education reforms. Concern that the 'subversive' tendencies of the global market-place will erode national and communal values has led some to suggest that these aspects should receive more attention in the formal curriculum. In Britain, David Hargreaves (1994), who is generally supportive of recent policies of diversification, nevertheless believes we should reassert a sense of common citizenship by insisting on core programmes of civic education in all schools. From a different perspective Green (1996, p. 59) also suggests that schools will need to regenerate social cohesion 'as the social atomisation induced by global market penetration becomes increasingly dysfunctional'. He argues that the current abdication on the part of governments to pursue goals of social cohesion will need to be reversed: 'With the decline of socially integrating institutions and the consequent atrophy of collective social ties, education may soon again be called upon to stitch together the fraying social fabric.'

How to bring about this greater emphasis on citizenship is problematic. It is unclear how far adding a component of civic education to the timetable, as Hargreaves (1994) suggests, will provide an effective counterbalance to the permeating values of the market-place. If much of the potency of the hidden curriculum derives from its invisibility, it would seem unlikely that its effects could be overcome by adding to the academic curriculum. And while Green (1996, p. 59) holds that '[t]he scope for education to act as a socially integrative force is not necessarily diminished or impeded by the forces of globalization and postmodernity', he himself provides few indicators of how education systems can be restructured and who will initiate such a process in a situation where responsibility for education is increasingly seen as a matter for individuals and families.

The development of state-initiated curricula might provide one source of response, but, certainly in the case of England, the current National Curriculum does not appear to hold much promise for a revitalised citizenry. Countering the power of the hidden curriculum seems likely to require the development of new sets of relations both within schools and beyond them, so that students can experience responses to globalisation other than the currently dominant neo-liberal and neo-conservative ones. More specifically, if we want students to learn democratic citizenship we need to put in place structures which embody those principles (Apple and Beane, 1999).

## CONCLUSION

It is clear that debates on the impact of recent reforms are highly speculative. The main arguments concern the nature of educational transmissions, rather than the extent to which they are absorbed, appropriated or resisted. Even if it were possible to identify the needs of the new global market-place, these would be mediated at the level of the school, which has its own grammar of accommodation and resistance. As Bernstein (1990) has argued, we need to look at the curriculum as more than just the carrier of external pressures. In common with other theories of cultural reproduction, many recent accounts 'appear to be more concerned with an analysis of what is reproduced in, and by, education than with an analysis of the medium of reproduction . . . It is as if the specialised discourse of education is only a voice through which others speak . . . itself no more than a relay for power relations external to itself; a relay whose form has no consequence for what is relayed' (Bernstein 1990, p. 166).

What has been clear thus far is that the policies and practices of schools within marketised systems display many contradictory elements and paradoxical tendencies. Bernstein (1990, p. 88) argues that the market-oriented pedagogy is 'a new pedagogic Janus' which 'recontextualises and thus repositions within its own ideology features of apparently oppositional discourses' – diversification locked alongside new emphases on traditional social values and social hierarchies. There have, of course, always been contradictory elements within schooling – at system and classroom level (Dale, 1989), but few have seemed as acute as those we are witnessing at the present time.

In this situation, we need to explore the relative impact of globalisation and the imperatives of the nation state and the relationship between the hidden curriculum of the market-place and the overt lessons on the timetable.

The recent work of Bernstein (1997) suggests ways in which such a task might be approached. He argues that the tensions that arise from the increasing deregulation of the economic field and the increasing regulation of what he terms the symbolic field are generating new forms of pedagogic identity. Education reforms are leading to the recontextualisation of elements of the 'retrospective' identity of old conservatism and the 'therapeutic identity' associated with the child centred progressivism of the 1960s and 1970s to produce two new hybrids, the 'decentred market' identity and the 'prospective' identity.

The 'decentred market' identity embodies the principles of neo-liberalism. It has no intrinsic properties, its form is dependent only upon the exchange value determined by the market. It is therefore contingent upon local conditions and is highly unstable. The 'prospective' pedagogic identity on the other hand attempts to 'recentre' through selectively incorporating elements of old conservatism. It engages with contemporary change, but draws on the stabilising tradition of the past as a counterbalance to the instability of the market. These two new pedagogic identities are therefore both complementary and contradictory. To some extent they can be seen to embody the tensions discussed within this chapter. While the decentred market pedagogy can be seen to foster 'new' subjects, the 'prospective' pedagogy seeks to reconstruct 'old' subjects, albeit selectively in response to the pressures of a new economic and social climate.

The extent to which such pedagogic identities are being fostered by the new reforms requires further theoretical and empirical explorations. Such explorations require us to look at both form *and* content, the message *and* the medium, the juxtaposition of different types of knowledge and the complex and differential ways in which school knowledge relates to the everyday worlds of school students. The complexity and contradictions of recent developments may make such a task even more difficult than it appeared in the 1970s, but it needs to be addressed if we are to understand the ways in which subjects are being positioned by current policies and develop effective strategies for fostering alternative forms of social cohesion.

## NOTE

1. An earlier version of this chapter was presented at the Annual Meeting of the American Educational Research Association, Chicago, April 1997.

# 3

## School Culture: Black Hole or Fertile Garden for School Improvement?

### LOUISE STOLL

> . . . notions of improvement reside in the heads of participants and observers. One viewer may judge a reform to be an improvement, while another judges that same change to be a step backward.
>
> (Cuban, 1990, p. 74)

Take five scenarios. The first two involve improvement attempts from outside of schools; the other three, from inside. First, the external efforts. In the attempt to drive up educational standards, a national or state government mandates that all schools will use a 'tried and tested' approach to teaching writing. This will be introduced through professional development and monitoring practices found to be effective when introducing changes elsewhere. A local education authority or district sets up a voluntary school improvement project for its schools in partnership with a university that offers considerable experience in such projects, drawing on an extensive knowledge base on the conditions that support school improvement. In both cases, the 'pill' works in some of the participating schools, but not in others.

Now for the three internal improvement attempts. In the first, a headteacher (principal), newly arrived to her second primary headship, sets up a scheme where staff will observe each other in classrooms and give each other feedback, on the basis that it was both popular and highly effective in her previous school. She receives a distinctly cool response. Elsewhere, an information technology (ICT) teacher goes on an exciting course where he learns about the benefits of and strategies for promoting literacy across the curriculum through ICT. Enthused, he returns and tries to persuade colleagues in other departments to 'get involved', but there is little interest and take up. In the third school, a new headteacher at a middle school observes that staff are not seen to be very involved in decision-making, forward planning is not systematic, and there is little emphasis on teaching and learning. Less than three years later the place is 'buzzing'. While three months after her arrival fewer than half the teachers agreed that 'teachers at this school believe *all* students can learn', as recorded in a teacher survey, two-and-a-half years later the survey is repeated with the same teachers and 90 per cent agree with the statement. Anyone who works in or closely with schools can remember exciting new initiatives that have started with enthusiasm, commitment, and energy, at least on the part of some staff members. Two years later they have disappeared never to be seen again. So, what is going on here?

As already noted, all of these scenarios are attempts at school improvement, whether they originate from inside or outside of the school. This chapter is concerned with the significance of school culture within school improvement and, in particular, why the cultures in some schools are black holes, in which school improvement efforts disappear, never to see the light of day, and others provide warmth and sustenance for school growth and development. In beginning to attempt to unravel this complex puzzle, it may be helpful to consider three different definitions of school improvement.

## WHAT IS SCHOOL IMPROVEMENT?

Until recently, a widely accepted definition of school improvement emanated from the 14-country International School Improvement Project (ISIP) that reached its completion in the mid-1980s. Participants in this project concluded that school improvement was:

> a systematic, sustained effort aimed at change in learning conditions and other related internal conditions in one or more schools, with the ultimate aim of accomplishing educational goals more effectively.
>
> (van Velzen *et al.*, 1985, p. 48)

Assumptions underlying this definition were that school improvement needs to be carefully planned, managed and implemented, even through periods of inevitable turbulence, until changes are 'embedded or built into the structure', where they are part of the school's natural behaviour (Huberman and Miles, 1984). Additionally, throughout stages of the change process, those involved must recognise the need for change, be committed to the particular improvement focus and feel they have ownership of it, for the change to have any 'meaning' (Fullan, 1991). While real improvement focuses on teaching, learning, the curriculum and conditions that support learning, successful school improvement also extends to other related internal conditions; supporting roles, relationships and structures needing to be directly addressed. Furthermore, while improvement takes place in the school, schools are also located within an educational system where benefits can be reaped by collaborating and co-operating with other schools and being supported by external partners and agencies. The ISIP project also identified a broad range of goals of school improvement, including pupil, teacher and school organisation goals.

If we fast forward a decade to the mid-late 1990s, in Britain and many other countries schools' external context is very different, with decision-making decentralised to schools within a centralised accountability framework. Recognising this shift, Hopkins *et al.*'s (1994) definition of school improvement in an era of change has particularly emphasised pupil outcomes, rather than broad educational goals. They succinctly define school improvement as '. . . a distinct approach to educational change that enhances student outcomes as well as strengthening the school's capacity for managing change' (p. 3), adding:

> In this sense school improvement is about raising student achievement through focusing on the teaching-learning process and the conditions which support it. It is about strategies for improving the school's capacity for providing quality education in times of change, rather than blindly accepting the edicts of centralized policies, and striving to implement these directives uncritically. (p. 3)

Based on our work in Canada, Britain and elsewhere, Dean Fink and I offer a slightly different definition of school improvement that also views its ultimate aim to be the enhancement of all pupils' progress, achievement and development in the broadest sense. We view school improvement as:

> a series of concurrent and recurring processes in which a school:
> - enhances pupil outcomes;
> - focuses on teaching and learning;
> - builds the capacity to take charge of change regardless of its source;
> - defines its own direction;
> - assesses its current culture and works to develop positive cultural norms;
> - has strategies to achieve its goals;
> - addresses the internal conditions that enhance change;
> - maintains momentum during periods of turbulence; and
> - monitors and evaluates its process, progress, achievement and development.
>
> (Stoll and Fink, 1996, p. 43)

Understandably, there are several commonalities between the three definitions, even within an eleven-year period and a changed external context. Notably, all draw out the intricate relationship between school improvement and change. The need to understand the complexity of change when engaged in school improvement is all too often downplayed. Hopkins and colleagues' definition and that of Stoll and Fink also overtly highlight the issue of capacity. Changing practice is notoriously difficult, requiring time and effort to develop new skills, as well as the will to change (Miles, 1987). Determining a school's capacity and readiness for change, therefore, is vitally important for internal and external school change agents (Fullan, 1993). Capacity is vital to school improvement but harder to achieve in some schools than others. Without attention to internal capacity at the earliest opportunity, real lasting changes impacting on teaching and learning are highly unlikely (Stoll and Fink, 1996).

There are, however, two distinctive differences about our own definition, apart from its detail and reliance on bullet points! The first is in our use of the words 'to take charge of change', which implies more than just managing change. Like Hopkins and colleagues, we believe it is essential that schools are creative and are able to accommodate external ideas within their own context and needs. Even within an externally determined framework, more successful schools are in the driving seat, setting their own direction, adapting mandates creatively to fit their vision, 'colonising' external educational reforms

(National Commission on Education, 1995). Successful school improvement is based on an ownership mentality, where schools define their own direction, irrespective of external demands. Essentially, real school improvement can only come from within (Barth, 1990).

The very nature of the change, however, may vary. It may be rational change, as I will argue many external reforms are. It may also be non-rational change in an 'era of uncertainty' (Patterson et al., 1986). Being able to take charge of change in such a situation is by no means easy to do, which leads me to the second fundamental difference in our definition. We explicitly maintain that an essential part of school improvement is that the school 'assesses its current culture and works to develop positive cultural norms'. Why do we place such emphasis on school culture in relation to school improvement? In the remainder of this chapter, I will examine school culture, and how it can either hinder or support school improvement attempts.

## WHAT IS SCHOOL CULTURE?

School culture is one of the most complex and important concepts in education. In relation to school improvement, it has also been one of the most neglected. Schein (1985) notes various interpretations of culture: observed behavioural regularities, including language and rituals; norms that evolve in working groups; dominant values espoused by an organisation; philosophy that guides an organisation's policy; rules of the game for getting along in the organisation; and the feeling or climate conveyed in an organisation. Whilst agreeing that these meanings reflect the organisation's culture, Schein does not believe that they are its basic essence. This he considers to be, 'the deeper level of *basic assumptions* and *beliefs* that are shared by members of an organisation, that operate unconsciously, and that define in a basic "taken-for-granted" fashion an organization's view of itself and its environment' (p. 6). These are the heart of school culture and are what makes it so hard to grasp and change.

Culture describes how things are and acts as a screen or lens through which the world is viewed. In essence, it defines reality for those within a social organisation (Hargreaves D., 1995), gives them support and identity and 'forms a framework for occupational learning' (Hargreaves A., 1994, p. 165). Each school has a different reality or mindset of school life, often captured in the simple phrase 'the way we do things around here' (Deal and Kennedy, 1983). It also has its own mindset in relation to what occurs in its external environment. Culture is, thus, 'situationally unique' (Beare et al., 1989) as can be seen in the example of two ostensibly similar primary schools, located in the same area and drawing from the same population, with the same number of pupils attending them. These two schools view these pupils, their work and the external constraints they face in very different ways.

A school's culture is shaped by its history, context and the people in it. The age of the organisation can impact cultural change. Schein (1985) identifies three significant developmental periods in a business organisation's life. Parallels can be drawn with schools. In early years of a new school dominant values emanate from its 'founders' and the school makes its culture explicit. It clarifies its values, finds and articulates a unique identity and shares these with newcomers, whether teachers, pupils or parents. Culture is the 'glue' that holds everyone together, and can be seen as a positive development force. As time passes, the culture moves into a succession phase where differences occur between conservative and liberal forces and new people take leadership roles. In 'midlife', the school is well established but needs to continue on a path of growth and renewal. Changes may have occurred to its external and internal contexts, altering strengths and weaknesses. The most important aspects of the culture are now embedded and taken for granted, and culture is increasingly implicit. Subcultures have also sprung up. 'Unfreezing' occurs if the school in some way does not meet its goals or if rivalries develop between sub-groups. Change becomes much more difficult because of less consciousness of the culture; it is harder to articulate and understand. 'Maturity and/or stagnation and decline' is most problematical from the cultural change perspective. This stage is reached if the school has ceased to grow and respond to its environment. Dysfunctional elements have surfaced, but challenge of old assumptions is resisted (Fink, 1997).

School culture is also influenced by a school's external context. Locally, a school's community, including the pupils' parents, may have their own conceptions of what a 'real school' is (Metz, 1991): in other words, 'a real school is what I attended when I was a child'. The Local Educational Authority (LEA) or school district can also help create an improvement mindset (Stoll and Fink, 1996), as well as having its own improvement orientation (Rosenholtz, 1989) and language (Birmingham City Council, 1996). Political and economic forces or changes in national or local educational policies are also influences. For example, the division of the National Curriculum in England and Wales into *core* and *foundation* subjects, and an external assessment system that focuses only on *core* subjects at primary level, influences what is valued in schools. Teaching unions are another aspect of the external context that can have an impact on the school culture and, thus, its orientation to improvement (Fink, 1997).

Furthermore, school cultures vary between primary and secondary schools (Cooper, 1988). In primary schools care and control have influenced their culture (Hargreaves A. *et al.*, 1996), such that when pupils leave primary schools there is a feeling that they have left a family (Rudduck *et al.*, 1996). In contrast, secondary school culture is influenced not only by their larger size and department structures, but by the very fundamental nature of teachers' academic orientation (Hargreaves A. *et al.*, 1996) – the difference between being, for example, an art teacher and a science teacher, often emphasised and compounded by subject teacher associations and networks – and the fragmented individualism (Hargreaves D., 1982; Hargreaves A., 1994) that pupils experience in moving from one subject and teacher to another.

School culture is also very much influenced by the pupils in the school and their social class background. Thrupp (1997) argues that the social mix of the school plays a major role in how it functions, in large part because of the cumulative effect of the reference group processes of the pupils. In essence, the very pupils who attend the school flavour it in a particular way, through their own pupil culture. This takes on added significance when they reach adolescence, which is at an increasingly younger age. At this time of development and maturation, their identities and values are shifting as they establish 'who they are, their place among their peers, and where they fit in the larger society' (Hargreaves *et al.*, 1996, p. 10). The potential for clashes of values between the adults and pupils in a school is considerable!

Changes in society pose challenges to a school's culture, whether they be related to learning, the pupil population, organisational management, rapid technological developments or the changing role of women (Dalin and Rolff, 1993). Such societal changes often demand rapid responses from a school, and yet while culture changes as participants change, it can also be a stabilising force, particularly for those who have been part of the culture for a longer period. It can therefore appear problematic for those in search of quick fix changes because it often seems as if it is an unmovable force. While it presents, therefore, the paradox of both being static and dynamic (Rossman *et al.*, 1988), in reality it is constantly evolving (Hopkins *et al.*, 1994) and being reconstructed (Angus, 1996).

## WHAT DOES SCHOOL CULTURE LOOK LIKE? WHAT CAN YOU SEE AND HEAR?

From an anthropological standpoint, school culture manifests itself in customs, rituals, symbols, stories, and language (Deal and Kennedy, 1983; Nias *et al.*, 1989; Hargreaves D., 1995) – the 'artefacts' of culture (Schein, 1985). Thus, whether religion or spirituality, pupils' learning, sporting achievements, or discipline are emphasised in assemblies provides a lens on one facet of school culture. Similarly, the school that has an annual picnic for staff, parents and pupils, and the headteacher of Springvale School who welcomes new entrants to 'the Springvale family' are making statements about what is considered important. Viewed more practically, MacGilchrist *et al.* (1995) argue that school culture is expressed through 'three inter-related generic dimensions' (p. 41): professional relationships, organisational arrangements, and opportunities for learning. In other words, school culture is most clearly 'seen' in the ways people relate to and work together; the management of the schools' structures, systems and physical environment; and the extent to which there is a learning focus for both pupils and adults, and the nature of that focus: central differences between 'learning enriched' and 'learning impoverished' schools (Rosenholtz, 1989).

Culture can take different forms. The focus of this particular chapter is school culture as a holistic concept. Within this, however, there may exist several cultures. I have already discussed pupil culture. There can also be a teacher culture, leadership culture, support staff culture, and parent culture. Teacher culture has received most attention in relation to school improvement. Andy Hargreaves (1994) highlights four existing teaching cultures:

- *Individualism* – these are bounded in metaphors of classrooms as egg-crates or castles, where autonomy, isolation and insulation prevail, and blame and support are avoided.
- *Collaboration* – teachers choose, spontaneously and voluntarily, to work together, without an external control agenda. Forms vary from 'comfortable' activities, such as sharing ideas and materials, to more rigorous forms, including mutual observation and focused reflective enquiry.
- *Contrived collegiality* – where teachers' collaborative working relationships are compulsorily imposed, with fixed times and places set for collaboration, for example planning meetings during preparation time.
- *Balkanisation* – where teachers are neither isolated nor work as a whole school. Smaller collaborative groups form, for example within secondary school departments, between infant and junior teachers, and class teachers and resource support teachers.

## WHAT CAN'T YOU SEE?

Norms are the unspoken rules for what is regarded as customary or acceptable behaviour and action within the school. Morgan (1997) explains, 'Life within a given culture flows smoothly only insofar as one's behaviour conforms with unwritten codes. Disrupt these norms and the ordered reality of life inevitably breaks down' (p. 139). Norms also shape reactions to internally or externally proposed or imposed improvements. It is, therefore, important for those working in schools and those supporting them from outside to understand their norms because the acceptance of improvement projects by a school depends on the fit between the norms embedded in the changes and those within the school's own culture (Sarason, 1996). Some norms are more sacred than others (Rossman *et al.*, 1988), for example some people's fundamental belief that ability is inherited – you either have it or you do not – and, therefore, some children are unable to learn, or a teacher's belief that teaching reading using a particular method does not work, based on twenty-five years of successful experience using a different method.

As a result of our work with schools in several countries and our reading of the literature on school improvement, Dean Fink and I have identified cultural norms that influence school improvement. These are described in detail elsewhere (Stoll and Fink, 1996), but are summarised in Figure 3.1. Because norms are frequently unspoken, catchphrases articulate their core messages.

These norms are interconnected and feed off each other. Many are basic to human rights of equity and respect. They do not just represent a snapshot of an

1. Shared goals – 'we know where we're going'
2. Responsibility for success – 'we must succeed'
3. Collegiality – 'we're working on this together'
4. Continuous improvement – 'we can get better'
5. Lifelong learning – 'learning is for everyone'
6. Risk taking – 'we learn by trying something new'
7. Support – 'there's always someone there to help'
8. Mutual respect – 'everyone has something to offer'
9. Openness – 'we can discuss our differences'
10. Celebration and humour – 'we feel good about ourselves'

Stoll and Fink (1996)

**Figure 3.1** Norms of Improving Schools

effective school that it is impossible to attain if you are currently in a school experiencing difficulties. They focus on fundamental issues of how people relate to and value each other.

One norm, 'collegiality', merits further discussion because of the attention paid to it in the school improvement literature over recent years. This much used but complex concept involves mutual sharing and assistance (Fullan *et al.*, 1990), an orientation towards the school as a whole (Nias *et al.*, 1989), and is spontaneous, voluntary, development-oriented, unscheduled, and unpredictable (Hargreaves A., 1994). Judith Warren Little (1990) identifies four types of collegial relations, the first three of which she views as weak forms: 'scanning and story telling', general 'help and assistance', and 'sharing'. It is the fourth form, 'joint work', that is most likely to lead to improvement. Examples of joint work include team teaching, mentoring, action research, peer coaching, planning and mutual observation and feedback. These derive their strength from the creation of greater interdependence, collective commitment, shared responsibility, and, perhaps most important, 'greater readiness to participate in the difficult business of review and critique' (Fullan and Hargreaves, 1991). An example of collegiality is given by a member of a secondary school improvement team involved in an LEA improvement project, who describes the rationale behind her school's chosen focus:

> In a sense our main aim is to change our classroom practice supported by our colleagues, and as a major part of that we want to be able to observe each other in the classroom, to be able to have someone who can be what we are calling a 'reflective friend' to whom you can talk afterwards about the things that went well, the things that didn't go so well.

## DO SCHOOLS HAVE DIFFERENT CULTURES?

Given the different contextual influences described earlier, it is not surprising that schools' cultures vary. What is particularly interesting, however, is that schools with similar contextual characteristics have different mindsets. Over recent years, typologies that describe and label different 'idealised' types of school culture have been created. While such typologies cannot capture subtle nuances of individual schools and possible sub-cultures within schools, they are useful, however, as a discussion starting point to help teachers consider different facets of their school's culture. David Hargreaves (1995) offers one such model based on two dimensions: the instrumental domain, representing social control and orientation to task; and the expressive domain, reflecting social cohesion through maintaining positive relationships. Four types of school cultures sit in different and extreme places on the two dimensions:

- Traditional low social cohesion, high social control – custodial, formal, unapproachable;
- Welfarist low social control, high social cohesion – relaxed, caring, cosy;
- Hothouse high social control, high social cohesion – claustrophobic, pressured, controlled;
- Anomic low social cohesion, low social control – insecure, alienated, isolated, 'at risk'.

A fifth culture is also proposed, that of an effective school, demonstrating optimal social cohesion and optimal social control, with fairly high expectations and support for achieving standards. Hargreaves emphasises these are 'ideal cultures' because real schools 'move around' and, indeed, departments within schools may fall within different parts of this model.

Rosenholtz's (1989) 'moving' and stuck' schools model, although simplistic, is powerful because it conveys stark contrasts. You can visualise two schools next door to each other, with similar intakes, in the same school system, facing the same external government mandates, and yet their mindsets are different. The moving school feels 'freedom to' focus on its priorities; the stuck school seeks 'freedom from' outside demands. Rosenholtz's dimensions have been expanded by Hopkins and colleagues (1994) into 'four expressions of school culture', sitting on two continuums; one of effectiveness and ineffectiveness in terms of outcomes and the other representing the degree of dynamism of the improvement process, from dynamic to static.

The model Dean Fink and I have created develops these ideas. We focus on the current effectiveness of the school, but more important, we argue that the rapidly accelerating pace of change makes standing still impossible and therefore schools are either getting better or they are getting worse. These two concepts allow us to look at school cultures on two dimensions, effectiveness-ineffectiveness, and improving-declining (see Figure 3.2). As in David Hargreaves' (1995) model, within most schools, one can find sub-cultures that exemplify several, if not all, of the types.

'Moving schools' are not only effective in 'value added' terms and for a broad range of pupil learning outcomes but people within them are also actively working together to respond to their changing context and to keep developing. They know where they are going and have systems and the 'will and the skill' (Louis and Miles, 1990) to get there. There is more than one type

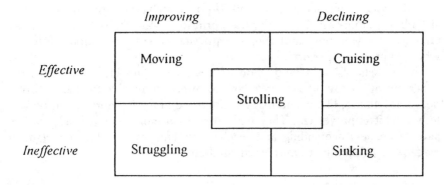

**Figure 3.2**   A typology of schools

of moving school. For example, if we look in terms of overall performance, there are some schools, usually located in more affluent areas, that are clearly 'high performing' as well as adding value. Others, in more deprived inner city or isolated rural areas, are making tremendous strides in extremely difficult circumstances. All, however, are underpinned by the norms of improving schools.

'Cruising schools' are often perceived effective by teachers, school community and outside inspectors because they appear to possess many qualities of an effective school. Often located in more affluent areas, their pupils achieve in spite of teaching quality. League tables and other rankings based on absolute achievement rather than 'value added' can give the appearance of effectiveness. Cruising schools are the 'good schools, if this were 1965' (Stoll and Fink, 1996), smugly marking time and not seeking to prepare their pupils for the changing world into which they are going. They possess powerful underpinning norms of contentment, avoidance of commitment, goal diffusion, being reactive, perpetuating total top-down leadership, conformity, nostalgia, blame, congeniality, and denial (Stoll and Fink, 1998). In such schools, if school improvement initiatives are to take hold, it will be essential to challenge and change these norms.

'Strolling schools' are neither particularly effective nor ineffective. Moving towards some kind of school improvement at an inadequate rate to cope with the pace of change, it therefore threatens to overrun their efforts. They have ill-defined and sometimes conflicting aims which inhibit improvement efforts. They may not show up on league tables or other similar indicators as 'disasters' but nonetheless they seem to be meandering into the future to the detriment of their pupils.

'Struggling schools' are ineffective and they know it, as a Lithuanian proverb highlights: 'If I don't know what I don't know, I know nothing. If I know what I don't know, I know something.' They expend considerable energy to improve. While there may be considerable unproductive thrashing about as they determine the what and how of the change process, there is a willingness to try anything that may make a difference. Ultimately they will succeed because they have the will, despite lacking the skill. Unfortunately, they are often identified as 'failing' schools which can suppress norms of responsibility for success, risk taking and celebration, and consequently act as a demotivational force to school improvement efforts.

'Sinking schools' are failing schools. They are not only ineffective; the staff, either out of apathy or ignorance, are not prepared or able to change. Isolation, self-reliance, blame and loss of faith are dominating norms, and powerfully inhibit improvement. They will often be in more deprived areas where parents are less demanding and teachers explain away failure by blaming inadequate parenting or unprepared children.

## HOW ARE CULTURE AND STRUCTURE RELATED?

There is a close link between culture and structure: indeed, they are interdependent. Most school improvement efforts focus on changes to structures:

- time – an example would be rearranging the school year into four or five periods with shorter breaks between;
- space – for example, moving the science and mathematics departments of a secondary school onto the same corridor to promote collaboration;
- roles and responsibilities – creating a post for a 'school improvement co-ordinator' or, indeed, a 'super teacher'.

This is because structures are relatively easy to manipulate and are visible, but for these structures to effect change, it is also necessary to attend to the underlying culture. Culture affects the structures put into place in a new initiative; for example a school may purchase two computers for every classroom, but because of norms of contentment, a lack of risk taking, collegiality or support, in many classrooms the computers stay in their boxes.

Structures can also, however, influence culture. As collaborative cultures can be fragile (Fink, 1997), offering extra pay and status only to certain 'super teachers' has the potential to destabilise them. If greater collegiality between teachers in schools is desirable, but the timetable does not allow teachers to meet during the day, this will act as a barrier. Andy Hargreaves (1997a) argues that it is no surprise that teaching is an isolated activity, because 'Structures of teacher isolation have their roots in schools that have been organised like egg crates since the mid nineteenth century' (p. 112). Collaboration does not just happen, however, and it is through structures – 'real tasks on which teachers can collaborate' (Hopkins et al., 1994) – that cultures can be modified.

## HOW CAN CULTURE BECOME A BLACK HOLE FOR SCHOOL IMPROVEMENT?

Thinking back to the scenarios that started this chapter, although all were well intentioned, most of them were ultimately unsuccessful. Many school improvement initiatives, particularly those introduced by national and other policy-makers, tend to emphasise what are described as empirical-rational change strategies (Chin and Benne, 1970). These are based on the fundamental assumption that schools are rational places and that the people within them will adopt proposed changes if it has been shown that it will benefit them. This 'research, development and diffusion' (R, D+D) model of educational change was first prominent in the United States in the Kennedy era because,

> it was believed that research for new knowledge and the proper technologizing and dissemination of that knowledge could solve technical, societal, indeed, *any* problems that might be encountered. It was primarily a matter of attention, application, and money – of engineering.
>
> (House, 1974, p. 225)

Such ideas emanate from Clark and Guba's (1965) linear analysis of four aspects of educational change (see Figure 3.3).

---

*Research* – to advance knowledge to serve as a basis for development
*Development* - to invent and build a solution to an operating problem
*Diffusion* – to introduce the innovation to practitioners
*Adoption* – to incorporate the innovation into schools

Based on House (1974)

---

**Figure 3.3** Clark and Guba's model of the stages of educational change

Current US examples of such an approach can be seen in various designs of the New American Schools initiative and attempts at their 'scale-up'[1] (String-field *et al.*, 1996). The recently introduced National Literacy Strategy in Britain (DfEE, 1997) is another example of such a rational model. Drawing on a range of research on effective literacy strategies and some aspects of the educational change and improvement literature, the model, while not compulsory, is intended to be implemented in every primary school in the country, as described on the front page of one national newspaper:

> Even the term during which children should learn each sound such as 'ch' and 'bl' is specified. So is the timetable for learning different spelling patterns. All primary teachers will be retrained to ensure that they can use the approved methods. (Judd, 1998, p. 1)

It is interesting to remind ourselves that the school improvement research knowledge base resulted in large measure from reflection on failed change efforts in the 1960s and 1970s, when a wide variety of changes were adopted by schools with little lasting effect (Fullan, 1991). In her revisit to the Rand Change Agent Study of the 1970s in the United States, McLaughlin (1990) concluded that 'the net return to the general investment was the adoption of many innovations, the successful implementation of a few, and the long-run continuation of still fewer' (p. 12). The failure of 'top-down' approaches and disappointing results of subsequent 'bottom-up' practitioner approaches which often did not lead to improvement in pupils' performance (Reynolds *et al.*, 1993) meant that by the 1990s, scholars were suggesting that change occurred best with a 'top-down, bottom-up' approach in which the larger system provided guidance and support while the actual change process was left to schools.

Research of House *et al.* (1972), among others, helps explain the inherent problem in the R, D+D approach: that 'situational constraints' are more important than the characteristics of particular change programmes. As House (1974, p. 235) explains, behaviour is determined more by the 'complex nature of the school as a social system', than staff development opportunities where teachers learn about and are demonstrated new teaching strategies. He concludes:

> *Avoid the primary pursuit of transferable innovations.* Distributed problems cannot be solved by a single innovation that will work in all local settings, for those settings are not only different and unpredictable in specifics, but they are also constantly changing . . . Different innovations will be more or less useful under widely different specific circumstances of their application. There is no Golden Fleece. (p. 245)

But how do we make sense of those 'situational constraints'? Morgan (1997) recommends using metaphors because they 'lead us to see, understand and manage organizations in distinctive yet partial ways' (p. 4). He argues that those who try to study or manage organisations drawing on a single perspective do not have a complete picture of the organisation:

> To illustrate, consider the popular idea that 'the organization is a machine'. The metaphor may create valuable insights about how an organization is structured to achieve predetermined results. But the metaphor is incomplete. For example, it ignores the human aspects. The metaphor is biased. For example, it elevates the importance of the rational and structural dimensions. The metaphor is misleading. For example, the organization is *not* a machine and can never really be designed, structured, and controlled as a set of inanimate parts. (p. 5)

Many approaches to school improvement, however, appear to overemphasise the machine metaphor. One of the metaphors Morgan applies is the cultural metaphor: 'It focuses attention on a human side that other metaphors ignore or gloss over . . . it shows how organization ultimately rests in shared systems of meaning . . .' (p. 147). It is an important metaphor, but it is important to remember that it is not the only one and that culture can interact with other metaphors.

One metaphor, however, that has been offered to draw together rational, structural and human aspects is that of an iceberg. It has been used to convey the difference between surface aspects and those below the surface when considering the management of change (Plant, 1987; Garrett, 1997). As all improvement is change, anyone who is trying to bring about improvement needs to understand how what goes on below the surface is likely to influence surface aspects of improvement. So, for example, the organisation, structures, roles and responsibilities, and necessary professional development opportunities for externally mandated literacy hours and school-selected technology projects are surface aspects. What is going on below the surface, however, is the real essence of school culture – people's beliefs, values and the norms that will influence how they react to these initiatives – as well as micro-political issues and the emotions people bring to their work (Hargreaves, 1997b; Fink, personal communication).

## SCHOOL CULTURE AND MICRO-POLITICS

Most observers of micro-politics in schools tend to view it as the underlying frame with which to view how schools change or stay the same (for example, Hoyle, 1986; Ball, 1987; Blase, 1991). Indeed, House (1979), reflecting on innovation over a ten-year period, separates the three perspectives that dominated thought on innovation at that time into the technological, the political and the cultural. While those who opt for technological change above the water's surface chart their course, below the surface of the water the different varieties of sea life congregate in different groups, with different customs and rituals and power relationships. Pollard (1985) is one who appears to see the link between two powerful undercurrents of school improvement. While he does not discuss school culture, per se, he chooses to describe the 'rather intangible "feel" of schools as organisations' (p. 115) as 'institutional bias'. In considering understandings of reality ('what a school is like') and normative behaviour ('what is done here') which evolve between teachers, pupils, parents and others, he rejects terms such as 'ethos' or 'climate' 'because of the unquestionable impression of cohesion which they sometimes tend to convey and because of their weak treatment of the issues of power and influence in a school' (p.115).

Micro-politics particularly come into play in relation to the issue of subcultures within schools. Indeed, it could be argued that the concept of one holistic culture is too simplistic, particularly in a large secondary school. While many models of school culture assume that the environment and cultural world of teachers in the workplace is 'a school level phenomenon' (Siskin, 1994), there are those who view it more as an agglomeration of several subcultures (McLaughlin *et al.*, 1990; Huberman, 1992). Any school may be composed of different and competing value systems, based on gender, race, language, ethnicity, religion, socio-economic status, friendship, and professional affiliation, all of which have the power to create 'a mosaic of organisational realities' (Morgan, 1997, p. 137). If role differences are added to these – between teachers, pupils, senior managers, support staff and parents – groups with their own common interests potentially could pull a school in several directions.

If we focus only on teachers, to take one example, in large secondary schools, but also in smaller schools, closer 'webs' are often formed by subsets of colleagues with different beliefs, attitudes, norms and social relationships (Siskin, 1994). Departmental divisions can prove powerful barriers to whole-school communication and collegiality. While Hargreaves (1994) argues that small group collaboration, itself, is not a problem, balkanised cultures are characterised by insulation of subgroups from each other; little movement between them; strong identification, for example, seeing oneself as a primary teacher or chemistry teacher, and with views of learning associated with that subgroup; and micropolitical issues of status, promotion, and power dynamics.

Essentially, 'Where two or more cultures coexist and interact, there will be conflicts of values in the day-to-day interaction' (Marshall, 1991, p.142). What this means is that even if one group of teachers believes that it is important to make a particular change to their teaching practice, for example adopting a new literacy approach or introducing Information Technology (ICT) across the curriculum, another group may have very different beliefs about the way to teach literacy or the importance of ICT. The school can then become a location for struggles for control, in-fighting and competition. Status issues are also involved, so in the case of the primary literacy initiative, the literacy co-ordinator may be seen as having assumed power while specialist subject teachers, for example music, may feel marginalised, especially once primary schools have flexibility to adapt the National Curriculum to focus on 'the basics'. Similarly, in a secondary school, certain departments may be favoured in the introduction of technology, whether it is through extra hardware and software, location of ICT laboratories next to certain departments, lowering of class size to accommodate ICT, or choice of staff to oversee implementation of the initiative.

Resolving these inter-group issues is often viewed as essential to the development of shared values, a necessary prerequisite of school improvement.

## HOW CAN CULTURE BECOME A FERTILE GARDEN FOR SCHOOL IMPROVEMENT?

Good seeds grow in strong cultures (Saphier and King, 1985). Understanding the school's culture, therefore, is an essential prerequisite for any internal or external change agent. Although helping practitioners to explore their own school culture is addressed in another chapter (see D. Hargreaves, Chapter 4), it is impossible to write about the significance of school culture to school improvement without referring to this issue. After all, as I have already discussed, 'assesses its current culture and works to develop positive cultural norms' is a central part of how Dean Fink and I have defined school improvement. In my work with teachers, headteachers and others involved in the improvement process, I frequently ask them to locate their school and parts of their school on the typology of schools (Stoll and Fink, 1996), and to explain why they have picked the specific location. I also encourage them to consider the norms, which three it is most necessary for them to address first in their particular circumstance, why, and to work with a colleague or partner to determine how they might go about this. Practitioners seem to find such typologies and norms help them understand the cultural processes and issues of their workplace.

Elsewhere (Stoll and Fink, 1996) we have also passed on practical guidance from Deal and Kennedy (1983) on three steps those in leadership roles can take. First, get to know their culture, by asking all involved participants what the school really stands for; noting how people spend their time; finding out who play key roles in the cultural network, and reflecting on the values they represent. As Morgan (1997) notes, a key way to understand culture and subcultures is to observe the day-to-day functioning as if one were an outsider. Second, consider how the school culture encourages or inhibits pupil progress, development and achievement, and accomplishment of school goals. To what extent is balkanisation evident? Third, arrange opportunities where people can discuss and re-examine their values. This third step, while appearing simple, is frequently neglected.

The role of leadership in relation to school culture is central. Leaders have been described as the culture founders (Schein, 1985; Nias *et al.*, 1989), their contribution or responsibility being the change of school culture by installation of new values and beliefs. Schein (1985) argues the possibility that the 'only thing of real importance that leaders do is to create and manage culture' (p. 2). Indeed, it is notable that the principals in Rosenholtz's (1989) stuck schools were described as adopting the posture of a 'burrowing animal'.

A primary deputy headteacher I knew, on starting at a new school, noticed that teachers sat in two groups in different parts of the staffroom. Before her first staff meeting, she rearranged the chairs so that everyone would be together in one group, then went out of the room to fetch some materials and return some telephone calls. Returning to the staffroom fifteen minutes later, she found the chairs had been moved back into their original positions. In this experience, she was given a quick lesson in the importance of 'priority on meaning before management' (Fullan and Hargreaves, 1991, p. 86).

## A WORD OF CAUTION

It has been suggested that collegiality as developed through 'site based' management and collaborative school development plans is just another way in which teachers are 'cajoled' into accepting external mandates (Smyth, 1991). Indeed, strong cultures are viewed by some as promoting dominant interests through managerial manipulation (Bates, 1987; Jeffcut, 1993); that culture becomes problematic when treated as 'a variable – as something "the organization has" which has to be manipulated and controlled' rather than 'something "the organization is" – as the product of negotiated and shared symbols and meanings' (Angus, 1996, p. 974, drawing on Meek, 1988). For example, within schools, senior managers may re-arrange the timetable, a structure, to enable to teachers to work together. Such a managerial arrangement can be seen as an example of contrived collegiality (Hargreaves, 1994) as described by one teacher in an LEA improvement project in which I was involved:

> Last year started well . . . even then, it got more difficult towards the end of the year; the enthusiasm wears off. This year we're still keeping the journals going, but they must be written in their own time, because our non-contact time is to work with our

partner, and so it's not non-contact time when you're actually going into their class, and somebody's covering your class.

Morgan (1997) helpfully distinguishes between the need to create networks of shared meaning, linking people around positive visions, values and norms and the use of culture as a manipulative management tool – 'values engineering'. He suggests that leaders and managers should ask themselves, 'What impact am I having on the social construction of reality in my organization?' and 'What can I do to have a different and more positive impact?' (p. 148).

Ultimately, however, the development of a fertile garden for school improvement is likely to depend on reculturing.

## RECULTURING

Reculturing is 'the process of developing new values, beliefs and norms. For systematic reform it involves building new conceptions about instruction . . . and new forms of professionalism for teachers . . .' (Fullan, 1996, p. 420). This is no task for the faint hearted. Indeed, Morgan (1997) maintains it is:

> a challenge of transforming mind-sets, visions, paradigms, images, metaphors, beliefs, and shared meanings that sustain existing . . . realities and of creating a detailed language and code of behaviour through which the desired new reality can be lived on a daily basis . . . It is about inventing what amounts to a new way of life. (p. 143)

For such change to occur, 'normative-re-educative' strategies are necessary (Chin and Benne, 1970). These emphasise the pivotal importance of clarifying and reconstructing values: 'These approaches centre on the notion that people technology is just as necessary as thing technology in working out desirable changes in human affairs' (p. 45). Most significantly, they focus on the need to improve problem-solving capacities of those within organisations, a key capacity for school improvement.

Returning to the link between culture and structure, in *Change Forces*, Fullan (1993) proposes:

> the interesting hypothesis that reculturing leads to restructuring more effectively than the reverse. In most restructuring reforms new structures are expected to result in new behaviours and cultures, but mostly fail to do so. There is no doubt a reciprocal relationship between structural and cultural change, but it is much more powerful when teachers and administrators begin working in new ways only to discover that school structures are ill-fitted to the new orientations and must be altered. This is a more productive sequence than the reverse when rapidly implemented new structures create confusion, ambiguity, and conflict ultimately leading to retrenchment. (p. 68)

If schools are to become professional communities (Louis, Kruse *et al.*, 1995) and to continue to be effective in the future, they will need to build structures which promote interrelationships and interconnections, and simultaneously develop cultures that promote collegiality and individuality (Hargreaves, 1994). Although it sounds paradoxical, not only must the school's culture promote group learning but it must honour individuals, 'mavericks', because creativity and novelty will be required to deal with an unknowable future and prevent 'groupthink' (Janis, 1972). In effect, cultures and counter-cultures will need to interact to find innovative solutions to complex and unpredictable circumstances (Fink and Stoll, 1998). Hargreaves (1994) promotes the notion of teachers flexibly and creatively engaged in different problem-solving tasks: the 'moving mosaic' (Toffler, 1990). Their orientation is one of continuous learning and improvement. They are characterised by collaboration, opportunism, adaptable partnerships, and alliances. Thus membership of groups overlaps and shifts over time to meet the needs of the circumstance and context.

Reculturing, however, needs to go beyond redefining teacher cultures; it must include pupil and community cultures as well. Pupils can be a conservative force when teachers attempt to change their practice (Rudduck, 1991; McLaughlin and Talbert, 1993). Similarly, as noted earlier, communities are often resistant to change (Fink, 1997). Change agents must therefore attend to both.

## CONCLUSION

Real improvement cannot come from anywhere other than within schools themselves, and 'within' is a complex web of values and beliefs, norms, social and power relationships and emotions. Changing schools is not just about changing curricula, teaching and learning strategies, assessment, structures, and roles and responsibilities. It does not just happen by producing plans as a result of external inspections or reviews, or by setting targets because data, even valid and sensitively analysed data, suggests that all pupils or certain groups of pupils could be doing better. It requires an understanding of and respect for the different meanings and interpretations people bring to educational initiatives, and the nurturing of the garden within which new ideas can bloom.

## NOTE

1. Scaling up involves the attempt to spread ideas from pilot schools to a much larger group of schools.

## ACKNOWLEDGEMENTS

I would like to thank Dean Fink for his feedback on an earlier draft, and Chris Watkins and the teachers involved in our school-based masters degree course for their insights.

# 4

# Helping Practitioners Explore Their School's Culture

## DAVID HARGREAVES

### INTRODUCTION

It is assumed in this chapter that the motive for exploring one's own school culture is to enhance effectiveness or as an element of a programme of school improvement. I assume also that you, the practitioner, are a headteacher or a senior member of staff engaged in such an endeavour.

As a school leader, you have in this regard three major tasks in relation to school culture – diagnostic, directional and managerial. The *diagnostic* task is that of finding a method or technique of diagnosing the present character of your school's culture. The *directional* task is that of deciding in what ways you want the school's culture to change. The *managerial* task is that of devising and implementing a strategy for moving the school's culture in the chosen direction. The three are, of course, inter-linked. To take the most obvious example, all the methods suggested below of diagnosing your school's culture are heavily value-loaded and your preference for one or other diagnostic tool will influence the way in which you solve the subsequent directional and managerial tasks. So observe how your own values shape your preferences and prejudices at the diagnostic stage.

### DIAGNOSING YOUR SCHOOL'S CULTURE

The initial questions you face are these.

*Who is to be involved in making the diagnosis?* You alone? The head and senior management? The whole staff? Governors? Students? Parents? Outsiders/critical friends, such as inspectors, advisers and consultants? The main arguments for involving as many people as possible is that you may uncover very different perceptions of aspects of the school's culture and this will affect subsequent action; and the involvement of people in the diagnosis may motivate them to engage in a later development of, or change in, the school's culture.

48

*How much time and energy are you prepared to give to the diagnostic task?* Simple diagnostic devices don't take much time, but they naturally lack depth. Indeed, simple devices often use the concept of school culture in simplistic fashion, whereas there may in reality be a staff culture (with its own sub-cultures) and a very different student culture (again with sub-cultures) as well as conflicting perceptions of both by governors and parents and outsiders. How much time can you afford for what degree of depth?

*Is your method of diagnosis direct or indirect?* I discuss direct methods below, but it's worth remembering that there are indirect methods, such as your school's internal review, the views of students and parents, an Ofsted report, and all such evidence that comes to you anyway as feedback on the character or ethos of the school, though the word culture may not be used. Such evidence is important, since it can be used to check on the validity of the perceptions of the school's culture emerging from the use of a more direct method.

Perhaps the simplest direct method is to draw on one of the 'two-by-two' typologies and ask those involved to say which type the school is closest to and then engage in the discussion that arises from attempts to classify the school in this way. For instance, by getting the participants to judge whether the school is broadly effective or ineffective, and improving or deteriorating, you can place the school's culture in one of the five cells in Stoll and Fink's (1996) ingenious typology (see Chapter 3). In my experience, participants find this difficult (except in extreme cases) since they judge the school is effective in some ways and not in others, and the same for the improving-declining dimension. Moreover, in a period of massive change in schools, few teachers feel the label 'strolling' to be appropriate to them. However, the basic concepts are easy to understand and could, with a brief explanation, also be handled by parents and many pupils.

A rather different four element typology of schools is suggested by Handy and Aitken (1986, pp. 83ff).

- *The club culture* (a spider's web) – the school as an informal club of like-minded people whose task is to achieve the mission of the head who is at the centre of things.
- *The role culture* (a pyramid) – the school as a set of job-boxes co-ordinated to execute the work of the organization, which the head manages through a formal system and procedures of a bureaucratic kind.
- *The task culture* (a grid) – the school as a friendly matrix of variably composed groups and teams which achieve a range of planned tasks to solve organizational problems.
- *The person culture* (a cluster) – the school as a minimally organized resource for the development of its members' talents and exercise of their skills.

Another four-element typology of teacher (not school) cultures is that offered by Andy Hargreaves (1994) – individualism, collaboration, contrived collegiality and balkanization (see Chapter 3).

Both these typologies could be turned into a diagnostic instrument in which teachers are presented with cameos of each culture type and use these to make a diagnosis of their own school culture. In practice, participants will rarely identify the school with a single type and will be influenced by the labels. Larger schools and almost all secondary schools, for example, inevitably display a degree of balkanization, and collaboration and individualism may characterize different parts of the school or different aspects of life in school. A collaborative culture sounds desirable, but the other three cultures are clearly objectionable. Although there is much insightful detail into teachers within the four types, they may strike some as rigid (can't a school be a mix of types?) and static (doesn't a school vary its mix of types over time or between situations?). Though to teachers a 'person culture' will probably have more favourable connotations than a 'role culture', the labels are more neutral in the typology devised by Handy and Aitken, who emphasize that a real school will rarely be of a single type. Successful schools, they say, get 'the right mix at the right time', an appropriately dynamic model of how school cultures work, but difficult to capture in a written diagnostic instrument.

At the other extreme are schemes and devices that are conceptually more complex but also much more time-consuming to use. Take, for example, two typologies I devised (Hargreaves D., 1995). The first assumes that all schools, like all social collectivities, face two fundamental tasks: one is to achieve the goals for which they exist, and the other is to maintain harmonious relationships. These two tasks are often in tension, in that pressure to achieve a key goal (e.g. student achievement) may be at a cost in relationships (e.g. making students work hard). Schools require *social controls* over teachers and students so that they work together in orderly ways, concentrate on teaching and learning and avoid the ubiquitous possibilities of distraction and delay. At the same time, schools have to try to maintain *social cohesion*, social relationships that are satisfying, supportive and sociable. This I easily turned into another two-by-two typology, in which there are four extreme types in the corners, according to whether the social control and social cohesion dimensions are high or low, as follows.

*The 'formal' school culture* (high social control, low social cohesion) puts pressure on students to achieve learning goals, including curriculum targets and exam or test performance, but with weak social cohesion between staff and students. School life is orderly, scheduled, disciplined with a strong work ethic. Academic expectations are high, with a low toleration for those who don't live up to them. To students, staff are relatively strict, though institutional loyalty is valued. The school is often 'a tight ship' fostering 'traditional values'.

*The 'welfarist' school culture* (high social cohesion, low social control) has a relaxed, friendly and cosy atmosphere. The focus is on individual student development within a nurturing environment and child-centred educational philosophy. Work pressure is low; so academic goals get a lower priority than, or even become displaced by, social cohesion goals of social adjustment and

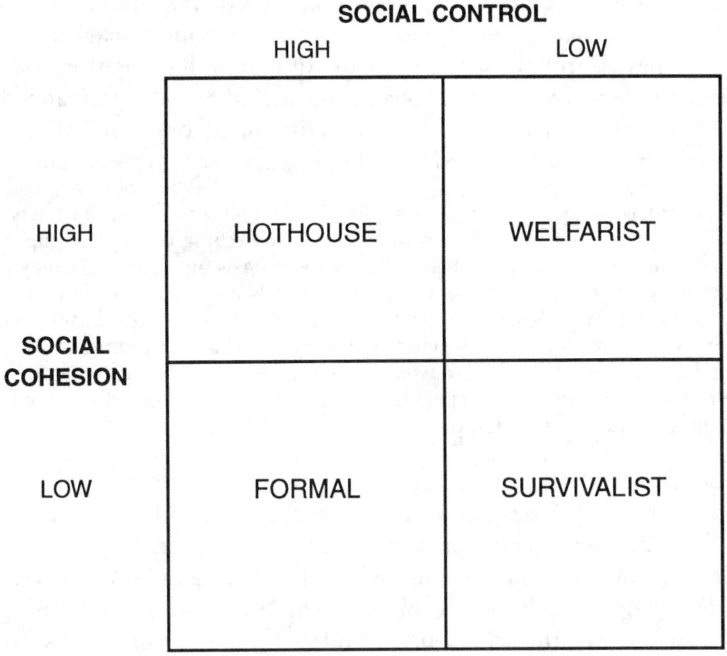

**SOCIAL CONTROL**

| | HIGH | LOW |
|---|---|---|
| **HIGH** | HOTHOUSE | WELFARIST |
| **LOW** | FORMAL | SURVIVALIST |

**SOCIAL COHESION**

Figure 4.1

life skills. The 'caring' inner-city school with a strong pastoral system ex-emplifies this friendly climate of contentment.

The 'hothouse' school culture (high social cohesion, high social control) is rather frenetic. All are under pressure to participate actively in the full range of school life. The motto is join in, enjoy yourself, and be a success. Expectations of work, personal development and team spirit are high. Teachers are enthusi-astic and committed and want pupils to be the same. It is a culture that is not overtly coercive or tyrannical, but teachers and students easily become anxious that they are not pulling their weight or doing as well as they should.

The 'survivalist' school culture (low social cohesion, low social control), in its most extreme form, veers towards the 'school in difficulty' or 'failing school' – social relations are poor, teachers striving to maintain basic control and allowing pupils to avoid academic work in exchange for not engaging in misconduct. Lessons move at a leisurely pace; students under-achieve. Teachers feel unsup-ported by senior colleagues and enjoy little professional satisfaction. Life is lived a day at a time. Many students feel alienated from their work which bores them. The ethos is often one of insecurity and low morale.

When this typology is turned into diagnostic devices (Ainscow et al., 1995), it is one in which all the staff of a school participate as an activity on a professional training day. Staff sit at tables in groups of four. On the table before them is the square of the typology, but it is divided into an 8-by-8 games board as for chess. At each corner is a different coloured marker, to indicate the four types clearly but without the use of names that might introduce bias. 'Players' are then given a set of four cards, each of a colour to match that on a corner, and on each of which is a description of one type of school. For example, the cameo of the 'formal' school (secondary version) reads:

> We regard ourselves as a well-disciplined sort of school, one that sets store on traditional values. The head runs the place as something of a 'tight ship' with high expectations of us teachers. There's a strong emphasis on student learning and we're expected to get good exam results and everybody's very proud when we do. We also like to do well in games and athletics, which is another important aspect of achievement. We expect students to be independent and to stand on their own feet whatever their background. We're clear what the school stands for and what we're about. We're naturally rather suspicious of new ideas and put more trust in what's been shown to work best through past experience.

Players are asked to think about their own school in relation to the four cameos by reading through the cards privately and without discussion. They then place their own school, *as it now is*, in one of the 64 squares and record this on a personal grid supplied to each player. This usually requires some hard thinking, as only rarely does a player locate the school exactly in a corner. Usually players see the school being pulled in different directions, so finding the extent of the 'mix', and thus the appropriate square on the grid, demands reflection. They are then asked to say in which square they would *ideally* like the school to be, and record that also on the grid. Each group then shares their private records and discusses as the issue. They are encouraged to try to reach consensus on the 'actual' and 'ideal' location of the their school. This group discussion is in itself a contributor to staff development.

The technique has been tried in some 150 schools – primary, secondary and special – in different areas of the UK and has never failed to be a professional development and/or research activity that staff enjoy. The culture of their school, as it is and as they would like it to be, is rarely discussed quite so explicitly in the everyday life of the school, but it's a topic on which staff have definite views. While staff take a coffee break, the individual records (*not* the group ones) are collated and transferred to two transparencies, one for 'actual' and one for 'ideal'. These are then revealed to the staff.

In some schools, there is considerable consensus as to the school's actual and ideal climate. In others, there is more agreement on the one than on the other. Figure 4.2 gives the results of the activity in a secondary school with 38 staff. The dots represent the actual school culture, and the stars the ideal. You can make sense of the patterns in various ways, of which the simplest is to divide the square into the quadrants closest to each corner. Only one teacher (a newcomer?) places the actual school culture in the survivalist quadrant, and it is no-one's ideal. Evidently most staff (25) locate the school in the formal culture quadrant, but only one teacher places the ideal here. A clear majority

HOTHOUSE                                                                                    WELFARIST

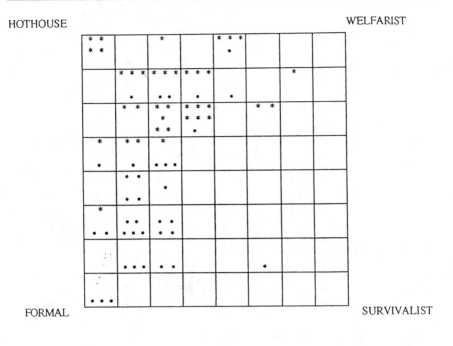

FORMAL                                                                                        SURVIVALIST

• = actual          * = ideal

**Figure 4.2**

(31) locate their ideal in the hothouse quadrant, and most of the rest are not far distant. Indeed, ten teachers think the school is already in this quadrant. Here is a case where there is greater agreement on where the school culture should be than where it is – a positive state of affairs on which to build. How do you interpret Figure 4.3?

Results sometimes come as a surprise, especially to the head and senior management teams, because they underestimate the extent to which staff may deviate from the management values and perceptions. As Alvesson (1993, p. 29) notes, 'Organizational culture and managerial culture are not the same', a fact of which staff are always conscious but about which management develops a convenient amnesia. Indeed, it is worth asking the SMT to sit on a separate table, since this both helps other players to be open in what they say and provides an independent record of SMT perceptions, which are sometimes out of line with the rest of the staff. 'Maps' of the school's actual and ideal cultures are worthwhile, but bear in mind their limitations. Remember the Handy and Aitken point that actual (and ideal) cultures are dynamic, being a mix of types that at the best will vary over time and by situation. This is occluded by the static maps, but the conversations of the teachers, both while completing the task in groups and while discussing the maps in the feedback session, are much more informative about how the culture of the school is understood and experienced by staff.

HOTHOUSE                                                     WELFARIST

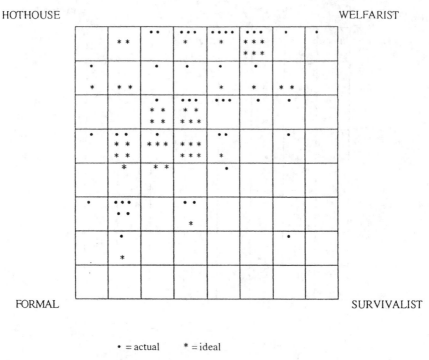

FORMAL                                                       SURVIVALIST

• = actual      * = ideal

**Figure 4.3**

There is no space here to report on the fascinating variety of outcomes of this activity; different patterns of cultures require different approaches to the follow-up. Where the staff are more agreed on their ideal culture than on the actual, the discussion can focus positively on what is inhibiting them from moving towards the ideal. In the few cases where there is low agreement on both actual and ideal, the follow-up needs to handled with great sensitivity.

For these reasons, it is probably best if the technique is led by an outsider, such as a consultant or an LEA adviser. Do *not* be tempted to lead it yourself: this will provoke suspicion and discourage honest responses and open discussion. NQTs and teachers who are new to the school should not have their views recorded on the collective version, for it has been shown that they tend to be 'deviant' and so reduce consensus: it evidently takes a year or two for teachers to be able to judge a school's culture with any accuracy. There is a student version of the technique, which works well with both upper primary and secondary students. This can be illuminating for a brave staff, not least because students tend to take a harsh view of the actual culture and see a greater gap than do staff between actual and ideal.

This diagnostic device has considerable potential. You can use the cameos developed in Cambridge manual (Ainscow *et al.*, 1994) or invent your own. Indeed, you can change the character of the basic concepts to suit your own purposes. For example, you could take the dimensions from the Stoll and Fink typology, write up four new cameos (effective + improving; effective + declining; ineffective + improving; ineffective + declining) for the corners but still use the grid and the approach with players working on the actual and ideal.

If you think this technique is too complex and time-consuming, but are unhappy with the very simple diagnostic methods, then there are devices that fall between the two. For instance, you can take any bi-polar set of concepts or practices relating to school culture, choosing whatever seems to fit your circumstances or preferences, and set them out on a scale of eight steps as follows:

| | | |
|---|---|---|
| warm and friendly | ● ● ● ● ● ● ● ● | cool and hostile |
| high expectations | ● ● ● ● ● ● ● ● | low expectations |
| professionally rewarding | ● ● ● ● ● ● ● ● | professionally unrewarding |
| exam-focused | ● ● ● ● ● ● ● ● | insufficiently exam-focused |
| strongly led by the SMT | ● ● ● ● ● ● ● ● | weakly led by the SMT |
| collaborative | ● ● ● ● ● ● ● ● | individualistic |

The staff simply mark the dot closest to their own view of where the school's culture now is, and where they would like it to be. The overall range and average scores, which are readily calculated, are then reported back for discussion and action planning.

A similar technique has been used by MacBeath (1998) in his adaptation of Stoll and Fink's teacher questionnaire as a tool for examining school climate and organizational health. The 54-item questionnaire is laid out as shown in Table 4.1.

The collated responses can be used to provide a diagnosis of the school's current culture and to generate a staff discussion of future directions and appropriate action plans.

One of my own models (Hargreaves D., 1995) adopted a similar method, as part of an attempt to develop a more systematic and sophisticated approach to school culture by assuming that it is more than a set of teacher attitudes or perceptions, but at the same time is not reducible to the two dimensions used in many typologies. Five dimensions or underlying structures are proposed – political, micropolitical, maintenance, development, and service. The **political structure** refers to the character and formal distribution of power, authority and status among the staff. The **micropolitical structure** is the informal network of individuals and groups who plot, plan and act together to advance their interests. The political and micropolitical structures interlock, often as a contest between the official functioning of the school and the unofficial manoeuvring of the staff groupings with distinctive subcultures. Maintenance and development (Hargreaves and Hopkins, 1991) are structures that arise from the school's dual needs for stability and change. **Maintenance structures,** such as standing committees and procedures, are often hardly noticed because of their sheer familiarity, but they are powerful in their impact. At the same time, the management of change requires **development structures** or temporary systems for specific, short-term development tasks. Maintenance and development structures, like political and micropolitical structures, are often in tension. The **service structure** forges the social relations, including rights and

**Table 4.1**

**The school now**                                                   **The effective school**

1 = strongly agree                                                   1 = crucial
2 = agree                                                            2 = very important
3 = uncertain                                                        3 = quite important
4 = disagree                                                         4 = not very important
5 = strongly disagree                                                5 = not at all important

| 1 | 2 | 3 | 4 | 5 | | 1 | 2 | 3 | 4 | 5 |
|---|---|---|---|---|---|---|---|---|---|---|
| 1 | 2 | 3 | 4 | 5 | Pupils respect teachers in this school | 1 | 2 | 3 | 4 | 5 |
| 1 | 2 | 3 | 4 | 5 | Teachers believe that all children in this school can be successful | 1 | 2 | 3 | 4 | 5 |
| 1 | 2 | 3 | 4 | 5 | Teachers regularly discuss ways of improving pupils learning | 1 | 2 | 3 | 4 | 5 |
| 1 | 2 | 3 | 4 | 5 | Teachers regularly observe each other in the classroom and give feedback | 1 | 2 | 3 | 4 | 5 |
| 1 | 2 | 3 | 4 | 5 | Standards set for pupils are consistently upheld across the school | 1 | 2 | 3 | 4 | 5 |
| 1 | 2 | 3 | 4 | 5 | Teachers share similar beliefs and attitudes about effective teaching and learning | 1 | 2 | 3 | 4 | 5 |

duties between the staff and the school's clients – students, parents and governing bodies.

This typology organises the possible variations in these five dimensions around two types of school, labelled as *traditional* and *collegial*. Staff are presented not with single words or phrases but short cameos. For example, the political structure reads:

*The real decisions in this school are made by the head and senior staff though there is consultation sometimes*  ● ● ● ● ● ● ● ●  *Before major policy decisions are taken there's full and free discussion by the whole staff and attempts are made to get full agreement*

and the development structure reads:

*This is a supportive place if teachers want to try out new ideas. There's often somebody to try them out with. Staff are encouraged by management who make time for teachers to do new things*  ● ● ● ● ● ● ●  *There are some good ideas around, but they usually come from management, not classroom teachers, so it's a bit of a top-down school. If you do something new, do it on your own in private*

As you will perhaps imagine, staff tended to locate the school's present culture (very much) more to the left than the SMT in the political dimension and more to the right on the development dimension. Indeed, the evident gap, sometimes considerable, between the staff's perceptions and those of head and SMT is in my view one of the more useful outcomes of these activities.

Again, you could use the Cambridge cameos or invent your own. Cameos are more interesting and thought-provoking for teachers, but you cannot be sure which elements within the cameo are being responded to. Using single words or phrases avoids this problem, but they are less interesting and, because one side is easily seen as the 'right' response i.e. the one favoured by management, they are less likely to elicit honest reactions. Whichever format you use, the activity is best presented as staff development led by an outside friend of the school rather than by you.

## CHOOSING THE DIRECTION FOR YOUR SCHOOL'S CULTURE

My advice is that whilst you are diagnosing the school's actual culture you also tap staff (and perhaps student) conceptions of the school culture they would like, but this assumes you trust them to choose a new cultural direction. If all or most staff can agree on a future direction at the time that they diagnose the present culture, there is a motivational spur to close the gap and to work out the positive strategies for so doing. Where the gap between ideal and actual is relatively small, there is a boost to morale; where the gap is relatively large, then means for devising strategies for change should be discussed immediately to prevent demoralization.

If you think staff would not make a prudent choice and/or you have your own strong views on what the future culture should be, you will prefer a diagnostic technique that does not entail stating a preference for an ideal culture. Your own view of the future direction of the school and the associated change in culture will normally be sufficiently loose to allow all the staff to believe that their ideas have much to contribute and that it is through discussion and debate that some of the shape and much of the detail will be determined. In other words, whilst you do not specify very precisely the culture you want, you may wish to enhance your understanding of culture in order to enrich your preference for the *kind* of organization and/or community you want the school to be.

School leaders tend, for understandable reasons, to want a culture that is clear, consistent and consensual. All the staff are pulling in the same shared direction, the argument goes, so we are more likely to achieve our goals. Indeed, this is the implicit line of much writing on school cultures, which in recent years have emphasized collaboration as a key to school effectiveness and improvement. In striving for such an ideal, school leaders risk blinding themselves to lack of consensus that characterizes organizations in real life and to exaggerating the negative effects of a lack of consensus. Of course, a school at war with itself is unlikely to be happy or successful or effective, but the alternative is not necessarily conflict-free consensus and collaboration.

Homogeneity is not always a sign of strength. Elements of dissent and ambiguity within a culture are potentially healthy, particularly when (as is generally true today) schools need to be highly adaptable if they are to prosper in a turbulent environment. Whilst ineffective schools resemble unhappy families in some respects, the 'happy family' model of school culture may not be as desirable as it appears at first sight. The most effective school leader may be a skilful *manager* of ambiguity and conflict rather than their *destroyer*. Where teachers feel they have to suppress their differences and dissent, especially from school leaders, there is a risk of creating the mere appearance of a happy family that masks a deeper discord. The cleverest heads learn how to channel dissent along positive paths that indirectly contribute to the school's goals – or at least into the harmless side-roads where most of us like or need to dawdle sometimes. In other words, their model of the school cultures is less one of *sub-cultural division of an organization* and more one of *multi-cultural diversity within a pluralistic community*. We can learn to apply the concept 'multi-cultural' positively more widely than to the school's ethnic composition (cf Hofstede, 1991, and Cray and Mallory, 1998). Wise leaders know which slightly deviant minorities to cultivate: one can never be sure when they might be needed.

School effectiveness arguably depends most of all on the classroom effectiveness of each teacher. For school leaders to provide conditions in which each classroom teacher is maximally effective in the art and science of teaching for student learning, a 'thin' school culture, or one that has a bare content requiring staff assent, may be all that is required. The current fashion is for a 'thick' school culture – lots of it, requiring consensus to its themes and close collaboration in its enactment. There is something to be said for a 'thin' culture that focuses on supporting high quality, somewhat individualistic, classroom practitioners, not least because such a culture may be more easily achieved by school leaders than the 'thick' cultures of many textbooks!

If you find these tensions as fascinatingly provocative as I do, you will enjoy Joanne Martin's *Cultures in Organizations* (1992), which outlines three perspectives on organizations – integration, differentiation and fragmentation – from which any particular organization, such as your school, may be interpreted and understood. Because she emphasizes that any organization can be looked at with profit from each perspective, you will come away not with simple recipes, but with an enriched understanding of how your school culture needs to be examined from these different perspective if you are to understand and shape it.

## MANAGING THE CHANGE TO THE NEW CULTURE

This, it almost goes without saying, is the most difficult of the three tasks, but is easier to accomplish if you have a clear diagnosis of the current culture and a sharp picture of the culture towards which the school is striving. School leaders don't always meet these basic criteria before setting about cultural change. I've known heads who have tried to change their school culture without taking steps to verify the nature of the school's actual culture and with only the vaguest of visions for the future culture.

As with the diagnostic task, there are direct and indirect methods of cultural change. In the direct method, there is a 'full frontal' attempt to change the staff's shared beliefs, attitudes and values at the core of an institutional culture. This approach seems to be encouraged in parts of the literature, as in Schein's (1985, p. 2) much-quoted contention that 'the only thing of real importance that leaders do is to create and manage culture'. This often leads to the assumption that the staff will be persuaded, on some kind of rational basis, to shed older beliefs, attitudes and values under the spell of the new ones offered by the leader's stated vision. In reality most people's beliefs, attitudes and values are far more resistant to change than leaders typically allow, and direct attempts to change them may stimulate increased resistance. Schools, especially secondary ones, function in part as sophisticated bureaucracies. That is good, insofar as bureaucracies entail rational decision making, orderliness and fairness – try feudalism as an alternative! Remember Max Weber's warning that:

> Once it is fully established, bureaucracy is among those social structures which are the hardest to destroy . . . And where bureaucracy of administration has been completely carried through, a form of power relation is established that is practically unshatterable (Gerth and Mills, 1948, p. 228).

It is prudent, then, to assume that only under rather unusual circumstances will staff beliefs, attitudes and values or operating systems be open to rapid change. Such circumstances include the following.

- *The school faces an obvious crisis.* It is not enough for the leader(s) to recognize the crisis or simply to announce to a sceptical audience that, as the saying goes, the *status quo* is not an option. The crisis must be evident to all. Examples include a highly critical Ofsted report or a rapidly falling roll which puts staff jobs or even the viability of the school in jeopardy. Acknowledging the need for change to resolve the crisis motivates staff to listen to potentially persuasive arguments about future directions and the steps that need to be taken. The lack of a crisis is the enemy of cultural change. Remember John Harvey Jones's (1988, p. 127) dictum that:

  > the engine of change is dissatisfaction with the present . . . It is much more difficult to change things when everything is apparently going well.

- *You are a charismatic leader/headteacher.* If you have real charisma, cultural change can be more radical and achieved faster, but most school leaders are not particularly charismatic and do not command instant trust, loyalty and followership. Unless you have powerful evidence to the contrary, assume charisma is not your strongest card. If you are entering your second headship, don't assume that any charisma attributed to you by the staff of your first school automatically carries over into a second. Charisma is more context-bound and situation-specific than some people imagine. Remember, too, that staff talk themselves *into* new beliefs, attitudes and values more readily than they let you talk them *out* of old values and attitudes.

- *You are the successor to a very poor leader/headteacher.* This can be almost as valuable as an obvious crisis. Staff will be looking for a change that is strongly led, either because the previous direction was mistaken or (more likely) the school simply lacked direction. For a few months at least staff will be unusually open to new ideas and arguments. If, on the other hand, you are following someone who was regarded as a very good leader/head, then it will be very difficult, if not impossible, to change the cultural direction in any speedy or direct way.

If none of these special conditions applies, assume that cultural change will be rather slow and will involve indirect methods.

The greatest obstacle to a new cultural direction may be the existence of a 'resistance group' or 'rump', varying in size from a small, hostile group to a sizeable proportion of the staff. Resistance groups are not the same as 'subcultures', which diverge either from the management culture or other subcultures in some regards, but do not actively threaten them. Healthy subcultures among a school staff do not challenge the school leaders' right to manage nor the right of other colleagues to take a different point of view. Resistance groups are *counter-cultures*, who are actively subversive of management and intolerant of differences between subcultures. Such a group saps the morale and commitment of the supporters of change, and exasperates the leader(s).

The most effect method of countering the resistance group is simply stated: get rid of them, or at least the most active and vocal ones. Such action is normal and unremarkable in a business or industrial setting, where there is an open rule that those who cannot work with a new management direction must seek work elsewhere. In schools, by contrast, this very notion is hardly mentionable. It is, of course, nevertheless done. Indeed, there are indications that it is a key measure used by heads whose task it is to turn round a school in difficulty. Peter Clark, the man brought in to deal in 1996 with the Ridings School (which the tabloids called 'the school from hell') lost around a third of the old staff. The new head of Newall Green School transformed the school between 1991 and 1993 and the Ofsted (1994) report of this success curtly notes that the reduction in some 20 per cent of the staff 'was achieved largely through voluntary redeployment, early retirement and severance'. I suspect from other very similar cases known to me, such as that of now famous Phoenix School in Hammersmith (see Whatford, 1998, p. 79), that losing some staff is a precondition of school improvement from a low base and this requires real determination and skill (including managing the short-term insecurity that will be experienced by the rest of the staff) as well as humanity towards those departing. There are ways of doing this that are compatible with preserving a teacher's dignity.

The selection and recruitment of new (or replacement) staff is crucial, of course. Some leaders see the key test as essentially ideological: do the candidates share the values of the school and will they fit in with the desired culture? Other leaders use an effectiveness test: are they first class in the classroom with stu-

dents? Ideal candidates pass both tests, perhaps. The danger is letting the ideological test outweigh more professional considerations, but this is done only by
weak leaders threatened by a degree of cultural diversity within the school.

If there is no resistance group, or a small one that can be ignored and
sidelined as occasion requires, then less drastic strategies for cultural development need to be considered. These can be no more than suggestions, based on
observation and experience. As other chapters in this book make clear, much is
known about the correlates of effective schools – or more strictly of schools
organized in currently conventional ways judged by rather narrow criteria of
effectiveness – but relatively little about the causes of effectiveness. And there
are so few high quality research studies of school improvement that knowledge
of what works in what circumstances, and for how long the improvement
endures, is largely lacking. My suggestions include the following:

- choose your style
- prioritize the focus
- change behaviour
- devise supportive structures
- monitor the effects and penetration of cultural change
- import assistance
- be your own culture.

## Choose your style

There are many different leadership styles for changing the culture. You should
choose one that has a reasonable fit with your personality, but make sure that
you're aware of the strengths and weaknesses of the one you prefer. The
different approaches are quite well documented. Take the following four (Bate,
1994).

- the *aggressive* style, imposed change by unilateral and autocratic methods.
- the *conciliative* style, the joint approach through discussion and
  collaboration.
- the *corrosive* style, which is unplanned, evolutionary and coalitional.
- the *indoctrinative* style, re-education through training and development.

No style is free from disadvantages, and few leaders manage change successfully with just one style.

## Prioritize the focus for your planned change to the culture

A school's culture, even a relatively 'thin' one, has many features. You can't
change everything at once, so don't be too ambitious. Decide which element of
the culture most needs attention, by asking:

- which aspect of the school needs to be changed most urgently?
- which will yield some tangible results quite quickly?

- which will win over, and be highly rewarding to, the staff involved?
- which elements of the culture need changing to promote all this?

If the school is 'failing' or 'in difficulty' then it is likely that the social order of the school and/or a concentration on better teaching and learning will become the priority and so a culture which supports these tasks has to be created.

## Change behaviour: attitudes follow suit

Culture contains mental elements – beliefs, attitudes, values – and behavioural elements – practices, routines, habits, ceremonials and rituals. It is commonly thought that changing the mental aspects is the obvious or even natural way of changing a culture. True, if the school staff can be persuaded to adopt new values, they may well change their patterns of behaviour to match their new values; but values are very difficult to change in a direct way. It may be easier to persuade people to adopt, perhaps on a trial basis, some new ways of working – new forms of pedagogy in the classroom; mutual observation in classrooms with a view to sharing good practice; forming a working group to explore how to get parents to be more supportive of students' homework. People then tend to adjust their beliefs, attitudes and values in line with their changed behaviour, and these become the seeds from which a new culture germinates.

## Devise supportive structures

Though you would not always realize it from the way some books and articles on school culture are written, cultures depend heavily on underlying structures. As Anthony (1994, p. 3) puts it:

> the attempt to manage culture without structural change is likely to be at best ineffective and at worst dangerous, [for] structure is not only a necessary accompaniment of cultural change but . . . it often provides the best means of achieving it.

There are two main types of structure – physical and organizational/social structures. Physical structures are hugely influential, not least on organizational and social structures, but are quickly taken for granted and so largely ignored in life in organizations. Think how the layout of classrooms, staff rooms, administrative corridors and the location of gymnasia, workshops and laboratories influence social relationships and the frequency and character of interactions. Social structures are characterized by the distribution of power, authority, status and influence.

The art of shaping culture includes maximizing the mutual modification of structure and culture and recognizing that it is often easier and more effective to change the structure than to change the culture directly whilst leaving the underlying structures undisturbed. Change often requires the creation of development structures, such as working parties and task groups charged with a particular mission – rather than trying to use maintenance structures, such as standing committees, where the culture and social dynamics are often directed to preservation of the status quo. So whenever you want to change an element of culture, especially beliefs, attitudes and values, ask yourself:

- what physical, organizational and social structures underlie and reinforce this aspect of the culture?
- in what ways do these structures inhibit cultural change?
- what (short-term) changes need to be made to the structures to promote cultural change?
- what (longer-term) changes need to be made to the structures to sustain the cultural change once it occurs?

The hardest thing for school leaders – especially men – is fully to recognize that the core of school improvement is what goes on in classrooms where individual teachers have maximal professional autonomy and that school cultures need to be transformed so that, in what may be a wide variety of ways, they empower and energize teachers to be better classroom teachers. This may well entail in part a change in the social structures concerned with the distribution of power. In the words of one of the United States' most sceptical and trenchant critics of recent reform movements:

> when teachers advocate educational reform, they almost never are referring to what they can or should do in their own classrooms . . . [A]ltering and supporting what goes on classrooms will require changes in the style of classroom and social governance. There are relationships between teacher and students, between teacher and parents, between one teacher and other teachers, between teachers and principal; when these power relationships change in ways that truly alter the decision making processes governing the composition and atmosphere of classrooms, desirable educational outcomes stand a better chance of being realised.
>
> (Sarason, 1993, pp. 19, 170)

## Monitor the effects and penetration of cultural change

The main work of schools occurs in classrooms, yet classrooms are the part of the school which school leaders are least able to influence and change. So it is important that leaders monitor the depth and effects of cultural change. Cultural change can occur at the managerial and staff levels, producing happier relationships or new attitudes, but without penetrating into classroom practices. School leaders need to explore their school's culture, but they also need to investigate the impact and consequences of cultural change, and in particular to check that when cultural change has beneficial effects, these are maintained over time. As Huberman (1993, p. 12) explains:

> Working together to accomplish the chief missions of the school is a desirable, even irresistible, objective. So desirable that we have to ask ourselves why so little of it appears to be going on at present and, when it has gone on, why it seems so difficult to sustain. Longitudinal studies . . . suggest that task-related collegiality – as distinct from contacts with no bearing on classroom practice – is much more evanescent, volatile and brittle than initial observations had suggested . . . Collegiality is not a

fully legitimate end in itself unless it can be shown to affect, directly or indirectly, the nature and degree of pupil development.

The commonly met advocacy for increased collaboration and collegiality as a (even the) key mechanism for school improvement – of which Huberman has been the outstanding critic – is usually not based on much evidence. This is a good topic for a researcher-practitioner partnership.

### Import assistance

Although many leaders like to think (in private, usually) that cultural change is largely their own work, it is sometimes prudent to use outsiders to do part of the work (including monitoring and follow-up) for you. If you select them well they will:

- legitimate most of your programme of change, as staff see that similar ideas are held by independent advisers/consultants;
- provide active help at teacher level, leaving you free for other things;
- divert some of the blame from you if some of the ideas don't work out;
- help to foster a climate of collaboration and experiment in the school.

### Be your own culture

Since every school culture is unique, there's little point in trying to turn your culture into any of those named above. In my view these are merely ideas against which to explore your own culture, both actual and ideal. I am not convinced that we know very much about the characteristics of effective school cultures – and there must be many forms of them – let alone how they develop. And it may be that some of the most effective school cultures of the past may not remain the most effective in rapidly changing societies such as our own. If you press me to take a more concrete position, I suspect that the core of the effective school of the future will be a form of what Quinn (1980, p. 58), in the field of business organizations, has called 'logical incrementalism', an idea which is much more attractive than its label. In such a culture,

> the organization probes the future, experiments, and learns from a series of partial, incremental commitments rather than through global formulations of total strategies.

This is not effectiveness by top-down management and control, nor is it managerial manipulation of the culture to serve management's ends. Rather it is a school where the teachers are encouraged to experiment or, in Huberman's happy phrase, to 'tinker' in their classrooms and to do so in loose association with colleagues in a climate that enables and encourages innovative playfulness in the search for more effective teaching and learning. In this way, the detailed direction of the school is shaped in part from below. As Kanter (1985, pp. 289f) puts it:

> major changes in large organizations are more likely to represent the accumulation of accomplishments and tendencies built up *slowly* over time and implemented *cautiously* [italics added].

Or as she expresses it more technically:

> An organization's total strategy is defined by the interaction of major subsystem strategies, each reflecting the unique needs, capacities and power requirements of local units. Even when it is impossible to fully guide the organization from the top – i.e. predict how these units will evolve – the right kinds of integrative mechanisms, including communication between areas, can ensure the co-ordination among these substrategies and micro-innovations that ultimately results in a company's strategic posture. In short, effective organizations benefit from integrative structures and cultures that promote innovation below the top and learn from them.

In my translation for schools:

> The school's development plan for its core mission of teaching and learning is defined by the relationships between individual classroom teachers, each of whom has unique needs, capacities and requirements for support and resources, and between the teams or departments to which these teachers belong. As each individual and team experiments with more effective ways of working, the task of senior management is not to predict outcomes but to maximize integration and communication between staff so that, as effective strategies emerge, they can shape the overall strategic plan of the school. In short, in effective schools the task of school leaders is to discover and implement those integrative structures and cultures that promote innovation at classroom level and learn from that.

The nature and process of the culture of the school as a learning organization are yet to be adequately explored, analysed and reported. It is usually said that such a school has a capacity for managing change and that indicators of this are features such as staff development or a focus on professional inquiry and reflection. Underlying such features as well as the culture of the effective school are, I suspect, three capabilities that lie at the organizational core. These are:

- a **monitoring capability**, or scanning the school's internal and external environment for pressures and problems, for opportunities and for partnerships. This capability provides the school with the skill of linking internal self-evaluation to external potentialities.
- a **proactivity capability**, or having a can-do philosophy, relishing challenge, and so looking ahead positively, taking into account the long-term as well as the short-term view. This capability generates optimism and confidence.
- a **resource deployment capability**, auditing the full range of the school's resources (human and intellectual as well as material and financial) and directing them to the key purposes of schooling. This capability breeds goal achievement.

If these deep capabilities – which reflect, respectively, the spatial, temporal and resource dimensions of organizational life – are visible through the school's culture, then the school is probably well placed to enjoy continuing effectiveness in an unstable and changing environment. The art is finding ways of checking whether they do indeed lie below the surface of the school's overt culture, which can be frustratingly opaque to those who seek to understand and influence it.

# 5

## Primary Teaching as a Culture of Care

### JENNIFER NIAS

The definition of culture that I find most helpful is 'what keeps the herd moving west' (Deal and Kennedy, 1983). It emphasises goal-orientation (beliefs, values, purposes) as well as the action (customs, habits, ways of behaving) which is caused and sustained by normative pressure (group agreement on goals and actions). Despite all that has been said and written about 'culture' in the past two decades, there is still a tendency to neglect values and the beliefs which underpin them and to focus instead upon behaviour. Yet to do this is to weaken the concept in two respects. First, it ignores the most fundamental attribute of school cultures, that is that they are rooted in a shared 'vision' or 'mission' which is itself the manifestation of jointly held and deeply internalised beliefs and values. Second, it distracts attention from the important task of trying to establish the educational significance of the beliefs and values which lie at the heart of particular cultures. In this chapter I attempt an analysis of the values which contribute to the widely-held view that primary school teaching is a 'culture of care'. I identify six ways in which 'care' is used by primary teachers and others in school and the tacit beliefs which accompany each of them. Three bear a strong resemblance to, though they are not explicitly derived from, the ethical thinking of 'relational' feminists. By contrast, two have socio-historical roots and explain 'care' as a matter of social conditioning rather than of morality. The last, which underpins all the others, derives from symbolic interactionism and stresses personal investment and self-esteem. Each of these beliefs about the nature of 'care' may be, and often is, in tension with the others. This in its turn adds to the stresses which teachers experience and so to the difficulties of their job. These are further compounded by the fact that the behaviours tacitly expected of teachers who 'care' are at odds with many of the conditions under which they work.

First, I make a general point. In my analysis I have used terms such as 'maternal' and 'women's work'. I do not wish thereby to imply that primary teaching is an unfit profession for men, nor that men do not 'care' every bit as much as women about their pupils and about their own professional competence. However, the fact that for a century or more there have been more women than men in primary schools has resulted in a legacy of beliefs about the nature of the job and of schools, the influence of which is still very powerful. As a result, cultural assumptions about women sometimes shape the way in which teachers of both sexes themselves perceive the job and interpret their responsibilities. Feminist thinking has much to contribute to the debate about 'caring' in schools, but does not apply simply to women.

## CARE AS AFFECTIVITY

Feminist writers have suggested for a decade or more that women use an ethic of care which stems from feelings rather than from rational principles. In particular, a number of psychologists and philosophers, sometimes described as 'relational' or 'cultural' feminists, have argued that women perceive, learn, reason and make moral judgements in ways different from those commonly practised by men (see, in particular, Gilligan, 1982; Noddings, 1984; 1992; Belenky et al., 1984). Women focus on affectivity and connected relationships, celebrate responsiveness, receptivity, empathetic behaviour and trust. They are more interested in collaboration than competition, in ensuring everyone's well-being than promoting the success of the few, in preventing conflict than resolving it. In Noddings' words, 'Ethical behaviour arises [in women] out of psychological deep structures that are partly dispositional and partly the result of nurturance. When we behave ethically, as 'ones-caring', we are not obeying moral principles.' (Noddings, 1984, p. 175)

These writers have been criticised for assuming that women 'naturally' have such values and ways of thinking, for making little allowance for diversity and change in 'women's ways' over time and for paying scant attention to the social contexts which may have formed them (see, e.g., Acker, 1995). Nevertheless, relational feminists have made a considerable contribution to our thinking about 'care'. For example, they take for granted the existence of feelings in teachers and learners and press the case for the education of the emotions. They challenge the idea that building and sustaining relationships between people are low-level, low-status activities. Instead they argue that the qualities traditionally associated with 'women's ways' (e.g. of working, managing, making judgements) should be celebrated and promoted as alternatives to established models, since these have almost always been shaped by 'men's ways' of thinking and behaving. Noddings (1992; 1994) in particular has vigorously argued that caring in this affective sense is not simply an adjunct or aid to the achievement of cognitive goals. Rather, it is central to teaching and should be consciously adopted as a moral basis for practice in classrooms and schools.

Teaching can readily embody the ethic of care described by Noddings and others, because it is an occupation saturated with feeling. Even though little attention is paid to the emotional aspects of their work (*Cambridge Journal of Education*, 1996), most primary school teachers are fond of children; indeed for many it is their chief reason for choosing the profession (Nias, 1989).

This is not always the case. Every teacher will be able to recall individuals whose personal characteristics they found disagreeable or offensive or whose behaviour was insupportable (as the current debate about exclusion suggests), and classes with whom a comfortable relationship was established only after repeated negotiation. Nevertheless, feeling positively towards children is the more or less universal backdrop to work in primary schools. Teaching and non-teaching staff who do not, in a generalised sense, enjoy working with children do not in my experience stay for long in the profession or, if they do, they become very unhappy people.

Some teachers move beyond liking into a deeper relationship with individual pupils or whole classes, although the extent of their involvement is normally masked by their assumed calm and what King (1978) calls their 'professional pleasantness'. Men and women use the words 'love', and less often 'hate'; they feel bereaved at the end of an academic year (Nias, 1989). There are individual and structural reasons for such intensity of feeling. For instance, it may meet the emotional needs of individuals. In any case, young children evoke strong, loving feelings in many adults, whatever their jobs. Further, the one-teacher-one-class system makes it easy for teachers to be isolated for long periods with 'their' children in what Grumet (1988, p. 85) describes as their 'kitchen-like' classrooms.

Whatever the reasons, if we accept as generalisations that teachers are affectively involved with children, and the proposition of the relational feminists that affectivity is the basis of an ethic of care, then it is easy to construe primary teaching as a 'culture of care' whose underlying values emphasise the importance of making children feel secure, happy and cared for. Indeed, many teachers set out in the classroom to achieve this, tacitly accepting both their 'love or natural inclination' (Noddings, 1984, p. 4) and their belief that children who feel secure in an adult's affection can concentrate on learning.

However, I have been in classrooms where the preservation of a warm social climate seemed to have become an end in itself (see also Broadfoot and Osborn, 1993 and for a similar perspective from the medical profession, Mackenzie, 1997), where teachers and children shared so much personal conversation, laughter and fun that little time was left for forms of learning other than the affective. Since the purpose of schools is to further children's learning in many areas, 'fun', used as a shorthand term for a range of affective activities, is a legitimate means to broad educational ends; it is not itself the only end of schooling.

Yet preserving a balance in classrooms between the affective and the task-centred is particularly important at the moment in view of the mounting evidence that it may be in danger (Pollard et al., 1994; Woods et al., 1997). Faced with a relentless intensification of their workload, teachers are reluctantly reducing the frequency of their affective interactions with children and classes and cutting back on shared moments of banter, joking and talk about personal matters. Time and energy for similar informal contacts outside the classroom are threatened by budgetary cuts, and the increase in teachers' curricular and administrative responsibilities. But teachers are not comfortable with these developments, feeling both that they reduce their own pleasure in the job and that they adversely affect children's motivation and sense of self-esteem. Viewed this way, the fact that teachers show their liking for children through their behaviour in school is not a sentimental self-indulgence but a necessary condition for the latter's learning. So, although we may question the amount of time some teachers devote to 'fun', we need to preserve its existence. If the time were ever to come when teachers felt too pressured to demonstrate to children their affection for them, the lives of both would be morally as well as emotionally and educationally impoverished. In particular, school may be the only place in which some children experience a sense of being cared for and valued in a consistent and predictable fashion, by adults who do not habitually put their own interests first.

## CARE AS RESPONSIBILITY FOR LEARNERS

In their consideration of ethics, relational feminists do not stress only women's natural inclination to feel for others. They also emphasise the priority that women attach to creating, maintaining and enhancing positive relationships. Gilligan (1982) and Noddings (1984; 1992; 1994) discuss in detail the inter-personal nature of caring and the importance of developing the attitudes and skills required to sustain caring relations. Viewed this way teaching is also a culture most of whose members 'care', in that they regard their relationship with their pupils as a personal rather than an impersonal, bureaucratic one.

Teachers are supported in this view of the teacher-learner relationship by the influence, albeit often unrecognised or unarticulated, of those philosophers who see education as an encounter between persons in which teachers make themselves available as resources to the learner. The idea that learning results from this kind of communication between persons and therefore that the teacher-as-person has an inherent importance goes back in Western thought at least as far as Socrates and, later, St Augustine and is present in the twentieth century in the writings of Martin Buber and Carl Rogers. It is still implicit in much educational discourse, not only in the primary sector. Many teachers feel that their relationship with individual learners lies at the heart of what they do.

It is when teachers become emotionally or intellectually engaged with pupils, or develop what Buber calls an 'I-Thou' relationship with them, that the inter-action between them becomes inter-personal. For teachers in the Cambridge Accountability Project (Elliott et al., 1981) moral accountability, which they normally described as 'responsibility', derived from two sources. Rationally, they saw it as part of their professional duty, that is, they believed that teachers ought to act with their pupils' interests in mind. But in addition it developed from their personal relationship with them. Indeed, some teachers used the term 'answerability' to describe their sense of moral responsibility for pupils, implicitly stressing its direct and individual quality. The introduction into education in the past two decades of the language of market forces and cost-effectiveness runs so forcefully against this ethical sense of inter-personal obligation that it has been a major cause of stress and burnout among teachers and headteachers (Woods *et al.*, 1997; Nias, 1998).

Although teachers' moral responsibility for children sometimes focuses upon their physical, social, emotional or moral welfare, they are primarily concerned with their pupils' learning. Throughout the age ranges and in all types of school, teachers judge their success by and draw their main job satisfaction from knowing that they have helped individuals to learn and to develop. Their aspiration is to be effective as practitioners. Pupil progress is at the heart of answerability.

Significantly, the chief complaint of the teachers studied by Evans *et al.* (1994) to the introduction of the National Curriculum was that it had undermined their sense of professional competence in the eyes of teachers, children and parents. Pollard *et al.* (1994) documented similar concerns among practitioners, centring on loss of freedom and a feeling of being forced into an 'unnatural way of teaching'. Drummond (1993), Campbell and Neill (1994), Alexander (1995), Croll (1996) all highlight the fact that teachers passionately want to have a sense of professional efficacy. In a longitudinal study of teachers I concluded: '[For  these teachers] to care for children was to teach well and to accept the need for continuing self-improvement' (Nias, 1989, p. 41). Put another way, technical skills and efficacy are not ends in themselves for teachers, but are the means by which they express their sense of answerability to learners.

Indeed, it is possible that the more technically assured teachers believe themselves to be, the deeper, and so more moral, their interpersonal relationship with their classes can become. Fuller (1969) suggests that teachers are not able to see through pupils' eyes the demands of the curriculum nor their own performance until they feel themselves to be professionally competent. Similarly, I found that as teachers mature, they become more relaxed and more self-confident in their teaching, more, to use their words, 'natural' and 'whole' (Nias, 1989). Arguably, then, the more able teachers are, the greater their sense of responsibility to children. As a result, but paradoxically, experienced teachers often feel more rather than less vulnerable than their younger colleagues, because they construe allegations, explicit or implicit, of technical ineptitude as attacks upon their ability to make sound moral judgements and so upon their professional identity (Kelchtermans, 1996).

There is another sense too in which moral responsibility for children's learning goes further than technical skill. It also requires from teachers an active engagement with individuals' minds. Drummond (1995), in a cogent and persuasive attack upon simplistic notions of 'competence' in teaching, reminds us, quoting Iris Murdoch (1985, p. 31) 'that to perceive clearly those with whom we have a relationship requires 'moral imagination and moral effort', the ability to see not just accurately, 'but also justly or lovingly' (ibid., p. 23). We cannot help children to learn if we do not pay close attention to them, in the sense in which Weil (1986) uses the word. Weil suggests that 'attention' conveys the act of putting 'oneself in someone else's place, listening for justice and virtue, being alive to truth and to affliction' (Drummond, 1995, p. 10).

Teachers, then, face a hard and unending obligation, to attempt to achieve a clear and focused vision of individual learners, of their perspectives, priorities, ideas and experiences.

This obligation is the more demanding in schools or countries where the influence of Rousseau, Pestalozzi and Froebel is still widely felt, because of its emphasis upon the need to pay attention to the 'whole child'. At one level this means that individual teachers feel themselves responsible for each pupil's emotional, social, moral, aesthetic, physical – as well as cognitive – development. At another, the notion of 'wholeness' becomes part of practitioners' thinking, as this excerpt from a teacher's letter suggests: '"Wholeness" is not an option, either desirable or undesirable, but a necessary corollary of the nature of personhood. In consequence, the whole child is always the object of the educational process whether the teacher recognises it or not. So the question is – is it safe to risk ignoring some aspects of the whole because we are – truly- overstretched?' (Bond, 1997).

As this comment suggests, the conditions under which many teachers work make it impossible for them to discharge the responsibility they feel for children's learning. First, there is an inherent conflict between answerability for the development of all aspects of a growing child and the demands of large, diverse, under-resourced classes. The work of educationalists such as Alexander (1984; 1992), Bennett *et al.* (1984) and Tizard and Hughes (1984) has conclusively shown that before 1988 the rhetoric of a 'child-centred' curriculum was not matched by the reality of practice in many English primary schools. Yet the assessment and reporting requirements of the National Curriculum, even in their revised (1993) form, tend to perpetuate the myth that it is possible for one teacher, often with dwindling material resources, to plan for and assess the cognitive, practical and social progress of every child, across nine subject areas and a number of cross-curricular themes, in classes which are often in excess of thirty. Add to this, the increasing number of 'mainstreamed' children with special needs, often placed in schools without adequate social or curricular support for teacher or child, the growing ethnic and linguistic diversity of many classes and a wide range of social and behavioural problems among all children, and the full extent of teachers' dilemmas begins to appear. Over the years primary teachers have been asked to take on moral aspirations, rhetorically described as 'care' and 'commitment', which it is beyond the capacity of any practitioner consistently to fulfil. Worse, they have accepted this definition of their task, have internalised expectations which cannot be met except under rare and ideal circumstances and then pass them on from one professional generation to another. Primary teachers continue to accept their accountability to everyone (Broadfoot and Osborn, 1993; 1995), their responsibility for everything (Nias, 1989; Evans *et al.*, 1994; Jeffrey and Woods, 1996), and, underlying all of this, the constant burden of guilt which Hargreaves A. (1994) sees as characteristic of the profession.

Second, there are the emotional costs of sustaining the interpersonal relationships which give teachers some of their main job satisfactions, but also provide many of their main pressures and anxieties. As significant others for teachers of all age ranges and of all lengths of experience pupils have always had the capacity to undermine teachers' self-confidence and self-esteem. Teachers' relationship with pupils is so central to the way in which they see themselves, as people and as practitioners, that when it goes wrong, it undermines their sense of who and what they are, sowing self-doubt and a deep sense of personal failure (Nias, 1989).

Third, there is a conflict between teachers' desire to have authentic relationships with children and the exhaustion which results. It is very tiring, physically and emotionally, to attempt to sustain individual and sometimes intense relationships with many people throughout a working day; teachers' chronic fatigue is legendary, as their partners and children testify. Of course, teachers are not alone in facing the emotional strains of 'people work', as Hochschild's work on 'emotional labour' suggests (Hochschild, 1983). Nevertheless, they engage in thousands of individual interactions during a working day (Jackson, 1968), many involving considerable self-control. It is small wonder that a large number of practitioners feel that their job has an adverse impact upon their domestic lives (Nias, 1989; Campbell and Neill, 1994; Jeffrey and Woods, 1996).

Teachers who 'care' in an interpersonal sense about their pupils' learning are faced with two further questions, deriving not so much from their working conditions as from the nature of the curriculum that they are required to teach. These are: What learning is it in children's best interests to acquire and to which children do we refer? These are moral questions requiring moral answers (Kelchtermans, 1996). Despite, or perhaps because of, the introduction of the National Curriculum and its repeated revisions, we need a continuing debate about values in the curriculum. Skinner has claimed: '[The National Curriculum] gives insufficient weight to values and experience through which students (of any age) grow and become critical persons. I refer to literature, music, drama, dance, art and even sport and physical activity'. (1996, p. 253). In North America, Noddings has steadfastly argued that the aim of education in Western society should be to produce citizens who 'care' in the relational sense about one another, intellectual ideas and the environment which they share with other species. Her curricular critique is even more fundamental and more general in its application than Skinner's: 'Liberal education is a false ideal for universal education . . . [It] puts too much emphasis on a narrow form of rationality and abstract reasoning . . . It neglects feeling, concrete thinking, practical activity and even moral action . . . It is largely a celebration of male life; activities, attitudes and values historically associated with women are neglected or omitted completely.' (1992, pp. 28 and 42). Unless we continue to call in question and to debate the nature of the curriculum to which children are exposed, it is possible to envisage a time when teachers would best meet their moral obligations to their pupils by teaching them less. More learning does not necessarily mean a better quality education.

## CARE AS RESPONSIBILITY FOR RELATIONSHIPS THROUGHOUT THE SCHOOL

In some schools 'care' is used in a third sense, to refer to the nature and quality of relationships within the organisation as a whole and to the idea that those relationships should be pursued as ends in themselves. In these schools teachers or headteachers have made a conscious moral choice to promote in their interactions with adults as well as with pupils a culture which embodies values such as trust, co-operation, tolerance and consideration; in Grumet's words (1988, p. 179), 'It is affiliation . . . that will bind us into an educational community.' The group is seen to be as important as the individual and attention is paid to collective as well as individual goals (e.g. whole school discipline policies, the state of the school environment). To be sure, a 'culture of collaboration' (Nias *et al.*, 1989) can arise in response to circumstances or changes in teachers' working conditions. For example, Acker (1995) describes an inner-city school in which the task of teaching was so stressful that teachers could cope with it only by depending heavily on one another. But even in this case much of their mutual support was due to the headteacher's leadership and the importance that she attached to interpersonal qualities such as compassion, empathy and appreciation of others' contribution to the work of them all.

Noddings (1984; 1994) argues that caring behaviour implies the capacity to be the 'one-cared-for' as well as the 'one-caring', that is, that children should learn not just to respond appropriately to being cared for, but also to care for others. I have been surprised in some schools by the level of care which pupils will show towards their teachers if they are encouraged to do so. Many primary schools make this kind of regard for interpersonal relationships central to their work and have been glowingly commended for this in repeated HMI and Ofsted reports.

Teachers' awareness of and concern for their colleagues have been enhanced in the past decade by their schools' response to legislative changes. In the past, it was possible for teachers to escape contact with anyone except pupils and, occasionally, their parents. Now, teachers attend frequent meetings. In many schools the amount of informal interaction has also grown dramatically, both in order to increase collective efficiency and effectiveness and, most importantly, so that teachers can give one another help and support. Of course, it is still possible for individuals to interact in a superficial, disengaged or purely task-focused way. 'Contrived collegiality' or more destructively 'Balkanised cultures', (Hargreaves A., 1994) persist, especially in schools with a history of isolation or inter-group rivalry. Nevertheless in general teachers are now frequently in contact with one another about a multitude of matters before, during and after the school day.

To the extent that through increased contact they develop an interpersonal relationship with their colleagues, they also therefore feel ethically involved with them. In the schools in which I have worked as an ethnographic researcher the interpersonal took precedence over the bureaucratic at all levels and in all forms of activity, even though there were also plenty of meetings and working parties. As a result staff members (teaching and ancillary) felt responsible for one another as people and mutually answerable for the work of the whole school. In the process they explicitly or implicitly strengthened one another's conviction that education was a moral activity not a form of accountancy.

Working in a school which unequivocally accepts the interpersonal basis of education and carries this emphasis through into adult relationships can be a positive experience for all its staff. It leads to the giving and receiving of practical assistance and emotional support, to the acceptance and remediation of weakness and failure (in oneself and in others), to shared laughter, to mutual appreciation, gratitude and praise. The resulting climate of emotional security and open communication can facilitate both risk-taking and the constructive resolution of personal or professional conflict. It can also contribute to professional development, for staff members are well placed to support one another through the uncertainties and fears of adult learning. In addition, when teachers feel mutually accountable for pupils' progress everyone feels free to contribute to decision-making and to one another's professional growth (Nias *et al.*, 1992). As a result, interpersonal relationships take on a developmental as well as an ethical dimension.

There is, however, another side to staff interaction. It may prove an additional charge upon over-extended teachers, especially when individuals feel obliged to 'care' more than they feel is possible. When teachers come to see meetings, even conversations, as taking precious time away from their own pupils or the fulfilment of essential professional duties, they may also perceive 'collaboration' and 'collegiality' as exploitative and potentially intolerable burdens. It is small wonder that some within the profession (e.g. Hargreaves, 1994; Campbell and Neill, 1994) are sceptical about the value of these developments. Certainly, without the backing of additional resources, thoughtfully used, teachers cannot be expected to become more involved with their colleagues or to seek to see them 'justly or lovingly'. If the expectation that teachers will assume responsibility for other adults in their schools as well as for children is propagated, unchallenged and without properly thought out provision, it will add to their burden of guilt and tension and exacerbate the problems it might otherwise relieve.

## CARE AS ALTRUISM, SELF-SACRIFICE AND OBEDIENCE

'Caring' behaviour in schools may, then, arise from 'love and inclination'. It may, by contrast, owe its existence to social conditioning, the historical roots of which are so well buried that most teachers are unaware of their existence. There are practical overlaps between care which has ethical roots and that which arises from socialisation; an observer in both cases would note similar behaviours and relationships. Nevertheless, there are important differences in emphasis which may affect teachers' levels of job satisfaction and of stress. In

particular, attitudes and actions adopted out of a sense of obligation or professional duty may exact a more damaging toll upon practioners than those
undertaken freely as part of an interpersonal relationship. As a result, pupils
may suffer. A 'culture of care' built upon the Protestant work ethic and values
derived from a hierarchical, patriarchal society is likely to have a different
impact upon its members from one which favours feeling and connectedness.

There are three main historical reasons why teachers have been expected to
'care'. First, most teacher education in England and Wales has religious
origins. Until 1870, the majority of schools were provided by the Anglican or,
less frequently, non-conformist churches or by charitable individuals with religious sympathies. Teachers were prepared for their work through apprentice-
ship in the schools, notably the pupil-teacher system, or in a handful of Church
of England Training Colleges. As a consequence, they were socialised early in
their professional lives into a view of their work as helping, serving and indoc-
trinating others. As a corollary, the satisfaction of their pupils' needs was
expected to take priority both over their own and over the likelihood of
material reward. Kay Shuttleworth, one of the most influential teacher educators in nineteenth-century England, spoke of the students at St John's College,
Battersea as 'a band of intelligent Christian men (sic) entering upon the instruction of the poor with religious devotion to their work' who would 'go forth
into the world humble, industrious and instructed' (Rich, 1972). This is a view
that has persisted. There are still plenty of teachers in the system whose
motivation is that of service or the pursuit of social justice (Nias, 1989; Osborn
et al., 1997b), and even more outside it who feel that teachers' dedication
should exceed their desire for reward or, in some cases, for reasonable working
conditions.

In practical terms, such altruism often leads to self-expenditure. Teachers
with religious or socio-political motives for their choice of career frequently
give themselves to their jobs without regard to personal cost, work very long
hours in and away from school, often give their occupational lives priority
over their domestic ones, are constantly preoccupied with individual pupils
and their well-being. In addition, they undertake many tasks which go well
beyond a strict definition of teaching, acting as social workers, counsellors,
home and hospital visitors, not to mention cleaning, redecorating and
renovating classrooms, unblocking drains, washing and dispensing second-
hand clothes, and performing a range of other practical tasks in the interests
of children's welfare.

The second reason why teachers work altruistically for their pupils is because they have come to see themselves in some senses as parents. Froebel and
Pestalozzi in particular did a great deal to establish a view of teaching as
facilitation and informed intervention rather than instruction, and of learning
as growth rather than memorisation. Their educational theories drew heavily
upon what they saw as 'natural', for example, play, development, intrinsic
motivation, the unity of mind, body and spirit. Accordingly they also stressed
the educational potential of parenting, arguing that teachers could promote

children's learning by consciously extending the 'natural' attitudes and actions of mothers, in particular. Empathy, close observation, tactful intervention, compassion, concern are qualities that many parents exhibit. They lie at the heart of the educational methods advocated by Froebel and his followers.

Froebel's ideas were initially developed in Britain by men (e.g. Robert Owen) and there have been, and still are, many outstanding male 'child-centred' educators. Nevertheless it is maternal language and imagery that are most often used in relation to primary teachers. This may be partly because Froebel's influence in this country was greatest in early years education, an area which has traditionally been the preserve of women. It may also be, as Grumet (1988) suggests, that, in the nineteenth century when women were reaching out towards independent employment, their claim to be morally superior to men supported their bid to become teachers. And, in time, sheer weight of numbers encouraged the elision of 'teacher' and 'she'.

Whatever the reasons, teaching young children is often perceived in Western countries as a form of mothering. According to some feminist writers (see, e.g. Lawn and Grace, 1987; Acker, 1995), 'mother's work' in its turn is a historically-constructed idea, the origins of which lie in the industrial revolution and the rise of capitalist society. The supply of cheap labour needed for industrialisation depended on men's availability to work long hours and so upon women's capacity to sustain the home and care for children. As a result, these activities came to be seen as the work of women and particularly of mothers. Feelings such as warmth, compassion and affection were readily associated with physical caring and these too became a mother's duty and prerogative. So girls were socialised early in their lives, as many still are, into the assumptions that theirs was a caring role within the home and that caring involved both doing and feeling, labour and love. Grumet's seminal book, *Bitter Milk: Women and Teaching* (1988) takes this argument further, emphasising both the dull, repetitive and tiring nature of much maternal work and the self-sacrifice that it involves.

To construe teaching as an extension of this kind of mothering is to convey a depressing, in both senses of the word, view of the profession: Teachers in primary schools will be women. They will cheerfully undertake tiring, repetitive, physical tasks on their pupils' behalf. They will willingly expend themselves for others to the point of exhaustion and often beyond. They will make do with scarce resources, be content with low status and few material rewards. In return, they will receive the satisfaction of knowing that they have done their duty and, if they are lucky, will be blessed with the affection, esteem and gratitude of their pupils. In this context early years' teachers face a particular problem. To allow or to encourage a view of their work as maternal is to play into the hands of those who avowedly see the education of young children as a less-skilled, lower-status – and so less well rewarded – activity than that of older pupils. In other words, the obligation teachers feel to care may open women in particular to exploitation and may in the long run make effective teaching for all children more difficult to achieve.

In addition, involvement in mundane, repetitive tasks and altruistic self-expenditure can, like the enjoyment of children's company, become a substitute for thinking or talking about the cognitive aims of teaching and how these can be achieved. Teachers who work selflessly for their pupils may deprive themselves of the time and energy they need to improve their own technical skill.

But the picture is not straightforward. Most teachers would themselves argue that children need quasi-parental warmth, reassurance, concern, vigilant attention, both in their own right as dependent human beings and because appropriate levels of self-esteem and security are necessary conditions for learning. Moreover, physical nurturing is at times an essential means to pedagogical ends. Further, many teachers gain pleasure and a sense of fulfilment from self-expenditure. When, twenty years ago, I asked teachers, 'Why do you let the school take so much of you?', the typical reply was, 'I enjoy giving it' (Nias, 1989, p. 197). Now, as then, many teachers seem most fulfilled by their work when they are most depleted by its demands. Lastly, as members of a troubled society we also have to consider what might be lost if teachers became less loving and altruistic, and whether there is still a place for lifestyles which model for children idealism and self-sacrifice.

The third historical reason why many teachers accept, and even willingly espouse, a broad definition of their role and a workload which expands without apparent limit is associated with the other two. From the start, teachers in the public education system, especially if they were women, were expected to live in social and economic dependence on their patrons and employers. Tropp (1957), Simon (1965) and Rich (1972), are among those who have vividly documented the low social status accorded to primary teachers in the nineteenth and early twentieth centuries, the control exercised over them by those who appointed, inspected or paid them, their struggle for professional status and recognition. These were partly gender issues; in a patriarchal society women were expected to obey and defer to men. The struggle was also, however, class-related, especially in the nineteenth and early twentieth centuries. Most primary teachers were of working class origins; after 1870 they often taught in areas with poor, labouring populations. In the interests of social control, it was felt necessary to encourage them in habits of deference and dependency. There is plenty of anecdotal evidence in the profession to suggest that these attitudes were still current two or three decades ago, and it is easy to interpret the legislation of the 1980s and 1990s, and the actions which have followed from it, as attempts to reinstate the status quo. The tenacious authority-dependence (Abercrombie, 1984) of primary teachers, itself a century-old habit of socially-induced obedience which can be traced back to the origins of English public education, works in this respect to the advantage of politicians.

## CARE AS OVER-CONSCIENTIOUSNESS

It is in the context of these three historical aspects of teachers' work – religious or social idealism, quasi-maternalism and authority-dependence – that Campbell's work on conscientiousness is particularly relevant (Campbell and Neill, 1994). It vividly and painstakingly documents the hours worked, at home and in school, by teachers at different Key Stages, ages and career stages, points out the inflating expectations which bear upon them without the protection (because of the open-ended nature of 'non-directed time') of contractual limits, shows the mounting dissatisfaction and increasing ill-health of many teachers and suggests that in some instances the quality of their teaching has declined. They conclude:

'Conscientiousness', whatever its benefits to the pupils, has acted as a mechanism, actual or potential, for exploitation of teachers. Driven by their sense of obligation to meet all work demands to the best of their ability, the majority of teachers found themselves devoting much longer hours in their own time to work than they considered reasonable, and attempting to meet too many demands in order to achieve government objectives for educational reform. This was despite the fact that some of the demands . . . . were structurally impossible. Others . . . . were confused and unworkable.

(Campbell and Neill, 1994, p. 223)

Pollard et al. (1994) and Croll (1996) have come to similar conclusions.

In addition, it is clear that however hard they work, primary teachers cannot successfully do all that is legally required of them. Campbell and his associates have documented the impossibility of meeting the time requirements of the National Curriculum, even in its revised forms. There are also the pressures of repeated curricular changes, of budgeting, assessment, record-keeping, inspection, reporting to parents and governors and all the meetings and informal interaction required by these and other growing responsibilities. All too often, those who try to meet the targets set for them wear out, burn out or leave the profession.

The situation is complicated by the large numbers of women in primary teaching and by their learnt reluctance to attend to their own needs. This reluctance arises partly from the manifold demands they face which leave them little time or energy for their own concerns. Many women now work 'double' or 'triple shifts', juggling work, home and the responsibilities of child-care (Acker, 1994) or of elderly relatives (Evetts, 1990). However, Eichenbaum and Orbach (1983) suggest another explanation for women's neglect of themselves. There is, they argue, a cycle perpetuated through child-rearing practices which results in gender-related differences in the extent to which men and women express their needs and have them satisfied. Simply put, girls are brought up by mothers in ways which make them aware of their needs, but lead them to expect that these will not be met. Boys, by contrast, learn that 'needs' belong to women; they therefore do not learn to identify or recognise their own. However, with the tacit collusion of their mothers, sisters and, later, wives they grow up expecting that their needs will be met, usually by women. If Eichenbaum and Orbach are right, there are two additional reasons why women teachers are prone to over-conscientiousness and open to exploitation. They do not anticipate that their emotional or physical needs will be met, sometimes even noticed, by those with whom they work and out of habit they therefore continue to take on additional burdens. At the same time, they are likely to protect and attend to others, especially if these are males, compounding with altruism their own neglect of themselves. That is, women staff members, like good mothers, put the children first and, like well socialised girls look after men second and themselves a poor third.

On the other hand, Campbell has convincingly shown that primary teachers are sometimes their own worst enemies. Notwithstanding the fact that the long hours of extra work which followed from the legislation of 1989 were 'damaging their lives, their health and ironically the quality of their pupils' learning and relationships with them' (Campbell *et al.*, 1991, p. 10), they continued to try to do all that the government asked of them. A decade earlier, I concluded that some of the stress and fatigue '(that teachers) experience is undeniably self-induced' (Nias, 1989, p. 133). Lortie's (1975) classic study of American elementary teachers draws on even older data but reaches similar conclusions. Evidently, many teachers in the Western world have been socialised over a long period into an occupational culture which leads them to expect of themselves long working hours and the attainment of high professional standards, whatever the personal cost.

## CARE AS COMMITMENT AND IDENTITY

Underlying each of the other forms of 'caring' is the individual teacher's personal relationship with his/her job. Primary teachers identify very closely with their work (Pollard, 1985; Nias, 1989). They care about their work in the dual sense that they invest themselves heavily in it and that, as a result, their self-esteem is intimately bound up with their sense of success or failure in it. The daily work of the classroom and the staffroom matters to them in part because it reflects upon who and what they perceive themselves to be.

Partly as a result of this personal involvement in work many teachers are 'committed' to it, in Lortie's (1975, p. 189) sense that they are 'ready to allocate scarce personal resources' (e.g. time, money, physical effort) to their jobs. Now, it will be clear that individuals may be committed in this sense to many different aspects of their work. Given the fact that there are never enough human resources to meet all the personality and learning needs of pupils in any school, what matters to teachers' colleagues, however, is not the precise nature of their values, but whether or not they are generous, hard-working and capable of self-expenditure. The focus of an individual's 'commitment' is of concern only when it obstructs others' aims or the school's progress towards generally agreed goals. In other words, to say that teachers are 'committed' is to reveal nothing about their individual beliefs, purposes or sources of motivation.

This imprecise use of the term is particularly unhelpful to teachers because it places no limits on individuals' self-expectations. In a comparative study of English and French primary (elementary) teachers, Broadfoot and Osborn

(1993; 1995; Osborn *et al.* 1997a) demonstrated that the latter felt their professional responsibilities were both more clear cut and more limited than the former's. English teachers imposed far more diffuse and ambitious goals upon themselves and shared less with parents, with the result that they took responsibility for a much broader range of outcomes than their French counterparts. In consequence they more often felt guilty or inadequate. Similarly, I found that teachers were often conscious of not living up to their own internalised standards, but had seldom asked themselves or others if their aspirations were realistic, attainable or even educationally justifiable (Nias, 1989).

## CONCLUSION

In this analysis of primary teaching as a 'culture of care' I have made a distinction between care as an ethical concept deriving from feeling and a sense of interpersonal responsibility and care which stems from deeply engrained, socially-conditioned habits of obedience, hard work and self-neglect. In practical terms it is often hard to tell the two apart: either or both may be adopted as part of the individual's sense of personal and professional identity and so his/her values are likely to remain unquestioned as long as pupils, and in some schools, adults appear to benefit. Yet the distinction between them has implications for the teaching profession, especially in the light of legislative and economic changes since the 1980s. The ethic of care has a continuing place in the education of children. By contrast, teachers are right to look carefully at obligations and professional habits formed in social conditions very different from those which apply today. To distinguish between them, individuals need to become more willing to question the motives of themselves and others, readier to examine their own sense of identity, especially in the contentious areas of self-neglect, over-conscientiousness and authority-dependence. It is also worth remembering that caring attitudes and behaviours sometimes reward the carer as much or more than the recipient. Until such questioning takes place, at both an individual and a professional level, the notion of 'care' will continue to confuse teachers, pupils, parents, governors and all those interested in education.

A debate over the senses in which teaching should be seen as a caring profession is the more urgently needed because the conditions under which practioners work are at odds with both their belief in education as an interpersonal process and their willingness to take on fresh burdens. Two consequences follow for teachers from this conflict. The first is guilt. Since moral responsibility within the profession is wide-ranging, diffuse, lacking in definition and its limits are left to the individual conscience, rather than arising from open discussion or negotiation, the possibilities for self-blame become endless. In addition, there seems no limit to the expansion of teachers' workload and to the sense of professional inadequacy which results. Hargreaves A. (1994, p. 145) argues that teachers' chronic sense of guilt arises from the fact that they are caught between four forces: job-intensification and increased accountability; the open-ended nature of the job; a commitment to 'goals of care and nurturance'; a self-imposed desire for perfectionism. They have little control over the first two of these. Social conditioning and a moral commitment to pupils' welfare and learning make it difficult for them to reduce the effects of the last two. As a result, although individuals recognise that their capacity for self blame exceeds what they know to be reasonable, they go on feeling guilty.

The second consequence is tension. This too has been part of teachers' lives for many years and results from similar conflicting pressures: tasks which multiply without apparent limit; over-conscientiousness in their execution; an ethical commitment to the welfare and development of individuals. In addition, however, teachers increasingly lack the power or resources with which to meet their felt-obligations or to act to reduce them. The pressures, dilemmas and paradoxes which are an integral part of teachers' lives are increasingly compounded by a sense of impotence.

The impact of teachers' inability, or unwillingness, to act has been aggravated by a change in the public discourse and of the value-system which it represents. The talk is now of cost-effectiveness rather than care, of accountability not service. Competitive pressures have increased, within and between schools, and the financial consequences of falling behind in the race for results, for pupils and for funding often face teachers and headteachers with stark choices about resource allocation and the fate of individual pupils or staff members. In particular, teachers have often to set what they perceive as the best interests of the individual against what is legally required or what is financially advantageous to the school (Nias, 1998). Although one main intention of the Education Acts of 1988 and 1993 was to make teachers and schools more formally accountable, their effect, paradoxically, has been to make the discharge of moral responsibility more difficult to achieve.

Briefly put, primary teaching cannot effectively continue as a 'culture of care' until there is greater clarity in the minds of individual practioners and of those with an interest in their work about the beliefs which implicitly frame the nature of teachers' tasks and of the values which direct their work.

# 6

## Visual Sociology and School Culture

### JON PROSSER AND TERRY WARBURTON

### INTRODUCTION

Culture is a way of constructing reality and different cultures are simply
different constructions of reality. Although people of different cultures live in
different worlds no person lives in a random world. That is, no culture's image
of reality lacks order. Researchers strive to classify phenomena, to look at
cultures in terms of categories and patterns to understand why people behave
the way they do. The methodology we employ is essentially visually orientated.
It enables us to identify visual categories, patterns, and meanings, and is an
important aid in understanding what constitutes an institution's culture.
Whereas other chapters in this book serve to expand our substantive knowledge of school culture, this chapter examines how visual sociology may be
used as a tool for exploring the culture of schools.

### VISUAL SOCIOLOGY

Visual sociology acknowledges that culture is displayed in ceremonies, rituals,
artefacts, non-verbal communication, and constructed environments. In
schools, these may take the form of assemblies, speech days, trophies, and
classroom layout, for example.

To explore these areas it draws on theoretical models, methodological
inspiration and practices offered by other sub-disciplines such as visual
anthropology, psychology, architectural studies, media studies and cultural
studies. In the past, by attempting to establish and verify its research creden-
tials, social science has adopted an objective, 'pseudo-scientific' approach. This
has led to a marginalisation of image-based research (Prosser, 1998) among
orthodox qualitative researchers and as a consequence images are often perceived as acceptable: as a way of breaking the boredom of the written text or as
illustration of objects, places, people or events that are fully (and 'more properly') explained by language. However, they are often perceived as unacceptable as a way of 'knowing' because they are ambiguous and polysemic
by nature. A secondary aim of this chapter, therefore, is to make a case for

the inclusion of visual sociology in educational research by illustrating the potential insights it brings to the study of school culture.

This chapter is divided into two parts that roughly represent the two main theoretical traditions within visual sociology. Visual research's insight into school culture can be differentiated into 'researcher-generated images' and 'found images'. These artificial sub-headings parallel an orthodox visual ethnographic stance where data are collected and interpreted by researchers in the field, and a semiological stance were analysis of images in the form of constructed sign systems such as photographs, film, landscape, cartoons, postcards and symbols, are made.

## RESEARCHER-GENERATED IMAGES

Visual sociologists employ a range of techniques including filming, video, photography, and drawings. Images are created throughout the research process and encompass: data collection and recording techniques; the illustration of objects, people, places and events; and the exemplification of ideas or substantive theory.

Cultural systems are learnt by people rather than being inborn. Once set in a person's mind, a cultural construction of reality becomes integral to their view of the world. Hence, important features of school culture are unquestioned as Schein (1992, p. 239) points out:

> To really *understand* a culture and to ascertain more completely the group's values and overt behaviour, it is imperative to delve into the *underlying assumptions*, which are typically unconscious but which actually determine how group members perceive think and feel. [original emphases]

Visually this means exploring standard cultural patterns handed down by past determinants of school culture such as: the constructed and natural environment; school architecture; the content and layout of rooms; the level of technology; dress codes of staff and pupils; behaviour patterns; gestures; ceremonies and rituals; significant objects, artefacts, signs and symbols; and staff and pupils' work. The adoption of an essentially visual approach is especially worthwhile for practitioners reflecting on their own practice or on the culture of their own institutions since the approach encourages perceiving that which is taken-for-granted as problematic. In addition there are advantages in being an 'insider' in that they may possess particular knowledge of places, rituals, traditions, objects, institutional history and, most importantly, have ease of access that is denied an 'outsider'. Nevertheless, visual sociology is not merely a framework for reflecting on what is visually taken-for-granted since it also offers a range of useful strategies, methods and techniques for exploring institutional culture.

### Data collection

Despite the taken-for-granted nature of school space we are often aware of its significance. How is it, for example, we can drive past a school, urban, suburban, new or old, and yet almost without a second thought know that the building is a school? If we go through the front entrance of a school we 'know' that within thirty metres there will be a secretaries' office, a headteacher's office, and a display of pupils' work. This begins to help us understand the meaning of history, territory and status for participants in a school. Similarly, a study of pupils' use of playground space or staffs' use of staffroom space will reveal consistent and ubiquitous features that constitute the taken-for-granted sub-cultures of school. These and other sub-cultures are unsurprising to pupils and teachers but difficult to change because:

> each social situation in which we find ourselves is not only defined by our contemporaries but predefined by our predecessors. Since one cannot possibly talk back to one's ancestors, their ill-conceived constructions are more commonly difficult to get rid of than those built in our own lifetime.

> (Berger, 1963, p. 101)

Amongst other things, visual sociology records visual elements that represent the underlying assumptions of participants. These underlying assumptions are the foundations of the culture of school. In raising questions about the significance of these images to participants, such as teachers and pupils, people are helped to confront their cultural assumptions which in turn and where necessary, allows them to begin to change the culture of a school.

It is common practice in image-orientated research to use cameras during data collection to record dynamic and complex everyday events such as classroom interaction. This approach uses the camera's capacity to record visual information accurately and with a camcorder some verbal information can also be captured. This allows the collection of data of complex events to be made more efficiently than observations recorded by hand. Still photography, for example, in the form of single images or sets of images may be used to examine proxemic data (i.e. data concerning the relationship of space and spacial patterns to material components and people, for example, people with high status in a cultural system often take up more space than those of lower status. It is visible in a school in a headteacher's separate office, and in a classroom with teacher's desk as reserved space. But it can also be seen in pupils who claim high status and take up a disproportionate amount of space.)

*Cultural inventories*
One type of proxemic data used by visual sociologists is referred to as 'cultural inventories'. Collier and Collier (1986, p. 45) explain the inventory approach:

> The photographic inventory can record not only the ranges of artefacts in a home but also their relationship to each other, the style of their placement in space, all the aspects that define and express the way in which they use and order their space and possessions. Such information not only provides an insight into the present character of people's lives but can also describe acculturation and track cultural continuity and change.

The layout and content of a room is not arbitrary or capricious but provides an insight into who that person is, what they do, and how they behave in their rooms. The layout of a headteacher's office or a teacher's classroom gives important clues to the significance of personal relationships and values, and provide insight into the culture of a school. For example in Photograph 6.1, a headteacher's values and beliefs in terms of interpersonal relationships and authority can be explored.

Evans (1974) suggests that the general layout of a headteacher's room could represent at least five degrees of authoritarianism. Alternatively, a micro-analysis of parts of the room may raise questions about the significance of particular artefacts kept there. Why, for example, are there six different types of bible on the shelf; what is the significance of the Royal Airforce memorabilia on the back wall? Cumulatively these questions provide an insight into the Head's values, beliefs and attitudes which, as many studies in leadership attest, are central to institutional culture. It is the artefacts and their spatial relationships which cultural inventories record. When analysed in the context of constituent data – information about the contexts in which the images were made – and the particular questions being asked of them, they provide important insight into the cultural patterns being sustained, in that they are an expression of cultural patterns. A content analysis, for example, of books commonly visible in headteachers' offices would enable a comparison between headteachers' rooms to be made in different schools. Alternatively specific items or artefacts or arrangements could be explored for their historical or aesthetic significance. Practitioners wishing to identify their own school's unique culture may find analysis of a cultural inventory of their headteacher's office invalu-

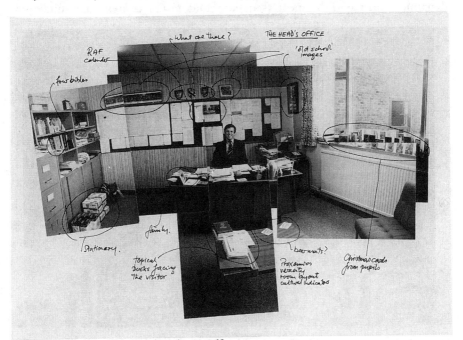

**Photograph 6.1**   The Headteacher's Office

able. However, as with any single set of data, emergent interpretations from cultural inventories require verification or repudiation by contrasting them with other methods or other sources of data.

### Kinesics

Both still and moving images can be used to record and examine dynamic everyday events, such as the relationship of body posture to space and materials in terms of the messages that such arrangements communicate. To focus on the complex components of body posture, body motion, and physical appearance at a 'critical moment' or a 'significant sequence' is to study important kinesic features of a culture. The components of body posture and appearance, like components of space or material culture, also relate directly to territoriality and status. The art of placing one's body on a particular spot or within a given area may be considered a claim to territory.

Photograph 6.2, 'The Evil Eye' is a simple example of a single 'critical moment' image. The photograph shows the deputy head displaying an authoritative and assertive stance, giving what is known in the trade as 'the evil eye' to pupils who are creating an unacceptable (to the deputy head) disturbance.

'The Evil Eye' is a 'critical moment' (Cartier-Bresson, 1952) photograph because it records movement and relationships at the height of their significance (see also *The Ritual of Knock and Wait*, Prosser, 1992). The analysis of still images of complex situations is problematic because they provide only a partial insight into visual elements of school culture. They leave untouched the dynamic world of movement, sequence and visual context that underpin

**Photograph 6.2**   'The Evil Eye'

veracity. On one level the image in Photograph 6.2 may be interpreted as evidence of a control system. Although teachers and pupils are arranged in their hierarchical positions and well trained in their appropriate roles, the performance of those rites is far from perfect. Despite norms of school culture being deeply embedded in people's minds, mischief, dissent, arguments etc. are common. Thus the photograph represents a certain form of behaviour aimed at exerting control over what senior staff perceive as inappropriate behaviour.

A series of photographs or a video of the event would have illustrated what Waller (1932) suggests is an important ability of a successful teacher – 'to know how to get on and off his high horse rapidly'. The notion of 'success' in this context is the ability to act in accordance with one's role and status.

Another way of 'reading' the behaviour of the teacher in 'The Evil Eye' is to contrast what is taken-for-granted but particular in a school culture, with what is normative in broader society. Teachers are aware that they construct an identity of a teacher – what Goffman (1956) calls 'face-work' – believing that they 'act' rather than 'live' that identity. Bertold Brecht (1965, p. 43) writes of this type of separation:

> Observe if you will, one thing: that the imitator never loses himself in his imitation. He never entirely transforms himself into the man he is imitating. He always remains the demonstrator, the one not involved.
>
> (From: *On Everyday Theatre*)

The construction of a teacher identity is as much a matter of visual representation of the self by, for example movement, posture and facial expression, as the spoken word. Teachers believe their teacher identity is a 'mask' which they put on and take off, and that 'mask' is related to, but different from their 'outside of school' self.

The act of making a visual record and using images to elicit information from teachers creates a context for exploring the 'mask', for understanding the relationship between what Sartre (1959) terms 'beings-in-themselves' (non-conscious 'things') and 'being-for themselves' (conscious beings).

*Photo-elicitation*
An important use of video and photography during data collection is as an interview device. This method, often referred to as 'photo-elicitation', involves showing excerpts of video or single or multiple images to individuals or groups in order to elicit a response (Collier and Collier, 1986; Harper, 1987; Schwartz, 1989). Images chosen for photo-elicitation may belong to the interviewees, have significance for interviewees, or they may be selected for their neutrality. The assumption is that images will be meaningful to interviewees who will provide their particular insight to the significance of the image(s). What is important is the capacity of images to dispose respondents to talk reflectively and to 'trigger' unanticipated comments. For example, trainee teachers can be helped to reflect on the quality of their teaching practice by viewing videotapes of their work with pupils; equally, videotapes of a department meeting could evoke a response about decision-making processes.

Apart from drawing on intrinsic ambiguities and bias within images that are known to interviewees, showing images that incite and are intended to be provocative in order to stimulate a response has also been used in educational research (Prosser, 1992). The provocative photograph stimulates interviewees sufficiently (1) to trigger a possibly previously suppressed response and to aid exploration of individual or group values, beliefs and attitudes; (2) so that they can be used as a 'watershed' device to map affiliations and role perspectives, or (3) to evoke insightful or unexpected comments from interviewees. Photo-elicitation used for these purposes must have appropriate 'punctum' (Barthes, 1984) to trigger emotive reaction and reveal individual disposition.

Photograph 6.3, showing a teacher in front of a class of third formers, was used to trigger a response from teachers. The students in the photograph have placed a note on the teacher's back – 'I'm a Wally' – without his knowledge. The objective in using this photograph was to examine an aspect of teachers' attitude to the increasing number of part-time and peripatetic teachers in schools. Images used in this way are suggestive of shock therapy in that they trigger personal memories unlocking associations and affiliations that traditional qualitative interviewing, or where images known to the interviewee are used, may not expose. There is an ethical issue to be addressed. Because photographs may show people's faces confidentiality of participants cannot be guaranteed. The original image was used only after the teacher in the photograph had left the school. What is presented here is not the original but a reconstruction with the same group of pupils in the same classroom for a similar lesson but with an actor as the teacher.

Photograph 6.3   'I'm a Wally'

## Images as evidence

The visual is not only important during data collection but also as data, evidence and 'another way of telling' (Berger, 1989). Images created within a qualitative research framework can contribute significantly to the 'portrayal' of school culture. Images, as far as research is concerned, will always need words but a number of contrasting paradigms now exists that help us understand the roles that images play in qualitative research.

An essential difference between these paradigms is explained via documentary photography. Documentary photographs may be seen as 'objective representations' or 'subjective representations' (Hall, 1997, p. 81). This is best viewed as a continuum. Although images can lie and so there is a need to understand the personal and procedural reactivity that is incumbent in image making, there is also a commonplace belief that photographs retain a degree of objectivity that goes beyond mere face validity. For example, the most primitive form of images as evidence – the illustrative or 'pseudo-objective' photograph – is known to be problematic because the choice of camera, lens, film, filter, lighting and framing all contribute to their inherent bias. So teachers using photographs to capture images of their classrooms inevitably make selections which may present a biased view of what has taken place.

The aim of the pseudo-objective image-maker is to limit such bias, make explicit choices, and take account of personal and procedural reactivity. Visual sociologists creating pseudo-objective photographs would use standard lenses, no filters, emphasise frontality of the subject and flatness of space, make images of people in their natural environment, print the negative full frame, and explain decisions, for example why black and white film is used rather than colour. Work of psuedo-objective photographers such as Sander (1986) held up as objective representations are no longer considered acceptable to the majority of visual sociologists who believe that photographs are subjective representations.

Over the past two decades, there has been a move by critical and interpretative visual anthropologists, visual ethnographers, and visual sociologists, to engage reflexively with the culture of those they study. This initially emerged out of classical criticism of image-based research and the need to take account of procedural and personal reactivity but expanded and diversified as critical theory, postcolonial and cultural studies gained momentum across a range of disciplines.

A significant trend among image-based researchers over the last twenty years has been the awareness of the need to take into account the way images are contextually bound and mediated by socio-cultural settings. For example, a photographic study of school culture would be made based upon issues as they emerged from the data. The interpretations created by researchers would be tested against the views of the participants, generating respondent validity. This might in time lead to an emergent substantive theory, at least for the location in which a study took place. Suchar (1997, p. 35) describes this approach which he appropriately terms 'grounded visual sociology'.

For an image-maker, as with a wordsmith, a substantive theory of school culture if it is to be insightful needs to be not only grounded in the data but also theoretically informed. Where interpretative photographs of school culture are insubstantial in terms of the analytical insight they provide, this may be due to lack of an overarching theory, as Becker (quoted by Adelman, 1998, p. 152) suggests:

> When social documentary photography is not analytically dense the reason may be that photographers use theories that are overly simple. They do not acquire a deeper, differentiated and sophisticated knowledge of the people and activities they investigate. Conversely, when their work gives a satisfyingly complex understanding of a subject, it is because they have acquired a sufficiently elaborate theory to alert them to the visual manifestations of that complexity.

## FOUND IMAGES

Images of quite a different order to those created by the researcher are 'found images' i.e., those images generated by those other than the researcher. For example, they may be treated as historical documents. Historical documents are useful for 'backward mapping' and provide a range of important information. However, all historical documents have limitations, for instance they often lack important contextual information. Given these limitations found images and historical documents with visual elements have been used to good effect in a wide range of sociological studies.

There are many kinds of found images in schools. One easily identifiable group – pupil graffiti – is found on desks, exterior walls, textbooks and pupils' notebooks, and toilet walls. These images are important in studies of school culture because they often provide insight into an important and remote sub-culture, that of pupil culture. Graffiti is a particular form of communication and important to researchers because it is, by its nature, unsolicited. A second kind of found image is printed documents, for example school prospectuses, old photographs of past events, whole school and class photographs, newspaper cuttings, icons, emblems and badges, and letters. The printed page may not contain discrete images but the pictorial information in documents such as the page layout, typeface, the texture of the paper used, all combine to provide a particular visual communication system that is representative of the culture from which it is produced.

There is insufficient space here to discuss meaningfully how the different media that constitute found images aid our understanding of school culture. Therefore, we will consider only cartoons: the first example draws on an orthodox qualitative research approach and interprets a 'found' cartoon within a known context; the remaining 'found' cartoons and photographs operate a broader context and apply a semiological analytical framework.

The first carton shown in Figure 6.1 – The Bank Executive – appeared in *The Guardian* newspaper in the mid-1980s and was found on a staff notice board in a secondary school.

THE GUARDIAN Saturday January 31 1987

**Figure 6.1**   The Bank Executive by Enzo Appicella

The cartoon depicts a bank executive watering school pupils as though they were plants. In his right hand is a watering can which he uses to sprinkle water on to a pupil-plant in its tub. The pupil-plants are interesting in themselves. At first glance they appear to be replicas of each other and fashioned entirely in the image of the bank executive who husbands them, though in a more youthful guise. This is an image which seems to symbolise success – at least success from the bank executive's perspective. The notion of success is reinforced by the rising profits graph on the office wall. Indeed the whole image exudes corporate respectability and achievement and confirms a very particular set of business values.

Why was the cartoon pinned to the staff notice board by a member of staff? The teacher concerned said he objected to 'exterior' (to the school) business values being applied to education (see marketisation principles in Chapter 2). Whilst this may be indicative of contemporary tensions between societal culture and school culture, it is important to understand the cartoon within the micro-culture of the school where the cartoon was found and to answer the question 'How does it reflect the culture of that school?'

The cartoon was placed on the staffroom notice board shortly after a visit by a school liaison officer for a well-known bank. During morning assembly for first year pupils the liaison officer had told the children that money left at home could be stolen and that they should place it in a bank – the liaison officer's bank. Pupils were told that if they opened a savings account they would be given geometry sets, a fountain pen, a sports bag etc. all with the bank's logo on. Very quickly the school abounded with the bank's artefacts sporting the bank's logo – the school's coat-of-arms was rarely to be seen. The teacher not only objected to the values implicit in the cartoon and reflected by the bank's liaison officer, but also to the 'tactics of bribery' and the school being used as a 'billboard for the bank'. The rhetoric of the cartoon had become, for the teacher, an unacceptable reality.

The cartoon is also a manifestation of the school's non-verbal communication system. It was one of a large number of cartoons on a variety of different topics placed on the notice board by various teachers suggesting not only that cartoons were a form of in-house visual argot, but also that humour was valued by teaching staff. In addition, the cartoons acted as a 'rallying point' around which controversial issues were raised and consensus was achieved (subsequently the school decided the 'hard sell' approach of banks would be discouraged in the school in future). The cartoon tells us, therefore, that teachers used this particular medium because it communicated complex but condensed messages which were representative of teachers' values; that cartoons were used as an aid for decision-making by staff; and that cartoons incorporated messages about the beliefs and attitudes of staff, and signalled their aspirations for the school's culture.

### Images of school culture for a wider public – a semiotic approach

Semiotics is the 'science of signs' and uses a very structured approach in analysing these. It involves the study of media such as newspapers, adverts, television and film, using a linguistic framework. Semiotics works from a mainly theoretical position rather than empirical methods and is used across a wide range of disciplines. So far we have focused our discussion of cartoons within a particular school, giving mostly an insight into that school's unique culture. At this point we want to move on to discuss cartoons in a much wider context. Schools do not exist in a vacuum. National and local cultures are part of the culture of all schools. Cartoon images of schooling are used to transmit messages about preferred school cultures to a wider public, providing a macroscopic viewpoint. The macroscopic viewpoint provides an insight into the values and perspectives which a wider society holds of schools and schooling. Transmitting messages to a wider public 'invests and imbues a particular form of existence on an image form' (Warburton, 1998).

Making an image public in this way brings three key factors to the fore: the messages an image carries, the stereotypes which represent a particular culture and the political processes inherent in communication. Using pictures to apprehend such social messages is ubiquitous. Kress and Van Leeuwen describe this process as 'social semiotics' (1996, p. 5). Cartoons as visual images used in the public media are representative in nature. What is communicated is not novel or introspective but rather the social world represented. Such images provide a new synthesis but a synthesis which is resonant and familiar, recognisable publicly. So images of schools which appear in the media either in news items or in fictional series tend to reinforce commonplace views of what schooling is, and what teachers are like. This is part of a much broader series of cultural processes which create, catalogue, characterise and code, as a common resource, public images.

Referring to these resources as 'the cultural cumulative text', Weber and Mitchell (1995, p. 6) point out that these images have the characteristic of being 'inter-generational . . . creating a multi-layered cumulative effect'. They are the basis of all stereotypes. Essentially, when an image is made public via a medium – and for most of us the press and television are key channels of access – they can be characterised as messages communicated as key moments and critical incidents depicted in a stereotypical landscape and peopled by key recognisable figures.

### Images and the political process – school culture re-cast in cartoons

Cartoons can be used to portray school cultural icons stereotypically to a large audience. A case in point relates to the publication of A-level results in 1996. Press coverage had been extensive and headlines such as the following from *The Guardian* (15 August 1996, p. 6) were typical: 'Row erupts over modular A-level success'. The *Daily Mail* (15 August 1996, p. 2) confirms this macroscopic view, using the headline 'Examiners accused on tarnished gold standard' and the sub-heading, 'Experts cast doubt on 86 pc pass rate in this summer's A-levels'. A scene is caricatured by JAK in the *Mail on Sunday* (18 August 1996, p. 31) following the publication of A-level results. It portrays the event repeated in 250,000 homes the previous Thursday.

A postman arrives with the results themselves. The drawing shows a stereotypical upper-class family seated on the croquet lawn, in front of a stately home being served tea in the time honoured fashion. The postman states 'Congratulations, I got six A-levels myself!' This suggests that the results he is delivering are the same as his own. JAK is insinuating that all-and-sundry are now obtaining good results, echoing the message of falling standards and rejecting the notion that A-level success rates have, in actual fact, risen.

Cartoons, as Warburton and Saunders (1996) argue are 'distinctive cultural artefacts' which 'rely upon the communication of stereotypes'. They transmit cultural narratives and amplify them.

Using cartoons and other images representing aspects of school culture to help transmit messages means that such images are not phenomenological but semiological in nature. Public pictures of this sort represent episodes in school culture indexically (i.e. they are a part of what they represent in the same way that smoke is an index of fire). They also become disconnected from the school, its culture and sub-cultures and act symbolically (i.e. they become regarded by general consent as naturally typifying or representative). Effectively, in becoming decontextualised from specific cultural episodes, images of

'Congratulations, I got six A-levels myself!'

Figure 6.2    JAK, *Mail on Sunday*

school culture gain an afterlife allowing stereotypical depictions of school events to become metaphors for other events.

The effect of education policy and other government decisions on schools are also depicted in cartoons, caricaturing key figures and events and on many occasions becoming sited in the classroom.

Figure 6.3, a cartoon by Dave Brown (*The Independent*, 22 May 1997, p. 19) depicts a tranquil classroom scene shattered by a bomb smashing through the window. Ignoring the bomb and other key signifiers for a moment, the classroom scene itself is an interesting portrayal. The traditional images of schooling, the tall windows drawn in the background; the metal light fittings added in the top right hand corner of the cartoon; the style of radiator drawn in the bottom left corner; the wooden floorboards drawn in the bottom right corner and the horizontal stripe running the length of the classroom at shoulder height, all help to form a particular perception of schooling. These images are familiar and commonly recognisable indicators of place and setting. Similarly, the pupils shown and the desks in which they sit are recognisably, if now anachronistically, depicted. This is true even down to the fountain pen which the boy at the front of the first row drops, spilling jets of ink, at the dynamic moment.

Returning to the key signifier of the bomb itself. Here, the Secretary of State for Education and Employment in the new Labour government of the UK after 1997, David Blunkett, is caricatured. His face is drawn in the shape of the warhead of the device. On the side of the weapon is the legend 'Special

**Figure 6.3**  Dave Brown, *The Independent*

Measures Action Recovery Team' written vertically, in respect of the bomb casing, so that the acronym SMART is clearly perceived, the initial letters emboldened so that this is not likely to be missed by the reader. The trajectory of the device delivers its 'payload' at its intended target, the teacher's desk – and by implication the teacher. Three key indicators signify the desk's identity as being the teacher's. First, the desk is drawn to face the class. Second, the chalk and its box are another signifier of identity. Third, the 'apple for teacher' is at one and the same time both iconic and symbolically stereotypical as an indicator of identity. The other elements, the book, the ink bottle and the ruler, all have an associated place but are less significantly obvious as badges of identity. The message is clear: teachers need a bomb under them in order to improve their practice. Readers are expected to engage with this view as an agreed macroscopic perspective on teachers and schools in England. Through this, the paper may be shaping its readers' opinions as much as reflecting them.

Two elements of narrative are denoted. In the first of these the cartoonist gives the Secretary of State utterance in a jagged speech bubble. Mr Blunkett, in the guise of the bomb, exclaims 'Direct Hit . . . . . . er . . . um . . . Sorry, I mean . . . Direct Help!' These words indicate both ambivalence and hesitation, and also emphasis, in how they are drawn, equally as much as in what they say. The second element of narrative runs as a wry editorial comment captioned in the bottom centre of the cartoon, overlapping the desk front, describing the opinion 'Not So Smart Bomb'. Implied common understanding necessary to 'read' this cartoon relates to the so-called Smart weaponry used in the Gulf war in 1992 by the coalition forces against the Iraqi opposition. This did not always hit its targets, and so was not always effective. The newspaper is therefore raising doubts about the efficiency of the Secretary of State's actions through the imagery of the cartoon.

Contextually, this cartoon relates to the formation of what press release 110/97 from the Department for Education and Employment calls 'an elite Special Measures Action Recovery Team (SMART), a team of experts with practical experience of turning around schools, who will be able to act as consultants to the management of failing schools'. Such teams have been constituted to demonstrate the Secretary of State's 'clear commitment to zero tolerance of underachievement'. Failing schools now have the opportunity to 'utilise the skills' of a SMART team. The press report then goes on to name the eighteen schools 'offered' such help. The ambivalence of the supposed words of Mr Blunkett, as drawn in the cartoon, portray the Secretary of State as being uncertain about how the measure is intended to be perceived, as support – 'help' – or as sanction – 'hit'. Indeed, the press release itself mixes the rhetoric of support and the rhetoric of sanction. It can also be argued that simply choosing the acronym SMART, however well-constructed by the DfEE to reflect expertise and advice offered to schools in a spirit of improvement, has the effect in the public perception of drawing to mind the alternative SMART epithet from the Gulf war, weaponry and defence domains. This creates an entirely destructive series of images and concepts, even if associated with high technology (hence expert) and precision in achieving objectives. Thus, the message made public here, through the medium of the image and stereotypes of school culture is that the Secretary of State has mishandled the implementation of this measure and is uncertain about exactly how to handle this or, at least, refer to it.

### Creating a dynamic with icons of school culture

Visual images communicate. They represent a reality existing elsewhere. Reading meaning into such images, decoding the messages they carry, is a cultural act – a social process. Making this communication process public entails using a medium. This imposes the conditions of reading and the bounds of interpretation. It disciplines polysemy. For this process narratives are formed using stereotypes. In respect of school culture, its public representations are used not only to depict episodes from school culture but also as part of a dialogue about schooling, illustrating, illuminating and locating debate. Images are also decontextualised and re-applied metaphorically. Not only is the process public, it is also political. As George (1959, p. 1) states, such images

> reflect the rhythm and tempo of national life, showing the immediate reactions to events and illuminating opinion and propaganda, with their myths and fantasies, catchwords and slogans . . . they illustrate, not the past, but a series of presents in a series of dissolving views . . .

This has major implications for teachers and head teachers about how they present and allow themselves and the processes of their schools to be represented in public discourse. It means that images of school culture have a very public afterlife. Becoming dynamic and useful they are now dialogic in nature, (i.e. the messages they carry become, and in some cases the images themselves are referred to as, part of the public debate), re-casting anew resonant images in a mythic and stereotypical culture of which we are all a part.

## Visual sociology as enquiry into school process

In this chapter visual sociology has been considered as a mode of enquiry into school culture by considering 'researcher-generated images' and 'found images'. Orthodox visual sociology, which draws on visual anthropology and visual ethnography, has been combined with contemporary visual sociology which draws on perceptions from media studies, cultural studies and particularly semiotics. Visual sociology provides a sound basis for the study of school culture by making visible through images of the juxtaposition of actions and artefacts within their narrative contexts the meanings, values and beliefs, which are usually taken-for granted by teachers, pupils and other people involved in and concerned with schools. In making these cultural artefacts visible, researchers and teachers are able to raise questions about the meaning and continuing efficacy of current practice. Arising from this is the need to explore the visual world of schools and seek ways of understanding how the visual can aid our understanding of school culture. This visual world can be explored both through 'researcher-generated images' and 'found images'. Both can be used in different ways to study school culture. It is their methodological congruence, in terms of the roles they play in the research process and the analytical insights they bring, that makes the case for combining orthodox visual sociology and semiotics in educational research so compelling.

## ACKNOWLEDGEMENTS

We would like to thank *The Guardian* and Enzo Appicella, The *Mail on Sunday* and JAK, and *The Independent* and Dave Brown for allowing us to reproduce cartoons.

# Schooling, Masculine Identities and Culture

MÁIRTÍN MAC AN GHAILL

## SOCIAL INEQUALITIES AND CULTURAL IDENTITIES IN CHANGING TIMES

Currently there is growing professional concern in education about 'white working class boys' schooling under achievement'. At the same time, popular representations are emerging in the media that position white working class boys as the new victims of institutional gender and racial discrimination. Implicit in these accounts is the notion of fixed gender and racial categories for girls and boys that are in the process of changing. In contrast, recent cultural and social theory has shown the limitations of earlier models of socialisation that operated with fixed gender and ethnic images. (Hall, 1992; Mac an Ghaill, 1996). It is suggested in this chapter that there is a need to draw upon this literature, in order to develop a more sophisticated framework of male identity formation in which schools are seen to make available a range of femininities and masculinities that young people come to occupy. In the 1990s schooling may be seen as a key institutional arena in which the changing nature of cultural difference is performed in the making and remaking of ethnic, national and sexual identities.

Early feminist and anti-racist work was very successful in placing issues of gender and race on the schooling agenda (Delamont, 1980). However, with its primary focus on gender and ethnic minorities, until recently questions of masculinity, sexuality and national belonging tended to be absent from such research in education. By the early 1990s, the old certainties had broken down and there appeared to be much confusion and uncertainty about how to interpret the effects on gender and ethnic relations of current changing conditions in 'new times'. These social transformations included: the cumulative effects of globalisation of capital and communication systems, the changing nature of labour processes and local labour markets, new school and work technologies, changing family forms, and the feminisation and racialisation of poverty. They were accompanied by the decline of the trade union movement and the success of feminist and anti-racist political struggles (Rees, 1992; Connell, 1995). Within this wider context, Wilkinson (1995, p. 15) argues that discrimination has become much more complex. She asks: 'What does it mean, for example, to provide positive discrimination for ethnic minorities when Indians are now the highest per capita income group in the US, when Koreans and Chinese are leaving whites at the starting gates in schools and universities, and when in Britain it's often white working-class young men who are as confused and alienated as unemployed young black men?' Currently, we are experiencing a political and cultural interregnum in which 'the old politics and identities have been in decline, but the new have still to emerge' (Rutherford, 1990; Wright, 1994).

What is often missing from anti-oppressive initiatives in schools is an under-standing of the changing social conditions in which young people are living. This requires a shift of perspective from 'simple' policy discourses of racial and gender inequality to the 'complex' policy discourses of social exclusion. For large sectors of working-class young people finishing school, the political-economic legacy of the 1980s is that of anticipating becoming unemployed or dependent on the low skilled central government training schemes for surplus labour. Young people are now part of a generation whose transition into adulthood as workers, citizens and consumers is being reconstituted as a result of high rates of unemployment, the de-regulation of youth labour markets and the withdrawal of financial state support for young people. Traditional sociological concerns with young people's transition from school to work assumed that preparation for work was the primary institutional space in which the formation of young people's identity would take place. Postmodern-ists argue that we need to shift away from class based sites of work to that of a wide range of consumerised life-styles, underpinned by individualisation and risk, in order to understand the complexity of contemporary identity forma-tions (Beck, 1992). Furlong and Cartmel (1997, p. 4) have recently examined the meaning of the impact of social changes on young people's lives. They argue that '. . . while structures of inequality remain deeply entrenched, in our view one of the most significant features of late modernity is the epistemo-logical fallacy: the growing disjuncture between objective and subjective dimensions of life. People's life chances remain highly structured at the same time as they increasingly seek solutions on an individual, rather than a collective basis'.

Together with these structural changes around work and consumption, there have been significant cultural shifts that schools need to address. For young people living in multicultural urban settings, we have moved beyond the era of post-war new commonwealth immigrants – the colonial paradigm – to that of English born ethnic minorities, such as Birmingham Irish, Leicester Asians, Liverpool Chinese, London African-Caribbeans. This marks a shift from the old certainties of colour as the primary signifier of social exclusion to more complex processes of regionally and institutionally based inclusions and exclusions. But, at conceptual, political and policy levels, the ongoing narrative

of post-war immigration and the settlement of Asians and African Caribbeans
is still being told in an older language of race and empire. This is not able to
grasp the generational specificities of emerging inter-ethnic social relationships
and their engagement with a different racial semantics.

## FROM SIMPLE SEX – ROLE SOCIALISATION TO COMPLEX SEXUAL/ GENDER IDENTITY FORMATIONS

A number of writers have persuasively presented the case against biologically-
based and sex-role socialisation theories that continue to inform much school
policy and practice in relation to gender issues (Davies, 1979; Connell *et al.*,
1982). They suggest that these are inadequate to explain the complex social
and psychological processes involved in the development of gendered subjectivities which are underpinned by institutional and social, political and economic relations. They argue that sex role approaches often take for granted a
definition of femininity and masculinity, which is implicitly assumed to be
ahistorical, unitary, universal and unchanging categories. Recent work highlights the way in which sexuality has been erased by subsuming it within a
broader discourse of gender.

The writers above suggest an alternative way of understanding the complexity of male and female students' gendered and sexual identity formation. In this
approach, the official and hidden curriculum do not merely reflect the dominant role models of the wider society but actively produce a range of masculinities and femininities that are made available for students collectively to
negotiate and occupy. For example, in *The Making of Men* (Mac an Ghaill,
1994a) I reported on the range of male peer groups that included the more
traditional working-class anti-school Macho Lads and the upwardly mobile
Academic Achievers, alongside the new middle-class Real Englishmen and the
working-class New Enterprisers. These peer groups provided a conceptual
map to begin to explore the range of student masculine formations that were
developing within the local site of the school.

A key area of research from this new perspective is an exploration of individual
and collective male student experiences, meanings and investments in different
masculine styles. The adoption of these varied styles is seen to be marked by
confusions, contradictions and ambivalences. Hence, contemporary modes of
school masculinity may be portrayed as highly complex and contradictory, displaying power, violence, competition, a sense of identity, and social support.
Earlier feminist studies in underplaying these contradictory functions of modern
schooling emphasised a static, ahistorical and over-socialised polarisation of gender differences. In so doing, they failed to incorporate a more dynamic perspective that sees schools as active agents in the cultural production of working-class
Anglo-ethnic masculinities (Wolpe, 1988; Davies, 1989).

More recently, feminist and 'queer' theorists drawing on poststructuralism,
psychoanalysis and cultural studies have provided new ways of thinking about
the formation of sexual subjectivities (Dollimore, 1991; Sedgwick, 1991;

Butler, 1993). This theoretical work is of particular value in helping to provide a framework to explore sexuality in schools. In *The Making of Men* I examined the cultural elements which make up heterosexual male students' subjectivity within secondary schools. These elements – contradictory forms of compulsory heterosexuality, misogyny and homophobia – were marked by contextual ambivalence and contingency. In order to understand how the students learn the sexual/gender codes that conferred dominant masculinity, it was necessary to bring together social structures, cultural processes and sexual subjectivities. As Butler (1993) points out, heterosexuality does not gain its form by virtue of its internal qualities, but rather defines itself against abjected sexualities, in particular homosexuality. What emerged is the way in which heterosexual male students were involved in a double relationship of disparaging the 'other', including women and gays (external), at the same time as expelling femininity and homosexuality from within themselves (internal relations). These were the complex and contradictory processes within which heterosexual male student apprenticeships were developed within a secondary school context. Such complexity is likely to have considerable impact on relationships between students in a school, particularly in their middle teenage years, and on relationships between teachers and students.

Schools treat student sexuality as a latent outcome of an emerging adult status. When sexuality does 'break into' the public arena, it is conceptualised as natural and normal. At the same time, it remains located within the private sphere, reflecting a popular conception of sexuality as being 'special' or 'exceptional'. Hence, it draws upon essentialist understandings of sexuality as an individual concern. In contrast to schools' attempts to erase sex and sexuality from the formal curriculum, I found that sexuality in schools can be seen as all pervasive, as it manifests itself in teacher-student relations, within disciplinary practices and within the curriculum (Wolpe, 1988; Skeggs, 1991).

Sex and sexuality reappear in an extensive repertoire of student-student interactions including name-calling, flirting, classroom disruption, harassment of girls, homophobic abuse, playground conversations, desk-top graffiti, students' dress codes as well as teacher typifications and student-teacher interactions. These wide ranging schooling activities are central in making available dominant and subordinate sexual subject positions. Equally important, the identification of sexuality as part of a wider schooling process reconceptualises sexuality as a key element of a public agenda that structures school experiences. Since sexuality is enmeshed in a set of power relations, it shows that the deployment of sexuality works within social relations of domination and subordination rather than being merely an isolated matter for individuals. Stressing that sexuality is part of a process, it is suggested that sexual oppression, violence and discrimination are a continual everyday phenomenon and not confined to extraordinary incidents or specific aspects of the curriculum. Sexual power relations are an implicit part of everyday schooling experiences. The sexual harassment of subordinated groups illustrate how these experiences embody normalised, dominant masculine (hetero)sexualities.

Recent theoretical work provides a useful framework within which to explore the interconnections between gender and sexuality as it is lived in schools. For example, it can help critically to explore the under-theorised question of the 'boys' under achievement' thesis. In structuring the attributes of being a 'real boy/real girl', the various forms of masculinity/femininity that are dominant in schools are crucially involved in policing the boundaries of heterosexuality alongside the boundaries of 'proper' masculinity/femininity. More specifically, to be a 'real boy' is publicly to be in opposition to and distance oneself from the feminine and 'feminised' versions of masculinity. At an institutional level, student identities are formed in relation to the formal curriculum and the categories it makes available, including the academic/ vocational split, the arts/science division and the academic/sporting polarity. These categories are highly gendered, with the 'soft feminine' academic and arts subjects juxtaposed to the 'hard masculine' vocational, scientific and sporting options. Similarly, involvement in sport can be read as a cultural index of what it means to be a 'real boy', while to not be involved in sport and its associated 'lad' subculture is to be a 'bit of a poof' (Mac an Ghaill, 1994b, 1996; Canaan, 1996).

Sexualised and racialised terms such as 'poof', 'lezzie' and 'paki' are key discursive resources in the acting out of homophobia and compulsory hetero-sexuality within schools (Cockburn, 1987). In highlighting the heterosexual presumption operating within schools, there is a need to address the contradic-tions of heterosexuality that impact on lesbians and gays. In a recent study of Asian and African-Caribbean gay students (Mac an Ghaill, 1994b) I examined the complex contingency of the way in which relations of gender, sexuality, age, class, race and ethnicity combine and interact at the local level of the school. The students discussed the links between the institutional and male peer-group surveillance, regulation and control of female and male gender and sexual reputations. They were surprised at the way in which male teachers and students conflated assumed gay behaviour with femininity in order to dis-parage the former: 'the worst thing a teacher could call a boy was a girl'. The assimilation of masculine non-macho behaviour to feminine behaviour was most evident in relation to the ubiquity of the term 'poof', which in 'denoting lack of guts, suggests femininity-weakness, softness and inferiority' (Lees, 1987, p. 180). Furthermore, the students linked this form of 'gay-bashing' to that of the use of the term 'paki' as a form of 'paki-bashing'.

Both these labels – 'poof' and 'paki' – have several meanings, sometimes they are used with a specific sexual or racial connotation; while at other times they are used as general terms of abuse. The notoriety and frequency of these labels acted as major mechanisms of policing gender and sexual boundaries with specific implications for African-Caribbean and Asian heterosexual and gay young people.

There is much work to be done to explore further the way in which a school's social relations of race simultaneously 'speak' gender and sexuality (for example, the way in which to be a 'paki' is also to be a 'poof', is to be a 'non-proper boy'). In examining these interconnections, while focusing upon the sexual majority, a key issue to emerge was the question of Anglo-ethnicity.

## THE PRODUCTION OF ANGLO-ETHNIC AND RACIALISED IDENTITIES: WHITE ENGLISHNESS, CLASS, GENERATION AND MASCULINITY

There is a growing body of evidence (e.g. Mac an Ghaill, 1994a; Back, 1996) that points to the contradictions, ambivalences and resistances of the popular cultures of racism amongst white youth. This work challenges anti-racist accounts that continue to project white racism as a homogeneous social phenomenon.

Until recently anti-racist policies have tended to focus exclusively on black people. In so doing, white ethnicity was made absent from critical analysis. There is an urgent need to investigate whiteness in terms of identity formation and racialisation (Brah, 1997). In *The Making of Men* I decided to make white English young men the object of my research, not only in terms of racial responses to others but also by focusing upon the problematic nature of white Anglo-ethnicity for a dominant majority in a 'post-colonial' era. What emerges is the range of fractured and contradictory positions that are 'taken up' by white English male students in relation to race, racism and culture. More specifically, I found that in exploring from within their own cultural logic the young men's construction of dominant white English ethnicities, I began to trace the links between institutional life in schooling and training sites, youth cultural participation, consumption patterns, *and* emerging nationalist identities and masculine formations as noted by Parker *et al.* (1992) among others.

Within contemporary urban spaces, highly complex racialised maps of inter-ethnic relations are being constructed, from which individual racial behaviour cannot simplistically be predicted or read off from the anti-racist black-white dualistic model. During my research, white male students illustrated the generational and intra-class specificity of racist discourses, challenging conceptions of a unitary working-class inheritance (Cohen, 1986). These young men who have diverse values, understandings and feelings as well as local cultural knowleges that they 'bring with them' into public sites, can be seen as active makers of ethnic identities.

A major flaw in much multicultural and anti-racist work, exemplified in the 'positive images' approach, has been a failure to conceptualise the complexity of youth identity formation. In this process, public institutions can be seen as crucial cultural spaces in which material, ideological and discursive resources are consumed. These serve to affirm dominant masculine ethnicities, while producing a range of subject positions that young men 'take up'. Most importantly, the subjectivities of these young men are multiple. These result in young men offering diverse and inconsistent explanations of racism, misogyny, homophobia and heterosexism that are not passively inherited in a unitary or total way.

Located within local ethnic, gender and sexual peer group cultures, different sectors of young men actively select from a range of socially oppressive constructs and in this process make their own individual and collective meanings (Gramsci, 1971). For example, among the working-class students, white non-socially mobile 'Lads' tended to adopt a proletarian stance, showing more continuity with their parents than other peer groups, with particular references to their fathers' arguments that 'blacks had taken our jobs' and 'taken over our area'. They appealed to varying forms of what Cohen (1988) refers to as the 'nationalism of the neighbourhood', emphasising the need 'to defend our territory'.

White English socially mobile young men, adopting a more liberal perspective, challenged this interpretation, claiming that black people could not be held responsible for mass youth unemployment. A number of inter-related elements can be noted here. African-Caribbean and Asian students' orientation to school and the accompanying masculine identities was particularly important for the white English young men's responses to them. Also important is that, unlike their fathers' generation, these young men have grown up with Asian and African-Caribbean young people. Such day-to-day contact does not necessarily lead to a decrease in white racist perceptions or an increase in predictable liberal practices.

This is because the institutional inter-ethnic social and discursive relations played out among the young men have historic roots within a *multicultural* as well as *multi-racist* society (Hewitt, 1986; Jones, 1988; Back, 1996).

Currently, much anti-racist thinking has failed to engage with broader theorising about contemporary social and cultural transformations. There is a continuing reliance on earlier theories that explain white racism in terms of predictable racial superiority. For example, there have been few attempts to locate explanations within the new conditions of late capitalism, investigating the impact of the restructuring of de-industrialising urban areas on relations between and within the ethnic majority and minority communities. Rather than feelings of superiority, within dislocating inner city areas of mass youth unemployment and fragmented family life, young white English people are reporting feelings of cultural inferiority (Wievorka, 1991).

A key emerging issue among white working-class English young men and women within inner cities, as part of a wider crisis in Anglo-ethnicity, is their claim that schools are racist in favouring African Caribbeans and Asians while discriminating against whites. In response to this, teachers maintain that the white students' comments are a result of their racism. If you ask head teachers what educational principles informed their schools' anti-racist policies, they argue that it is very important in a multi-ethnic community that the curriculum addresses students' diverse cultural needs. I found evidence in the selection of curriculum material of positive representations of minority cultures, particularly that of African Caribbeans and Asians. But there appeared to be little awareness of the needs of other ethnic groups, including Irish students, who were often the main ethnic group in schools within the West Midlands area.

Equally significant was that white English working-class students' cultural needs did not appear to be addressed. Asking the teachers about this absence, they replied by asking me: have white English working-class students got any culture? These comments highlight the conceptual limits for public sector professionals, working within an anti-racist framework. In this, white racism is assumed to be a homogenous social phenomenon, and the representation of blacks and whites is juxtaposed within a 'simple' framework of oppressed and oppressors. If the defining characteristic of the white English working-class as a social collectivity is their 'whiteness', then, within this reductionist black-white dualistic model of oppositional structures, 'whiteness' speaks power – 'blackness' speaks powerlessness. Hence, the public sector professionals are unable to respond to white working class accounts of feelings of exclusion, except to read it as further evidence of their racist stance, that is structurally pre-given. Anti-racist policy informed by a principle of exclusivity is unable to address the ethnic majority's current experiences, concerns and anxieties.

This projection of the Anglo-ethnic majority's fears illustrates the complexity of dealing with racialised institutional spaces in English inner cities in the 1990s. White English young people are appropriating the language of racialised oppression within the specific context of compulsory state schooling, in which they feel that those in authority are culturally excluding them. Their teachers make clear the dominant institutionalised response to white working class young men in terms of a class cultural deficit view. Here we see the success of new social movements' development of anti-racism and anti-sexism, in providing political minorities with counter-discourses to name their collective experience of hostile and exclusionary public spaces. They are in a position to provide, to themselves and to others, an alternative explanation of their own experiences of alienating institutions.

White English working-class young people are unable to draw upon similar discursive resources to name their experience of class marginalisation. Hence, their class-based experiences come to be spoken through the language of racism. These tensions and contradictions are likely to increase during the 1990s within the wider political picture of a discursive shift in the media from the racial problems of social minorities to those of social majorities and accompanying discourses of the 'new white male victims'.

## THE REAL ENGLISHMEN: IN SEARCH OF A NATIONAL(IST) IDENTITY

Much has been written by social scientists about working-class male youth forms of racism. However, middle-class young men have remained invisible. In my own research a most interesting subcultural group of English middle-class male students was identified. They called themselves The Real Englishmen. Their name served as a triple signifier, with reference to their parents' political position on gender, sexuality and ethnicity. These were highly problematic inter-generational issues for them. They were in the process of constructing a positive Anglo-ethnic identity. At times their talk of nationality appeared obsessive. They explained the significance of their name with reference to white English ethnicity. More specifically, they were developing a young masculine identity against what they perceived as their parents' denial and suppression of English nationality and nationalism. They pointed to the need for a local sense of ethnic belonging that older generational notions of internationalism and Europeanism failed to provide. Furthermore, they highlight that an older generation's preoccupation with colour as the primary signifier of difference and differentiation prevents their parents from engaging with what they consider to be the 'real' contemporary mechanisms of exclusion that operate through culture. The Real Englishmen in their defence of what they saw as a declining English masculine ethnic identity, nostalgically appealed to the demise of 'English culture'.

Who are the English? is a key question for British sociology of racism and ethnicity in current conditions of 'post-colonialism'. In many ways, this has always been a key question in an earlier colonial period. But for many English people, from different political and ideological positions, it remains submerged beneath questions of the 'special needs' of minority ethnic groups, represented as either problems or victims. Critical theory reminds us that this is familiar ground in exploring relations between dominant/subordinate social collectivities, where the focus is exclusively upon the lives of the latter. Schools need to move beyond a conceptual framework that begins with making minorities the focus of attention.

A major concern developed during my research was the question of what constitutes white Anglo-ethnic identity. More specifically, I became interested in the cultural elements making up dominant modes of white English subjectivity, that informed male students' learning to act out 'being English' within a school arena. These elements consisted of contradictory forms of inherited imperial images, new cultural forms of racism, and liberal counter-discourses, that were marked by contextual contingency, ambivalence and anxiety.

It is becoming evident that Anglo-ethnic identity is a highly fragile socially constructed phenomenon. The question that emerges here is: how does this fragile construction become represented as an apparently stable, unitary category with fixed meanings? It is suggested that schools, with other state institutions, attempt to administer, regulate and reify unstable ethnic/racial categories. Most particularly this administration, regulation and reification of ethnic/racial boundaries is institutionalised through the inter-related material, social and discursive practices of staffroom, classroom and playground microcultures. In turn white English academics have reinforced the reification of the ethnic majority with their own representations.

This younger generation of white English young people raise a critical issue that is often absent from anti-racist programmes: the question of how English ethnicity fits into the complex configuration of inter-ethnic interpersonal relations at an institutional level in civil society. Furthermore, implicitly they raise questions about whether we can begin to construct contemporary forms of progressive English national identity to counter the New Right's appropriation of the discourse of nationality with its projected atavistic representations of the strong, exclusionary British state. In such a process it may be possible to work through the question of why 'there ain't no black in the Union Jack' (Gilroy, 1987). Hall (1992, p. 258), writing of current shifts in black cultural politics, refers to this title and suggests that: 'Fifteen years ago we didn't care, or at least I didn't care, whether there was any black in the Union Jack. Now not only do we care, we must.'

Within the context of the increasing criticism against anti-oppressive initiatives, such as feminism and anti-racism, these young men as a gendered, sexual and ethnic majority embody central contradictions in providing a critique that may help to point a way forward. They suggest the need to revisit the question of culture. Most significantly, the students raise key questions about the assumptions of cultural fixity involved in processes of inclusion and exclusion that underpin anti-racist representations of urban school life.

## SHIFTING INTER-ETHNIC TENSIONS AND ALLIANCES: CULTURAL INVESTMENTS AND SEXUAL SUBJECTIVITIES

Rattansi (1992, p. 27) has outlined the contextual contingency of racialized discourses, arguing that shifting alliances and points of tension may emerge from different arenas. He writes:

> of the ambivalences generated for many white youth by the attractions of Afro-Caribbean, Afro-American and African musical forms, and their admirations for some aggressive forms of Afro-Caribbean masculinity, have resulted in alliances in particular schools and neighbourhoods between white and Afro-Caribbean youth against Asian youth, where in some schools black-white conflicts remain submerged the dominant form of racist insult occurs between different ethnic minority groups, for instance Asian and Afro-Caribbean or Cypriot and Vietnamese.

In my research I found similar inter-ethnic shifting tensions and alliances were present within a continually changing situation. For example, there was no fixed pattern of white or black inter-ethnic response in the different year groups. Rather, different student sub-groups assigned high status to particular individuals or peer groups in which different hierarchies of ethnic masculinities were competitively negotiated and acted out. During the research period this was highlighted in relation to English-born Asian non-socially mobile 'Lads', who racially insulted year seven students who had recently arrived in the school from Pakistan. Here, we see the lived complexity of shifting processes of racialised inclusions and exclusions. The English-born Asian 'Lads' drew upon older hierarchies of ethnic masculinities, in which low status is ascribed to 'feminised' Asian boys. At the same moment, their public performance in distancing themselves from this ascribed social category is circumscribed by a shift from colour to that of cultural difference as the signifier of racialised exclusion. Within this specific institutional space contradictory discourses of exclusion positioned the new arrivals as not belonging to the 'local community' of the school and surrounding neighbourhood. Similar practices of exclusion were experienced by Arab and Vietnamese students.

Student inter-ethnic relations were a mixture of race specific elements and a broader range of social and psychic phenomena located within the school and linked to other social arenas. They involved specific emotional investments and cultural attachments, around popular cultural forms, such as music and sport, that were of central significance to their creative explorations of the shifting contours of cultural and political identities among and between ethnic majority and minority young people (Gilroy, 1987). As in the work of Hewitt (1986) and Back (1996), these young men were involved in constructing new syncretic versions of transculturally based identities. This is a long way from the fixed ethnic categories of much anti-racist and multicultural discourses on the racialisation of institutional arenas.

The complexity and contingency of the student inter-ethnic relations within the school appeared most visible in relation to sexuality. This was made most explicit by the Macho Lads. The white Macho Lads adopted a range of contradictory racial and sexual discourses. At one level, there was a strong public masculine identification with the Asian and African Caribbean Macho Lads. The peer group constructed a hierarchy of sexual prowess in which they positioned themselves as the most successful with young women. This self-representation was worked out against conformist students, who they publicly derided for their assumed sexual inexperience. At another level, individual white Macho Lads privately spoke to me of the African Caribbean Macho Lads' perceived heterosexual success with young white women as illegitimate. Female students from the school were labelled as 'slags', if they were seen with African Caribbeans or Asians from other schools, who were constructed as 'monstrous others' (Willis, 1977; Fanon, 1967).

Similar contradictions operated with the African Caribbean non-socially mobile 'Lads', who combined a public solidarity with the white Macho Lads and privately a general criticism of white men's sexuality. They positioned themselves as sexually superior both to white and Asian students and to conformist black students. More specifically they spoke of themselves as the main producers of popular style, which they claimed made them attractive to young women. This could not be simply read in terms of youthful boasting. The African Caribbeans appropriated discursive themes from dominant ambivalent white student representations of themselves, in which black male students' behaviour was over-sexualised. As for white male teachers, this consisted of contradictory cultural investments, of desire and jealousy in the highly exaggerated ascription to the black non-socially mobile 'Lads' of stylish resistance, sporting skills and 'having a reputation with girls'.

In order to enhance and amplify their own masculinity, the black and white non-socially mobile 'Lads' were overtly sexist to young women and female staff, and aggressive to male students who did not live up their prescribed masculine norms. They adopted a number of collective social practices in their attempt to regulate and normalise sexual/gender boundaries. The black non-socially mobile 'Lads' were particularly vindictive to African Caribbean academic students, who overtly distanced themselves from their anti-school strategies. In response the African Caribbean 'Lads' labelled them 'botty men' (a homophobic comment). Mercer and Julien (1988, p. 112) point out how, black men 'incorporate aspects of the dominant definitions of masculinity in order to contest the conditions of dependency and powerlessness which racism and racial oppression enforce'. Ironically, the African Caribbean 'Lads', in distancing themselves from the racist school structures, adopted survival strategies of hyper-masculine heterosexuality that threatened other African Caribbean students, adding further barriers to their gaining academic success. Consequently, this made it more difficult for academic African Caribbean students to gain social mobility via a professional job and the accompanying middle-class mode of masculinity. At the same time, white teachers' social positioning of black males as aggressive were reinforced (Gillborn, 1990).

## THE WAY AHEAD?

The foregoing argument is not support for regressive social policies which blame anti-racism and feminism at a time when, across European nation-states, there is a convergence between anti-racist and racist discourses (Balibar and Wallerstein, 1991). For example, the young middle-class men's accounts may be interpreted as supporting the 'white flight' from inner-cities, as white middle-class parents search out 'good' schools for their children (Cohen, 1993). Alternative readings are possible: a younger generation is responding to an inherited legacy of anti-oppressive reformation, which, they would argue, has positive as well as negative effects. These young people point out that these issues are far more complex than their parents 'rationally imagined'. They provide important criticisms of a cultural world that progressive educators, underpinned by New Social Movements – anti-racism and feminist theory – have attempted to construct. The young men point to the internal contradictions of the complex interrelationship of different forms of social divisions. More specifically, they graphically illustrate that the attempt to address one aspect of multiple oppressions may have unintended consequences for other aspects. Within an anti-oppressive framework there is little sensitivity to the way in which in particular social contexts, such as educational sites, inter-ethnic relations exist at the intersection of a range of social relations, and influence these in a variety of ways. For example, power relations of subordination and resistance need to be understood as being actively produced as well as reproduced, as a result of shifting boundaries between different social groups within specific public institutional spaces. This has clear implications for schools' policies and practices in the structuring of the curriculum and the creation of an inclusive school culture.

Schools do not exist on their own as locations for the cultural production and contestation of masculinities but rather in complex interrelationships with other cultural sites, including the family, labour markets, the legal system and popular culture. However, perhaps as Connell (1989) argues, contemporary schooling is the most strategic site, as it offers a condensed range of experiences in a sustained and mandatory fashion. It is also necessary to emphasise that schools do not produce masculinities and femininities in a direct, overly deterministic way, but that the construction of students' identities is an active process of negotiation, rejection, acceptance and ambivalence. In turn, these processes are circumscribed by wider sets of social relations at a time of 'the hardening of class inequality' in late capitalism (Westergaard, 1994).

# 8

## The 'Darker Side' of Pupil Culture: Discipline and Bullying in Schools

PAMELA MUNN

### INTRODUCTION

It is generally accepted that education, or more accurately, schooling, is concerned with more than pupils' academic learning. Nobody would dispute that such learning is important, vital even. To the extent that a pupil's life chances in terms of entry to higher education and employment are significantly affected by performance in public examinations, clearly such learning is a fundamental purpose of schooling. Even if one did not accept such a narrowly instrumentalist view of schooling, academic learning is important. As Pring (1997, p. 84) suggests:

> 'Emancipation' is a useful metaphor, for education is to be contrasted with the kind of enslavement associated with ignorance and with the lack of those mental powers, without which one is so easily duped and deceived.

He goes on to illustrate the meaning of emancipation in terms of understandings, knowledge, skills and dispositions in a range of areas such as the physical world around us, the aesthetic world, the moral world and so on. In short, academic learning is a worthwhile pursuit in itself, part of what it means to be an educated person.

However, academic learning, certificated or not, is only part of the story. Schools also have a role to play in the wider socialisation of their pupils. Indeed some philosophers such as McMurray (1958, quoted in Fielding, 1996, p. 162) would contend that education is about conducting human relationships.

> The principle that we live by entering into relations with one another provides the basic structure within which all human experience and activity falls, whether individual or social. For this reason the first priority in education – if by education we mean learning to be human – is learning to live in personal relations to other people. Our ability to enter into fully personal relations with others is the measure of our humanity. For inhumanity is precisely the perversion of human relations.

111

McMurray goes on to argue for a particular conceptualisation of community, 'the reciprocal caring for and enjoying someone for their own sake; it is not about using others to achieve one's own fulfilment'. Thus in asserting that schools have a role to play in pupils' socialisation, one immediately bumps up against the question of what kind of relationships ought pupils be socialised into. Are relations to be based on contracts and provision of services with interactions based on roles and functions as in typical notions of Gesellschaft? Or are the relation to be based on notions of personhood, humanity and the like, as in notions of Gemeinschaft? The tension between individual autonomy and independence on the one hand and the desire for belonging on the other is a well known phenomenon of contemporary society (e.g. Putnam, 1993).

These tensions are being played out in schools. The emphasis on academic learning as expressed in public examination results and attainment targets imply a Gesellschaft approach. Teachers are there to provide an expert service to pupils. If they fail to deliver, or indeed, if pupils fail to respond, the contract can be terminated. In one sense, then, depending on one's value position, this is the darker side of pupil culture. However, schools might also be seen as adopting a kind of Gemeinschaft strand through that part of the explicit curriculum which is called personal and social development, where there are opportunities to discuss relationships.

Personal and social development also takes place through the informal curriculum, activities such as participation in voluntary work with the old or very young, membership of school clubs and societies and taking part in school events such as plays and concerts all contribute. In these contexts, as in regular academic work, personal and social development is typically not the explicit primary goal. Rather it is a by-product of the activity itself. As is well known, the hidden curriculum of the school is also a powerful influence on pupils' socialisation although commentators vary in the meanings they ascribe to the term, hidden curriculum. (For example, Meighan, 1981; Bottery, 1990; Barr, 1997.) In general it may be described as the messages, intended and unintended, which are transmitted about the culture of the school. For example, through policies such as streaming or setting, the school may convey messages about the value and esteem in which pupils are held; or again, the way a school communicates with parents can indicate whether they are valued as genuine partners in their children's education, or as interfering busybodies, or as people to blame when a child has learning or behaviour difficulties.

Thus the personal and social development of pupils takes place in many different ways in schools and, of course, schools are not the only influence. A pupil's home, friends, work-mates and the media all contribute. Schools, however, are distinctive in that they are one of the few places where children and young people regularly spend most of their time with large groups of people of the same age. In this respect they provide particular opportunities for peer pressure to operate for good or ill. As formal institutions, schools can  convey the meanings of power, status and hierarchy to pupils.

The remainder of this chapter is concerned with the 'darker side' of pupil relationships. As such it necessarily operates at a level of generality which skims over the positive and affirming influence of school culture. Pupils helping each other with homework, engaged on joint projects, befriending new students to the school and supporting each other in adversity are all somewhat neglected in the account which follows as are the positive and friendly relations experienced between many pupils and many teachers.

The first part of the chapter focuses on school discipline as an area which can throw light on relationships between pupils and teachers and amongst teachers themselves. It concentrates on three main aspects: exclusion from school; teacher perceptions of discipline; and bullying. The second part identifies a range of strategies which schools can adopt to promote positive relationships between teachers and pupils and among pupils themselves. The chapter does not deal with broader philosophical and political issues of the kind of society we are educating pupils for. Rather it starts from the assumption that personal relationships are vital, that schools have a role to play in educating people about personal relationships and that school discipline provides a prism through which these can be viewed.

## DISCIPLINE IN SCHOOLS

What counts as 'good' and 'bad' behaviour in schools is difficult to measure given the importance of context. Teachers, for example, vary in this respect and even the same teacher may not apply the same standard of discipline depending on such circumstances as the ages of the pupils, the time of the day or year and his or her own mood. What counts as good discipline with first years on a Monday morning may be rather different from last thing on a Friday afternoon. Likewise the standards of behaviour seen as acceptable from five year olds would not be appropriate for ten or twelve year olds. This means it is difficult to obtain a valid and reliable picture of discipline in schools across Britain and hence of the general relations between teachers and pupils and among pupils themselves.

Such evidence as we have presents a worrying picture. Permanent exclusion from school in England and Wales has risen dramatically over the last six years. Parsons (1996) estimates that over 11,000 pupils were permanently excluded from secondary schools and 1,800 from primary schools in the school year 1995/96. The absolute numbers are worrying in themselves but of greater concern is that numbers are growing with a 45% increase between 1993–94 and 1995–96 in primary schools and an 18% increase over the same period in secondary schools (Parsons, 1996; Lawrence and Hayden, 1997). Furthermore boys are around four times as likely to be excluded as girls and African-Caribbean pupils are excluded between three and six times more often than their white peers (Commission for Racial Equality [CRE], 1996). The situation in Scotland is different as some local authorities do not permit permanent exclusion and, in any event, the English legislation stipulating the maximum number of days in any one term for which a pupil can be excluded does not apply. Nevertheless there is concern. Research revealed that in a sample of around 200 schools, of the 4,500 pupils who were excluded in an eight month period, most were excluded only once, for three days or less and returned to their original school. A substantial minority, however, 30%, were excluded for longer and over 1,000 young people had been excluded for six days or more (SOEID, 1997).

What impact does exclusion have on pupils and their families? Research in this area in Britain is necessarily small scale and relies on interviews and questionnaires with young people and their families or carers. A fairly consistent picture emerges. One theme is that of the unfairness of the exclusion. In the study for the Commission for Racial Equality (1996) half of the twelve people interviewed said that their exclusion was unfair. Cohen et al., (1994) in their study for Barnardos report a similar story, parents and children feeling that they had been unfairly labelled as troublemakers by teachers. They report (p. 76)

> [Unfairness] came through particularly strongly in cases of Black pupils who also pointed out that when they retaliated to racist name calling and other forms of racial harassment this could provoke a series of events which led to exclusion.

The issues of name calling, through not in a racist context, and of labelling, also featured in Scottish research involving eleven frequently excluded pupils and their families (Cullen et al., 1997, p. 48)

> They [other pupils] call you names and nag at you and you end up just striking back because you get sick of them and then it's not the other person that gets into trouble, it's me.
>
> (Jean A, Coruisk School)

> The teachers shout at you for wee things, even if somebody else did it, they ken that you're always in trouble so they give you worse than what the other person got that's hardly ever in trouble.
>
> (Michael N, Gairloch School)

This study showed that the pupils concerned were well aware of the consequences of 'getting a reputation', yet for some their behaviour was viewed as part of them and impossible to change. This passivity was quite striking. This might be interpreted as a way of absolving themselves from any responsibility for their actions – it was the teachers or school provision or organisation which had to change. Alternatively it might be seen as a recognition that they were destined not to be a valued member of the school community, forever beyond the pale as it were, unable and maybe unwilling to accept school norms and values.

This latter interpretation is borne out to some extent by reports of feelings of low self-esteem, stupidity and general lack of worth by some excluded pupils. A number of psychological studies in the USA have shown the association between these feelings, aggressive behaviour and youth crime. (See Goleman, 1996, pp. 234–7 for a useful overview; Cullingford and Morrison, 1995,

p. 548.) In the CRE (1996) study, some pupils were relieved to be excluded, perhaps because it removed one site in which such feelings were experienced. However, another theme emerging from the small number of studies which contain excluded pupils' voices is that of boredom, of missing school and of wanting to return.

These same studies report the stress which exclusion can cause in families. The CRE research (1996) involved interviews with 27 parents, 17 of whom used words such as stress, strain and worry, perhaps unsurprisingly, to describe the effects of exclusion. In a small number of extreme cases there were reports of illness, nervous breakdown and having to give up work. Other studies paint a similar picture, highlighting the other stresses often being experienced by families including poverty, bad housing, bereavement and illness (e.g. Cohen *et al.*, 1994; Lawrence and Hayden, 1997). Effects on the family are likely to be more intensely felt when the exclusion is permanent or long term and no alternative provision is made.

The impact of exclusion upon the generality of pupils is more difficult to gauge. Teachers' explanations of the purposes of exclusion often refer to their responsibilities for the general welfare of all the children in the class(es) as well as the individual welfare of troubled and troublesome pupils (Cullen *et al.*, 1996). Thus teachers contend that a 'cheer goes up from the silent majority of pupils' when a disruptive pupil is excluded. We might also speculate that exclusion sends messages about the kind of behaviour which would not be tolerated in school, reinforcing the existence of unequal power relationship between teachers and pupils and the nature of the implied contract between them. More subtly, perhaps in terms of socialisation, exclusion is sending messages about the nature of communities, their shared assumptive worlds of norms and values as a defining characteristic and, as far as schools are concerned, the importance of conforming to norms and values. A sense of belonging is thus premised on being alike rather than on understanding or even living with difference.

A different source of evidence about the darker side of pupil culture, albeit an oblique one, is that of surveys of teacher perceptions of indiscipline in schools and classrooms. As indicated above, the context dependence of behaviour makes it difficult to collect valid, reliable and statistically generalisable data about (mis)behaviour in schools. A postal survey carried out by Gray and Sine (DES, 1989) for the Elton Committee's investigation of school discipline in England and Wales tried to root responses in what actually happened in schools and classrooms in a given week. Some 4,400 teachers were involved, over half of whom were in secondary schools. The survey was repeated in Scotland in secondary schools only involving 900 teachers (Johnstone and Munn, 1992) and this survey was re-administered to the same schools but not the same teachers in 1996 (Johnstone and Munn, 1997). A new element was that the most recent survey involved primary (825) as well as secondary teachers (561). The survey listed a number of behaviours which teachers might encounter in their classrooms and around the schools and asked teachers, among other things, to note the frequency with which they encountered the behaviours, whether they were difficult to deal with, whether there were particularly difficult pupils and classes and the kinds of strategies they used in dealing with difficult behaviours, pupils and classes.

The consistent picture which emerges from these three surveys is that it is the 'drip, drip' effect of seemingly trivial behaviour such as talking out of turn, avoiding work and hindering other pupils which seem to be most wearisome to teachers. Physical aggression towards teachers was rare – reported by six teachers in 1996. Teacher perceptions of relations amongst pupils, however, tell a different story. Physical aggression between pupils in the classroom had to be dealt with by about half the sample of secondary teachers in both England (42%) and Scotland (50%) and by 74% and 69% of the respective samples of primary teachers. Approximately two thirds of all teachers over the three surveys reported encountering and dealing with general verbal aggression from one pupil to others. Tables 8.1 and 8.2 give more precise information.

The picture which emerges from these tables could be worrying. We do not know the exact number of pupils involved, nor the contexts in which physical and verbal aggression occurred nor indeed whether pupils were intimidated, upset or took such behaviours in their stride. Nevertheless, as a society we presumably want to encourage interaction based on reason, respect for others and basic courtesy. Taken together with the substantial proportions of staff (data not shown) indicating that talking out of turn, work avoidance and lack

**Table 8.1** Pupil-pupil behaviour encountered by teachers at least once during the survey weeks: Elton Report

| Type of Behaviour | In Class | | Around School | |
|---|---|---|---|---|
| | S*N = 3,200 % | P*N = 1,200 % | SN = 3,200 % | PN = 1,200 % |
| physical aggression towards other pupils | 42 | 74 | 66 | 86 |
| verbal abuse towards other pupils | 62 | 55 | 76 | 71 |

**Table 8.2** Pupil-pupil behaviour encountered by teachers at least once during the survey weeks: Scottish Research

| Type of Behaviour | In Class | | | Around School | | |
|---|---|---|---|---|---|---|
| | 1990 SN=883 | 1996 SN=561 | 1996 PN=825 | 1990 SN=883 | 1996 SN=561 | 1996 PN=825 |
| physical aggression towards other pupils | 50 | 50 | 69 | 67 | 69 | 77 |
| verbal abuse towards other pupils | 66 | 69 | 64 | 75 | 77 | 65 |

S* = Secondary teachers                    P* = Primary teachers of concern for others were daily occurrences, we do not get a picture of a well motivated and eager-to-learn pupil population. For some pupils, no doubt, coping with such an environment is part of growing up and poses few real problems. For others, however, such an environment can be threatening and ultimately destructive as research on bullying shows.

## BULLYING

Bullying has been taken seriously by schools only comparatively recently. Over the last ten years or so there has been a growth in research, in the development of support packages for schools and in organisations offering advice to victims and their families, via helplines and other means. Some packages offer advice on peer support/counselling to help bullies empathise with their victims and hopefully make them remorseful and so stop bullying behaviour. Attention to bullying can partly be explained by a small number of tragic cases in Britain which have resulted in the murder or suicide of victims. These high profile cases have generated questions about school discipline, programmes of personal and social development and the responsibilities of home, school and local community. Bullying is also an important issue in Japan and the United States where some victims have pursued litigation against the school district (Tattum and Tattum, 1992). Long term interest and action had been evident in Scandinavia. The Norwegians invested in a five year campaign of research and development in 1983–88 and have continued to be involved in developments designed to counteract bullying (Roland, 1988; 1989).

There is a lack of consensus in the literature as to what counts as bullying. Bullying can take many forms including physical aggression, threats, intimidation, extortion, rejection, name calling and teasing. Cullingford and Morrison (1995) identify three issues on which many writers focus, repetition, intentionality and unequal power relationships. In essence the behaviour has to take place more than once; the intention is to intimidate, threaten or exclude; and the bully or bullies are more powerful in terms of age, physique or numbers. Cullingford and Morrison (1995) argue for a broader definition, suggesting that more subtle manifestations of bullying tend to be ignored in the literature, by a concern for quantification. They assert that all children are involved in relationships in which some form of bullying takes place and call for a conceptualisation of bullying that focuses more clearly on the effect on the victim rather than on the behaviour of the bully. They point out that one-off incidents may be perceived as harmless by the perpetrator while having lasting psychological effects on those who experience them (Cullingford and Morrison, 1995, p. 551).

Victims' accounts of their feelings convey something of the loneliness, misery and terror which being bullied can generate.

Farana:          Some people hurt me in my class. They swear, sort of. They call me names. Sometimes they don't like me because I'm Pakistani. They don't like me. They think I'm *just* a Pakistani.

| Interviewer: | Do you ever feel lonely? |
| Farana: | Yes, when I've no friends – when Joanne is not my friend, when my sisters are inside school. |
| Interviewer: | Have you tried to be friendly with them [others in the class]? |
| Farana (quietly): | Sometimes. They won't be my friend. |

(Cowie *et al.*, 1992, p. 89)

I have been picked on. People think I am nothing and say anything they want to me. Every day I feel rejected. It's not that people use violence against me but I feel as if I am treated as a dustbin.

(Mellor, 1993, p. 11)

When I was at primary school I got picked on non-stop for two years. No-one talked to me. I hadn't done anything to get blamed for. I used to cry myself to sleep at night. This all happened in primary 6 and I have lost nearly all my self-confidence and hate being on my own.

(Mellor, 1993, p. 5)

Bullying has been given as an explanation for non-attendance (Reid, 1988; Johnstone and Munn, 1992) as well as leading to feelings of isolation and inadequacy.

## WHAT CAN SCHOOLS DO?

It is one thing to describe the darker side of pupil culture; quite another to offer prescriptions for counteracting it. Moreover the connection between research and practice is tenuous and contested (Hargreaves D., 1996; Hammersley, 1997; McIntyre, 1997) to say nothing of the problems in bringing about educational change (Fullan, 1991; 1997). This section provides a brief description of interventions which schools might make, categorised in terms of school level, classroom level and individual pupil. See Lloyd and Munn (forthcoming) for a fuller discussion. Standards of proof as to the effectiveness of these interventions are certainly not equivalent to evidence based medical studies. Indeed a major gap in the research literature exists in this respect. A good deal of innovative and imaginative work is taking place in schools but more needs to be done both to disseminate the work and to evaluate its effectiveness. Recent research suggests that 'some things do work, sometimes!' (Lane, 1994). Defining what effectiveness means in terms of socialisation is problematic and school effectiveness research has taught us a great deal about the need for longitudinal studies employing multi-level modelling techniques if one wants to make robust claims about what works.

### School level

The generally accepted association between school ethos and pupil behaviour suggests that schools wanting to counteract the dark side of pupil culture should develop a positive ethos. (The terms ethos and culture tend to be used interchangeably in the literature. Ethos is used here as it is the term used generally in Scotland to describe developments aimed at improving school culture). Of course encouraging schools to develop a positive ethos is glib and much easier said than done. Nevertheless, there are examples of schools trying to do just that. In Scotland the association between ethos and behaviour has been taken seriously and HMI commissioned researchers to develop 'ethos indicators' as part of a general strategy for school improvement. This strategy emphasises that the key to improvement is school self-evaluation and so researchers and HMI working together offered schools a support pack suggesting both a substantive focus for improving ethos (e.g. physical environment; pupil morale; teacher morale; parental involvement) and tools for collecting evidence about ethos. The tools emphasised the need to seek information from pupils, parents and staff and to involve them in identifying and taking forwards developments. As schools began to experiment they wanted to share ideas and experiences with others and so the Scottish Schools Ethos Network was born. Over 1,000 schools are now members. They receive a newsletter, case studies of action, the opportunity to attend a series of seminars and there is a high profile national conference once a year. An initial concern with technical aspects of collecting information in a valid and reliable way has now developed into a focus on substantive issues such as ways of involving pupils in decision making, making constructive use of the playground, the advantages and disadvantages of buddy systems and using praise and rewards to promote positive behaviour. There are therefore practical and low cost steps which schools can take to investigate pupil culture and to help its darker side.

A particular aspect of the darker side of pupil culture is bullying. As mentioned above, there has been a burgeoning of resource packs and advice on this topic. A prior condition for any development here is that senior staff take the issue seriously and are prepared to acknowledge that bullying teachers as well as bullying pupils exist. Mellor (1995) provides a comprehensive account of the diversity of approaches developed in Scotland.

### Classroom level

There are a number of strategies which teachers can use in the classroom to help counteract the darker side of pupil culture. Circle time is increasingly used in the primary class as a way of promoting positive group relationships. It is based on the thinking of social group work and uses many of the methods developed for use in youth work and 'intermediate treatment' in the 1970s and 1980s (Button, 1982; Mosely, 1995).

Co-operative learning is an umbrella term for a number of approaches to group work which are claimed to enhance academic achievement and interpersonal skills. Although the substantive focus and particular approaches to group work vary, co-operative learning techniques share four common characteristics which set them apart from other approaches to group work. These are i) pupils work in small heterogeneous groups, e.g. different social and ethnic backgrounds, skill levels and gender; ii) pupils are interdependent, to succeed pupils need to be concerned about the performance of all group members; iii) there is high individual accountability, e.g. each group member has to understand his or her responsibilities within the group; and vi) pupils work to develop interpersonal skills and small group skills, for example of negotiation, task allocation, turn taking. The research and development work underpinning this approach is associated with Johnson and Johnson (e.g. 1981, 1984, 1996) in the United States.

Circle time and co-operative learning derive from theoretical perspectives emphasising self concept and aim to enhance self-esteem. Other approaches assume that teachers could be more effective in preventing and responding to indiscipline in the classroom (e.g. Chisholm *et al.*, 1986; Wheldall 1987). Others again restate the right of the teacher to be in charge of the classroom (Moss and Rumbold, 1992). Clearly values questions underpin whatever approach is seen as appropriate, as do questions relating to the substantive focus of concern. A focus on teacher-pupil relationships would direct attention towards teacher behaviour and skills while a focus on relationships among pupils would direct attention to methods such as circle time or co-operative learning. A troubled classroom may require many different kinds of intervention but teacher-pupil relationships would seem to be the logical starting point for improvement. Techniques such as circle time are predicated upon a basic level of trust and respect between the teachers and pupils in the class.

### Individual level

A range of strategies is available to help an individual child or young person suffering as a consequence of the darker side of pupil culture. A number of factors will influence the selection and use of a particular strategy. Key among them is the reason for the suffering. The teacher may see the child as generally disaffected from the norms and values espoused by the school, or as having individual psychologically based problems which make it difficult for the child to conform, or as having learning difficulties, or a combination of these. Responses to individual pupils also vary according to the age and stage of the child, the confidence and competence of the teacher, resource availability and the theoretical interests of any external professionals involved, such as educational psychologists or doctors (Lane, 1994). Responses may also be influenced by whether the difficulty is seen as 'curable' or enduring (Allan, Brown and Munn, 1991). Thus approaches include counselling, anger control, learning or behaviour targets, the prescription of Ritalin (for Attention Deficit and Hyperactivity Disorder), brief therapy and the like (Lloyd and Munn, forthcoming).

### CONCLUSION

This chapter has suggested that one way of exploring the darker side of pupil culture is to consider research evidence on school discipline, exclusions and bullying. This evidence tells us something about the relations between teachers and pupils and among pupils themselves. There are relatively few studies in this area which focus on pupils' experience of schooling from the pupils' perspective and those which do tend to be small scale. Our understanding of what it means to be a pupil and whether there is a significant variation within and across schools needs to be enhanced. Since schools consist of large numbers of young people and relatively few adults one aspect of the darker side of pupil culture is that of how the individual pupil who does not 'measure up' or conform to the standard set by adults – whatever that may be – feels and is treated. Emphasis on the individual is deliberate as a number of studies describe the formation of anti-school, typically male, sub-cultures among groups of pupils who see school as a social centre, to meet friends and have a laugh. These studies to some extent map a male, working class, adolescent sub-culture (Hargreaves D. *et al.*, 1975; Willis, 1977; Corrigan, 1979).

If one interpretation of the dark side of pupil culture is social isolation and loneliness then the individual who does not conform to academic, sporting, artistic or behavioural standards set by adults surely experiences the dark side. Those who do not conform to these kinds of standards but are able to identify with others in the same boat, so to speak, can find solace, or dignity or esteem from the group. This is what makes a lonely child in school so poignant. We know from studies of pupil-teacher interaction how easily children's self-esteem can be dented by teachers deliberately or unconsciously valuing some pupils more highly than others. To have this compounded by feelings of isolation from or rejection by one's peers is dark indeed. Children have to go to school and thus some have to cope with such feelings on a daily basis.

Rejection and isolation can be seen as one kind of bullying but other aspects of peer relationships can be characterised as the dark side of pupil culture. These include physical violence and intimidation, verbal abuse and other more subtle pressure to conform to cultural norms of dress, general appearance and behaviour. There are two senses in which peer pressure can count as the dark side of pupil culture.

The first sense is when an individual is forced to behave in ways they do not wish to or cannot. This includes pressure to achieve academically as well as other things. The second sense is when the behaviour of the group is anti-social involving say extortion, theft or drug abuse.

Another sense in which the dark side may be conceptualised is those aspects of the reality of school which do not conform to the idealised notion of teachers teaching happy, well motivated children, most of whom are well behaved in the classroom, around the school and in the playground.

Cultures, dark or light, are not static. Pupils' cultures derive from and interact with that of teachers and of others working there. All these cultures are in a constant state of flux. This is only part of the story, however. Pupils and teachers and other school staff have lives outside school, easy though this is for each to forget in the demanding experience of being a teacher or pupil. The ways in which these interact dynamically to construct and reconstruct what it means to be a pupil is something that still eludes us. We know enough, however, to recognise that there is a dark side to being a pupil and to begin to develop strategies and interventions intended to make the dark side brighter.

# 9

## Inclusivity and School Culture: the Case of Special Education

JENNY CORBETT

### INTRODUCTION

The term 'special' implies something distinct which removes it from the dominant culture. Examining the case of special education aids our understanding of the complex relationship between sub-cultures and the dominant culture, both in the broad social context and in the community of the school. Whilst taking this sub-culture as a case study, it is important to conceptualise special education as just one of many other marginalised sub-cultures, each struggling for anti-discrimination legislation and equality of opportunity.

This chapter will begin by setting the case of special education into the current legislative and political context. In this sense, it is exploring the way in which special education is seen in relation to education generally, in particular the debates upon standards and effectiveness. The chapter will then focus upon institutional cultures which include or exclude certain individuals and groups and explore the ways in which consumer choice and a market economy have influenced special education priorities. The relationship between new concepts of inclusivity and familiar notions of integration will be analysed in order to consider whether elements of the latter are retained in the former. Finally, peer cultures are examined in relation to the degree of inclusion which they can offer to those who are seen as different. In taking this approach, the arguments will develop sequentially from the macro to the micro cultures of social, structural, institutional and individual value systems.

Four key questions, relating to inclusivity within a school culture as perceived in the case of special education, are going to be addressed in this chapter. These are:

- How can schools create an inclusive culture in a climate of effectiveness?
- Are the concepts of entitlement and inclusion incompatible?
- What does inclusion actually involve?
- What specific practices help individuals to feel included or excluded?

In drawing upon evaluations of government initiatives and legislative policy-making as well as insights provided by ethnographical methodology and practitioners' reflections, there is a deliberate attempt to illustrate the layers of influences from different sources which combine to form the cultural climate of any school community. By 'climate' is meant that unwritten code of habitual practice, procedures and power relations which forms the composition of every institution and makes each one similar yet unique. What unites these different sources is their common concern for values, fairness and equity; what may divide them is the different roles, status and cultural capital each brings to the process.

Special education has often been seen as a separate provision, removed from the norm. Recent policy documents from the new Labour Government suggest that this oversimplified distinction persists (DfEE, 1997b; Barber, 1997). A separatist perspective offers a narrow interpretation of special need which is focused upon difference, rather than recognising the ways in which needs are common to all learners and that some individuals will have very specific needs, requiring particular responses. There are multi-dimensional aspects of need: those educational needs shared by all pupils; those which arise from exceptional characteristics, such as impairment or particular abilities; those which are unique to individuals and distinguish them from all others.

Differentiation is a concept which has become confused in the current, assessment-focused context. It is concerned with developing effective teaching skills to meet the individual and group needs of diverse learners within the mainstream classroom. It is a multi-level process which has to address the divergent cultures of different schools, the class grouping within schools and the organisation of teaching within classes. Designing a common curriculum for all has to take account of difference in a broad cultural sense and not just in relation to learning difficulty and disability. This means recognising that learners bring unequal levels of cultural capital into their school lives, reflecting their social status and sense of worth in relation to social norms. Where they and their families experience social exclusion beyond the school community, they are likely to bring this feeling of exclusion into the school context and differentiation needs to allow for different degrees of social acceptance. The new Government Green Paper, 'Excellence for all children: Meeting Special Educational Needs' (DfEE, 1997a) raises many interesting and important issues for inclusion. It is supportive of the principle of inclusion and calls for all children to be in mainstream schools unless there are compelling reasons for them not to be there. It wants children to be fully included within the curriculum and to be taught by methods which accommodate their varying needs. It seeks ways of celebrating the success of those schools which improve their ability to provide for a wide range of needs and even to develop a 'kite mark' for schools which reach the required standards. It is a document which refers to co-ordination and co-operation as key elements of the inclusive educational service it wishes to see for the future, in which 'By 2002 . . . a growing number of mainstream schools will be willing and able to accept children with a range of special educational needs' (DfEE, 1997a, p. 9). This is exciting rhetoric and a welcome encouragement for those who favour inclusivity in education. However, it rests uncomfortably with some other aspects of recent educational initiatives which have increased competitive elements between schools and fostered an exclusive school culture.

## HOW CAN SCHOOLS CREATE AN INCLUSIVE CULTURE IN A CLIMATE OF EFFECTIVENESS?

This question refers particularly to the dominant dogma of school effectiveness and school improvement and its implications for those learners whose needs are seen as special. Although advocates such as Sammons, Hillman and Mortimore (1997) claim that schools which are effective raise pupil self-esteem, create high expectations and maximise learning time, critics like Davies (1997) suggest that the narrow emphasis upon examination success makes an 'unproven assumption that what is good for competitive or individualized tests will also be good for cooperative or social learning' (p. 31). Inclusive school communities are difficult to create within an individualised model of achievement. It is the very nature of inclusivity that it supports community rather than individualised values, in establishing goals of social responsibility, active citizenship, solidarity and co-operation.

Inclusivity needs working at; it takes time. As White (1997) recognises, school effectiveness research tends to be concerned primarily with short-term outcomes and signs of tangible results. It often under-values social and affective progress in relation to academic outcomes, yet it is in the areas of social and emotional development that much special education is mainly concerned. A child who is very withdrawn and refuses to speak in class may gradually begin to speak with the therapist, on a one-to-one basis, after many slow and painstaking sessions in which there were minimal signs of progress. That this child is now using language to communicate and will respond to verbal requests may, in real terms, be a highly significant measure of progress, learning and personal growth. However, it is not measurable in external, examination terms and is unlikely to be conceived of as effective in relation to the cost of specialist input and the laboriously slow time it has taken to develop. Yet, if a school community espouses inclusive values, this has to imply that time spent on one individual whose exclusion results from difficulties which can be addressed is time well spent.

There are evident tensions between alternative conceptions of what constitutes an effective school. The dominant ideology within the school effectiveness movement appears to be that schools are effective if they attain high examination results and come near the top of the league tables in the national press. Other schools are seen as being effective in relation to 'value added' measures, which take into account their location, intake and recent history. The league tables do not differentiate between schools with very few pupils who have learning disabilities and those with substantial numbers requiring additional support. Viv Wakeham, Head of West Horndon primary school in Essex which has a special unit for speech and language disorders, made a legal challenge to the format of the tables which she lost. She commented to *The Times* in 1997: 'Schools are already increasingly reluctant to admit children with special educational needs because they are expensive to educate and have a potentially damaging effect on the league table position. Including the results of children in special units will deter most schools from agreeing to have one.'

It may be argued that the most easily created 'effective' schools are going to be those with the most motivated, industrious, high-achieving and socially advantaged pupils. In the current political climate, where schools are set in competition with one another, there is little incentive for schools to promote their commitment to supporting less able learners if it means that the parents of the more able will select alternatives. Inclusivity rests uneasily with a notion of effectiveness which seeks to level all learners to a measure of achievement which excludes a significant minority. Hamilton (1997) offers an extreme critique of school effectiveness research in which he suggests that it cloaks 'school practices in a progressive, social-darwinist, eugenic rationale' (p. 125). If a culture which promotes effectiveness and improvement truly results in a struggle for the survival of the fittest and a deprecation of those who fall outside the norm, it is an exclusive culture. Advocates may argue that, far from exclusive, it is actually setting high targets for all and not merely for a small elite.

However, critics like Hamilton (1997) claim that the manifestations of a culture of academic effectiveness 'are shaped not so much by inclusive educational values that link democracy, sustainable growth, equal opportunities and social justice but, rather, by a divisive political discipline redolent of performance-based league tables and performance-related funding' (p. 129). Whilst his views may reflect the most radical critiques of this influential aspect of British educational culture, they contain elements which indicate how difficult it is to achieve inclusivity. The dominant aspects of our current educational culture represent key elements of our social, economic and political life: competitiveness; accountability; an emphasis on national comparisons; the end of traditional work patterns; the emergence of personal portfolios; market values; the fragmentation of family and social support structures. They encourage individualistic rather than community values to develop. Within this context, it is not surprising to discover that a concept like 'entitlement' has become so familiar within the vocabulary of 1990s British special education.

## ARE CONCEPTS OF ENTITLEMENT AND INCLUSIVITY INCOMPATIBLE?

I have begun to feel increasingly that what distinguishes the concepts of entitlement and inclusivity is that the former is pragmatic and the latter idealistic. Some might suggest that entitlement is realistic whilst inclusivity is impractical. Others would challenge those who prefer entitlement as reflecting individualistic rather than community values. It might be supposed that inclusivity is about entitlement to participate in mainstream school culture and that, therefore, the two are inextricably linked and clearly compatible. However, when legislative restraints and funding limitations are accounted for, the issue of who is entitled to what often becomes fiercely contested. Entitlement is about actually getting the resources or placement which an individual requires; inclusivity is about working towards a cultural climate which celebrates all learners regardless of levels of need. It is a significant difference and a major shift from the practical to the philosophical.

Inclusivity has become a much debated issue. At a broad cross-cultural level, Reynolds (1997), who is a key founder member of the school effectiveness movement, suggested that 'what is interesting for both sets of societies – West and East – is the extent to which any blend of practice may be achievable without major cultural change in the wider society' (p. 17). This is exploring inclusion in its widest sense, as is happening within a global market enomony, in which what works for one country is eagerly adopted as valuable for another. Yet, as Reynolds acknowledges, without changing the national culture mere changes of practice are likely to be ineffectual. This must surely also be true of the culture of schooling. Superficial claims to inclusivity do not change the deep culture of schools as micro-societies. This is a theme I shall develop in the chapter, as the focus moves from legislation and concepts to peer interaction and individual experience.

Inclusion and exclusion have become political issues, related to concepts of equality and social justice. Estelle Morris, the education junior minister, expressed concern at the high percentage of ethnic minority pupils who were seen as school failures. She recorded that in 1995 only 44% of Black pupils reached five or more GCSEs at A to C grades (Morris, 1997, p. 25). Only 5% of gipsy and travellers' children were still registered as regularly attending school by Key Stage 4. The effective schools movement claims that effective schools can make a difference of up to two GCSEs in academic terms relative to other less effective schools, yet they cannot compensate for society (Barker, 1997). Where effectiveness is dependent upon intake, where does this leave special schools and sink secondary schools in which expectations may be very low and opportunities for social inclusion severely restricted?

The rapid rise in the rate of exclusions has become something of a national scandal as Ghouri (1997) testifies in revealing that exclusions have risen by 450% in five years with the fastest increase being in the primary sector, 30% in the last year alone. The national charity, The Children's Society, has piloted a new scheme called SHINE (Schools Have Inclusive Education), which offers children at risk of exclusion one-to-one support at school. Their findings are that Afro-Caribbean boys are four to six times more likely to be excluded, often rendering them unemployable, dependent on benefits and at risk of offending. It seems to me to be important to recognise the political dimensions of school inclusion or exclusion. Underlying the surface issues of working towards high achievement in numeracy and literacy, there are other more obscure yet invidious messages which some children receive, telling them they are outsiders and unwanted. Many parents would say that they did not receive the educational entitlement they were due because they lacked the insider knowledge to work the system. Others feel that their children were labelled as having an 'emotional and behavioural difficulty' instead of 'dyslexia' because they were black. Just as exclusions have disproportionately been applied to certain groups rather than others, so entitlement to resources and funding has not been shared equally.

The recent ruling that a woman, who had not received the 'dyslexia' diagnosis by the LEA educational psychologist early enough for it to have led to appropriate remediation, was to be awarded high damages was regarded as a landmark in legal history (Pyke, 1997). It indicated the minefield which special education professionals tread in a blame-culture of consumer choice, complaint and competition. Perhaps this example illustrates, more than any conceptual debates on inclusivity, that entitlement is about each individual getting as much out of the legislative frameworks as they possibly can, disregarding the fact that this will leave less available to share with others. In an interesting, reflective interview, Baroness Warnock suggested that the 1981 Education Act, whilst implementing aspects of the 1978 Warnock Report, was not very successful in its present practice and that it was effectively the 'last gasp of the welfare state' (Warnock, quoted by Peter, 1997, p. 11). She said that it was lack of money and lack of earmarked funds which made its impact so negative. She goes on to say that she was never a supporter of integration, certainly not of transferring children from special into mainstream schools. As regards entitlement, which is legitimated within the statement of special needs, her views are that 'unless someone is brave enough to bring to an end what I regard as our – my – greatest mistake, namely statementing, money will still be squandered in the same way as it is now' (p. 13). She regards the problems arising from statementing and the work of the Special Educational Needs Tribunal as being almost insoluble and very expensive.

The new Labour Government's Green Paper on Special Education (DfEE, 1997a) has also suggested that the practice of statementing should end, thereby addressing a problem which Warnock perceived as critical. They also seek to extend inclusive provision and to close more special schools. Immediate responses from supporters of parents' rights groups challenge the loss of entitlement to services and some teachers' unions have expressed concern that more inclusion will lead to an increase in teacher stress. Both reactions reflect the difficulty in balancing entitlement and inclusivity. They also suggest that inclusion is generally understood at the surface level only. It has to be seen as a multi-layered process, in which each stage leads to more complex and critical understandings.

## WHAT DOES INCLUSIVITY INVOLVE?

In 1978, the Warnock Report defined integration as comprising three distinct levels: locational, social, and functional. Locational involved merely being situated in physical proximity to mainstream students. It was the most rudimentary form of what constituted integration. Social integration meant sharing meal-times, recreational and non-academic activities. This was seen as a next stage towards increased participation. Functional implied full integration, in that it was about some modifications of the curriculum to include all learners and full participation in classroom tasks (Table 9.1). These stages became highly influential among special educators in that stage 1 and 2 were seen usually as unproblematic but stage 3 as very difficult to achieve. Inclusivity may be seen to start at stage 3 as a basis.

**Table 9.1**   1978 Warnock Model of 3 Stages of Integration

| |
| --- |
| Locational (sharing a base) |
| Social (mixing for recreation) |
| Functional (full curricular inclusion) |

The language of inclusion is more polemical and passionate than that of integration. Low (1997), for example, distinguishes between three types of inclusivists: 'hard ones, soft ones and stupid ones' (p. 71) in which he sees the pressure for full inclusion as a snare, a delusion and an expression of elitism. Barton (1997) says that 'inclusive education is part of a human rights approach to social relations and conditions' in which 'the intentions and values involved are an integral part of a vision of the whole society of which education is a part' (p. 234). Thomas (1997) is extremely optimistic in feeling that 'an inclusive philosophy is rising again and prospering' and that 'inclusion will certainly happen increasingly over the first part of the new century' (p. 106). What seems to be common to all authors talking of inclusion is that they see it necessitating change. It is not about fitting into the status quo.

It is about changing the culture of an educational institution (be it school, college or university) to make it become more responsive to difference, receptive to change and sensitive to language, imagery and the presentation of ideas. Integration is about them fitting in with us. If individuals are to successfully integrate, it is they who need to adapt and assimilate themselves into the dominant norms which are accepted as intrinsically superior to marginalised cultures. Inclusion is about us creating a climate which welcomes, supports and nurtures diverse needs. An integration metaphor could be that of the square peg struggling to fit into the round hole accompanied by the caption, 'Come in, but only if you can fit'. An inclusion metaphor could be that of a circle containing many different shapes and sizes, all inter-relating within the whole, and the caption reading, 'Come in. We celebrate difference here. You can be yourself and not struggle to be normal.' It is that struggle which can be debilitating and create additional disadvantages to those already marginalised within the system.

Lindsay (1997), in a detailed analysis of research on inclusive provision and reflections on the distinction between integration and inclusion, concluded that 'an inclusive system need not imply every school is inclusive' and that whilst 'the latter may be an ideal, cutting down on travel, facilitating out of school contact,' he reflected that 'it is possible to have a system which is inclusive but focuses resources' (pp. 102–3). His suggestions link closely to views expressed within the new Government Green Paper (DfEE, 1997a) which reflect the awareness that carefully planned support structures need to exist if vulnerable individuals are not to become what I would refer to as inclusion casualties.

My observations on examining the process of educational integration over the last fifteen years are that it contains elements of the following features: the individuals being integrated are expected to have reserves of courage and tenacity beyond what could usually be considered reasonable to expect; most educational institutions create their own cultural norms which define who is achieving and who is failing. Given this reflection on the progress of integrationist practices, it seems to me that it is the culture of inclusivity which has to be addressed, rather than policy and curricular developments alone. This culture forms the deep, third level of inclusivity (Table 9.2). Level 1 is the surface inclusion, led by policy and notions of school effectiveness and Level 2 is the structural modifications to the school curriculum. Only Level 3, the deep culture, will address the hidden curriculum of fundamental value systems, rituals and routines, initiations and acceptance which form the fabric of daily life. This is described as 'deep' culture because it is often obscure, difficult to grasp and impossible to understand without a lengthy emersion. Like exploring the bottom of the ocean floor, a dip into the deep culture of an institution can reveal unexpected treasures and submerged dangers. It is within this level that children feel either included or excluded, whatever the policy or structural processes of inclusivity may offer them.

**Table 9.2**   1997 Culture of Inclusion

| |
| --- |
| Surface (policy/effective schools) |
| Structural (curriculum) |
| Deep (culture) |

Part of the deep culture in mainstream and in special schools is the intangible process whereby children are taught to see themselves as either valued or devalued group members. For teachers, it is a considerable challenge to discover strategies by which they can help a child to feel included, when that child is quite clearly different from their peers in perceptible ways. If there is a deep culture of ownership and shared responsibility, this can avoid too great a reliance upon either early statementing of special educational needs or exclusion. Estelle Morris (Morris, *TES*, 1997), in a response to the Green Paper, suggested that massive increases in the number of children being statemented and in parents going to appeal was an indication that the system lower down was not working. Don Foster the Liberal Democrat education and employment spokesman, said that the emphasis on market forces coupled with shortages of support services meant that too many schools were turning to exclusion as a preventative measure.

These reflections from politicians and charitable groups illustrate the cultural context of special education. There are social groups who are being excluded from schools just as there are social groups being excluded from the wider society. Exclusion of specific individuals is often justified on the grounds of their inappropriate behaviours, disruptive effect on others and general unacceptability. It may be nothing more than their difference from the dominant culture which causes offence. Some educationalists, like Hamilton (1997), would postulate that a recent drive for increased effectiveness and efficiency in education has accentuated notions of what is 'special', in order to foster a new generation of competitive high-achievers.

If the goal posts are constantly moving to accommodate new definitions of national average, this places more and more low-achievers into the penalty area where they risk relegation. It seems to me to be a fairly accurate analogy to compare the current education scene to football divisions: the first division attracts the high-flying players and the sponsorship in the form of parent power; the fourth division is struggling to maintain its stability, with a demoralised and insecure team and falling gates. Success attracts success; failure tends to lead to more failure. The potential for a crisis in exclusions is surely a reflection of the current rise of education as a market and the cult of the winners.

## WHAT HELPS INDIVIDUAL CHILDREN FEEL INCLUDED OR EXCLUDED?

Starting with what happens in the classroom, inclusion must also involve behaviours in both the playground and within the group friendships which make up informal school cultures. In their recent research findings on what works in inclusive education, Sebba and Sachdev (1997) say that 'there is a fundamental tension between the levels of support demanded by some schools faced with pupils who have increasingly diverse needs and the limited effectiveness of the current support provided, especially in secondary schools' (p. 41). They found in their investigations nationally that pupil participation and learning is helped by high expectations, drawing upon pupils' past experiences and maximising peer support. However, they also noted that it is hindered by rigid setting by ability. The latter finding is reflective of some recent confrontations between London teachers and Ofsted in which Ofsted has recommended setting for pupils aged eleven to fourteen and the teachers, through their unions, have sought the retention of mixed-ability teaching (Wolchover, 1997). From these research findings and the practitioner concern, it is evident that elements of our current climate of efficiency militate against the development of a high level of inclusivity.

Another critical issue to be addressed in any examination of inclusive school communities is that of peer acceptance or rejection. Children may be accepted by the headteacher and their needs explored by the classteachers but if they are then tormented by their peers, they do not feel included. In a recent research project on inclusivity in primary education, Vlachou (1997) revealed that disabled children were teased and, in their words 'tormented'. She observed that 'picking on' disabled children was just part of the complex power struggles within the deep culture of a school. Everyone got picked on according to their changing image and status within the group. Some of the disabled children were liked because their peers enjoyed helping them whilst others were seen as too disruptive.

These findings are interesting in relation to recent reflective comments made by a group of headteachers of special schools for pupils with moderate learning difficulties, whom I met in September 1997. They observed that, particularly at secondary level, it could be very difficult for their pupils to gain peer acceptance on their re-integration into mainstream schooling. One black girl, who was outstandingly skilled at running, gained a high level of approval when she first moved from her special school into her new mainstream school but, when she went on to beat the 'Queen of the May' in the end of year race, she was victimised by peers. It seems to link somewhat with Vlachou's findings that children liked to help disabled peers; they did not necessarily want to be outperformed by those who came in from the special school sector.

At its most extreme, the rejection of children with special educational needs can lead to suicide. This was the case with Kelly Yeomans, aged thirteen, who killed herself because she could no longer bear the torments of gangs of youths who waited for her outside her house in Allenton, Derby. The newspaper report on the suicide said:

> According to her sister Sarah, Kelly was persistently bullied at school – she was a fat girl in glasses, and bullies love to hate fat girls in glasses. She was taunted. She did not dare show herself in her PE kit. Someone poured salt over her school dinner. But, says Michael Shaw, the Principal at Merrrill College, the school was not aware of problems. Merrill is a grant-maintained technology college with a wide catchment area – some of the most deprived areas of Derby (Margaret Beckett's constituency) and also the leafy suburbs (what, until May, was Edwina Currie's constituency). In its 1996 Ofsted report, it was found to be 'acting satisfactorily' with its anti-bullying policy: 'procedures are set out and used to deal with the few instances of bullying' . . . Mr. Shaw said Kelly was 'an average pupil . . . She did have difficulty in some areas. She had great difficulty with reading. She was on the SEN (special educational needs) register'.
>
> (Gerrard, 1997, p. 18)

This example is given in some detail because it seems to me to be illustrative of just why inclusivity can be such an elusive concept and so difficult to implement through mere policy. Here was a secondary school with an anti-bullying policy and a good Ofsted report on its procedures. Yet, a child like Kelly was able to slip through the net because her persecution went largely unnoticed.

The public perception of the classic 'special needs' child tends to be focused at opposite extremes of disability imagery: either that of a physically disabled child in a wheelchair or using specific aids; or that of a violent and disruptive child whose behaviour challenges boundaries of acceptable behaviour. Kelly was neither of these extremes. She was quiet and well behaved, came from a family where all had been subjected to intimidation by a gang of local youths, and was aware that she did not fit in with her peers at school. Her lack of inclusion within the school context was a reflection of her family's lack of inclusion in the wider social situation. They were seeking the kind of inclusivity which it is almost impossible to create without changing the nature of society in a profound sense.

Barton (1997) recognises the complexity of working towards an inclusive society when he asks, 'What form of "democratic context" will support collective responsibility and thereby challenge individual self-interest?' (p. 240). For a vulnerable child, the experience of inclusion or exclusion does not just take place in an institution called a school but in the streets, the shops, the home and in various public spaces. Making schools more inclusive means taking into account these connecting areas and helping children to feel able to be different without fearing peer rejection. It is a daunting task for already very hard-pressed teachers and support staff. Actually accessing the deep culture which conceals examples of bullying such as that of Kelly is only the first step.

## CONCLUDING REFLECTIONS

Just as integration as defined in the Warnock Report could only be regarded as partial if it remained at the locational or social level alone, so inclusion at a surface or structural level has to be considered shallow and limited. As the special school headteachers told me, despite very careful preparation and planning, policy guidelines and curriculum modification, the surface and structural frameworks for inclusivity may be unable to counteract ultimate bullying and rejection from peers. Therefore, it is at this level of deep culture that true inclusion has to occur.

Precisely because the deep culture is below the surface, it is difficult to determine. With so much emphasis upon the culture of a school in the school effectiveness and school improvement literature, it is necessary to look into this culture in order to observe what is happening to special education and look to improve conditions. The future of special schools, according to the New Labour Government's 1997 Green Paper on special education, is likely to become that of resource centres attached to mainstream schools whilst many will be closed in the move to greater inclusion. Where mainstream schools are competing with others for those pupils who will enhance their league table results and attract the 'right kind' of parent, they are unlikely to actively seek children with special educational needs. It seems to be a strong possibility that 'special' mainstream schools will continue to evolve, in which those who are not wanted elsewhere end up. Theirs is likely to become a 'failing' culture, using Ofsted criteria, in which the inclusion of a disproportionate number of children with significant difficulties leads to a disempowered school climate.

Perhaps it should be a required criterion of any school which calls itself effective that it demonstrates an awareness of what exists within its deep culture and where some of the dangerous currents reside. Protection of the most vulnerable individuals can only begin when the special educational needs of the school culture are acknowledged and addressed.

# 10

## Boys and Literacy: Gendering the Reading Curriculum

GEMMA MOSS AND DENA ATTAR

This chapter draws on case study research funded by the ESRC under the heading 'Fact and Fiction: the gendering of reading in the 7–9 age group'.[1] The project was designed to throw light on boys' development as readers. Gender differences in reading are well documented: boys do less well at reading than girls, a discrepancy which begins early and intensifies with age; they also read less than girls; they read more non-fiction. These facts are well known, and have been well documented through quantitative research whose findings have remained remarkably consistent over an extensive period of time (Barrs and Pidgeon, 1993; Whitehead, 1977; Gorman *et al.*, 1988; Children's Literature Research Centre, 1966). Whilst the general picture may be clear enough, such work does not explain how such gender differences emerge in relation to reading. Given the resurgence of interest in a 'biological' basis for gender differences – ranging from claims that boys in early years are physically less able to sit still to renewed assertions about differences in brain function between boys and girls in respect of language – it seems urgent and important that those of us committed to understanding gender-differentiation in terms of social and cultural behaviours should be able to offer an alternative account. With this in mind our own research uses a case study focus to examine how boys and girls gender reading for themselves in the classroom and in the context of their own leisure time; and how reading is gendered for them through their interactions with adults at home and in school. In this piece we will concentrate on reading in the school. Below, we set the context for current concern over boys' underachievement at reading before going on to describe our own study.

### BOYS' UNDERACHIEVEMENT – THE MORAL PANIC

Much of the current discussion of boys and literacy has the flavour of a full blown moral panic, so famously identified by Stanley Cohen. Cohen describes moral panics as 'the mobilisation of public opinion, the orchestration by the

133

media and public figures of an otherwise inchoate sense of unease' (Cohen S., 1972). In other words, the focus for the immediate moral panic stands in for something else altogether more diffuse. Certainly the ways in which boys' underachievement has been identified and highlighted in the media would seem to indicate a much broader set of concerns than how well boys do at school. Worries about 'boys' attainment in school' stand in for wider anxieties about the nature of masculinity, and its identification with yobbish antisocial be- haviours; fears about the breakdown of the social fabric in the new contexts for employment which seem to offer few opportunities to the (male) unskilled worker; difficulties posed by the hard-won changes in women's role and status. Moral panics work by switching attention from the general and nebulous to an easily identified target. Once a target has been established the moral panic seeks rapidly to identify who is to blame, and equally swiftly, to pronounce quick fix remedies. Our own collection of press stories collected during the lifetime of the Fact and Fiction Project include the following headlines: CHAINED MALES: How boys are held back (*TES*, 16/5/97); Fathers blamed for boys' bad marks (*Guardian*, 13/1/98); Fathers prefer surfing to homework (*TES*, 16/1/98); and under the headline: Whatever happened to the lively lads?, an article with the following summary: 'Boys like to run and shout, says Anabel Dixon, who argues that their exuberance must be turned to educa- tional advantage if they are not to turn their backs on learning for good.' The article itself begins with the sentence 'Primary schools ooze with feminine culture'. This kind of angle on the problem with boys can also be phrased the other way round. An article in the *TES* about special classes for boys taught by men showed a picture of some boys reading with the following caption: 'Boy- zone: the reading skills of primary-age boys could be affected by the dearth of male teachers'.

In the media accounts, if boys are the problem, then by and large the blame can be variously ascribed to female teachers, who unnecessarily feminise the English curriculum, and/or deficient dads who, through absence or inade- quacy, fail to provide appropriate role models of good masculine behaviour by rarely reading with their children. Failing these, then girls' own achievements can be made the scapegoat, or assumptions about boys' innate ineducability. The *Panorama* documentary, Is the future female?, drew on both these sup- positions, and set the tone for much of the subsequent debate. Unfortunately, academic and professional literature on the topic doesn't always distance itself from these kinds of prescriptions, and indeed may positively subscribe to some (the headlines about fathers quoted above stem from reporting of Ted Wragg's work in the area). In the scramble to come up with easily identifiable causes and instant solutions there is little incentive to pause and reflect on the politics of this kind of agenda of blame. There should be. Blaming the most obvious suspects in such a superficial way is unlikely to lead to much positive new thinking. Moreover, such a reaction, fuelled by the sense of urgency engen- dered by a media-fed moral panic, is likely to reinforce crude sex stereotyping, in itself enormously counter-productive.

What is the evidence for an increasing gender differential in achievement in English? The most recent figures for 1997 show a steadily increasing gender gap in levels of achievement as schooling progresses. At Key Stage 1 in English, 7% more girls than boys achieve level 3; at Key Stage 2, 12% more girls than boys achieve level 4; at Key Stage 3, 19% more girls than boys achieve level 5; at GCSE 22% more girls than boys achieve grade C or above. Taken in the round, the figures certainly amply demonstrate why this is an issue schools should address. What they hide is the variation between schools; and the variation between groups of pupils within schools. In addressing underachievement, gender is by no means the only factor to keep an eye on, particularly if too glib an assumption is made that all boys must have a problem and no girls will. At the very least social class and ethnicity will cut across a straight gender divide.

Reacting as if all boys are doing badly and all girls are doing well would be fundamentally to misread the evidence. Moral panics demand instant solutions, but to date we have no clear explanations for the patterns of boys' underachievement. Schools should not be bounced into taking hasty action without considering the full evidence, nor encouraged to rush ahead with common-sense prescriptions which may simply compound the underlying problems. Above all, 'solutions' to boys' underachievement need to recognise variation amongst the school population as a whole, nor should they be achieved at the expense of a negative impact on girls' progress. Whatever it is that schools do about gender and underachievement needs considering in the round, in relation to the spectrum of achievement amongst girls and boys.

## FACT OR FICTION: BOYS AND THE READING CURRICULUM

The Fact and Fiction Project focuses on the seven to nine age group because that is the point at which children begin to read independently for themselves. The data presented below come from four case study sites: two schools in London and two in Hampshire. The schools were chosen to reflect broad differences in the social class of their catchments and also in their own ethos (one is a denominational school). This has enabled us to examine other variables such as resources, use of leisure time, community/school involvement which could intersect with gender in their impact on reading. Data collection in each case study site has included a period of intensive ethnographic observation in one year group, tracking a cohort of children through the school day. This period of observation has been used to document how each school constructs the reading curriculum through the routine interactions which take place during the school day and how children re-work these forms of regulation for themselves. It was in these social interactions that we expected to see the gendering of reading going on.

There were two points of particular interest to us. In the argument articulated in and through the moral panic about boys' underachievement, one strand sees as a major stumbling block to their success women teachers who in the early years are responsible for promulgating a culture of femininity (see Chapter 5) which excludes boys' more masculine pursuits and interests. This culture of femininity is often assumed to revolve around the fiction curriculum through which reading in the early years is taught (Barrs and Pidgeon, 1993). With this in mind, we wanted to account for the ways in which fiction and non-fiction texts are demarcated as part of the official school curriculum. We also wanted to see if the structuring of the school curriculum could throw any light on boys' preference for non-fiction and whether in turn such a preference had any bearing on boys' progress as readers. Our own initial hypothesis was that maybe boys' preference for non-fiction books led them in the early stages to seek out texts which were actually more difficult to read. A few would make it through, at the expense of the many who would not. Either way, we should take a closer look.

## SCHOOLS AND THE READING CURRICULUM

Our case study schools differ from one another in many respects – how they perceive their own educational role; their relationship with parents; their expectations of their pupils; school organisation and management; staffing profiles. Any account of the schools' culture per se might well want to highlight these differences. But in relation to the reading curriculum there was a good deal of uniformity across sites, as well as variation. We will begin therefore, by outlining what our four case study schools shared, in terms of the organisation of the reading curriculum. Despite different inflections in local sites, these remained key structuring features, which everywhere seemed to leave their mark on pupils.

Broadly speaking, in each site we observed a tripartite split in the reading curriculum. On the one hand there was what we call 'procedural reading' – reading to get things done, where although reading takes place, it is background to some other kind of activity which holds the attention of teachers and pupils. Reading here accomplishes some other purpose, rather than being an end in itself. Worksheets, letters home, incidental writing on the board as part of another subject, these all suggest the kind of literacy events we have in mind. Alongside there was the official reading curriculum. Here reading is highlighted and largely undertaken as an activity in its own right. The official reading curriculum has two different aspects: those activities which highlight what we call 'reading for proficiency', where how well the child reads is paramount; and those activities which highlight 'reading for choice', where the emphasis is more wide ranging, and centres on notions of enjoyment and interest. This same division between proficiency and choice is also there in the organisation of the English National Curriculum, and, with different emphases, survives in the National Literacy Strategy management of the literacy hour.

Each of these slots – procedural reading; reading for proficiency and reading for choice – leads to different forms of activity, often conducted around different kinds of texts, and occurring in different social settings. Take work-sheets as a simple example. For our purposes these exemplify procedural read-ing. Some worksheets are sufficiently embedded within the routine activity of the class to need no introduction. Often handed out without comment, they are used as a means for controlling activity in the class whilst the teacher gets on with other jobs. By contrast, worksheets which are more pivotal to the lesson content in particular subject areas are carefully framed by teacher talk. The teacher may well read through the actual words on the worksheet, but will also explain the text to the class: commenting on what the text means, what it requires the children to do and how they are to deal with it. The teacher talks the children through the text. When children begin work on the worksheet themselves they are then entitled to seek help from other children in 'reading' the text. Even in classrooms where this kind of group activity is not endorsed, they are usually expected to seek help from the teacher if they get stuck. 'Reading' in this context becomes a collective enterprise, where the capabilities of the group rather than the individual can be called upon to solve the prob-lems the text poses. Solving the problem leads to some other kind of, often written, outcome. This is not the case for all texts, and indeed the official reading curriculum is often predicated on a rather different set of rules. Sus-tained, private and often silent reading is generally held up as the model, even if in practice rather different kinds of things go on. One interesting point about the advent of the National Literacy Strategy is that it will refocus the official reading curriculum away from the view that reading is individual, largely silent and internalised mental activity to something more collaborative. The actual impact of that change in practice remains to be seen.

What our data make clear is that reading is framed differently in the class-room according to the context in which it takes place, the resources which are made available and how they are mobilised in particular literacy events. There is no one school literacy, resonant of a particular school culture. Rather, contradictory views of what reading is and what it can do for you are on offer to the children in each site. If the schools in our database share this general tripartite structuring of the reading curriculum, where they differ is in the relative weightings they give to one kind of reading over another. And here what teachers say may have little bearing on what they do. Talk to teachers about reading, and the most confidently articulated view you get back is about choice. Watch what goes on and 'choice' seldom holds as much sway in the classroom as the rhetoric would have you believe. This is a salutary point at a moment when the Government would claim it is reintroducing notions of proficiency to the school curriculum.

## MASCULINITY, FEMININITY AND THE READING CURRICULUM:
### THE OFFICIAL VIEW

For the rest of this chapter we will concentrate on the contradictory ways in which the activities which make up the official reading curriculum frame reading. We will examine both what schools themselves put on the deck, and what boy and girl readers do with this knowledge in our different case study sites. We will argue that it is precisely in this re-working of what's on offer that much of the gender politics of literacy lies.

Ethnographic observation of the official reading curriculum at Key Stage 2 shows a sharp distinction between those activities, and accompanying texts and settings, which are angled towards concepts of proficiency; and those activities, and accompanying texts and settings which are angled towards concepts of choice.

Children themselves know this. As part of our research, we logged what children were reading during quiet reading time (under different headings and with varying degrees of organisation, this curriculum slot was to be found in all our case study schools). In practice this meant touring the class and writing down the details of the texts we found in use. Go up to a child and ask the name of the book they were perusing, and in many instances the child would immediately reply: 'This isn't my reading book' and then proceed to take out another text altogether from their book bag or tray. By their reading book, children meant the book which they would take to the teacher if she asked to hear them read aloud – the prime means for judging proficiency. This book would shuttle to and fro between home and school, generally accompanied by some kind of record book, used to mark the proficiency of the child's performance. Whether this book was actually what children considered themselves to be reading depended, but they recognised its official status.

For some children, their reading book might be a severely constrained 'choice'; only some children in each of the classes we observed were deemed to be 'free-readers' – a term in widespread usage by the pupils in our case study sites indicating those whose choice of text was not in itself monitored by teachers (teachers seemed to prefer the term 'independent reader' here, but they designated the same thing.) Children who were free readers could choose what they liked from the class library as their reading book; children who were not yet free readers could not. Instead they would be still working within the constraints of a reading scheme – books arranged by publishers or, in one instance, the school itself, in a sequence of difficulty. Readers were expected to match themselves to a text according to their agreed level of proficiency. If you're on Stage 10 of a reading scheme you can't chose a book from Stage 11 or 13 (neither can you opt for Stage 4). Moreover, in the context of reading aloud to the teacher, the teacher can dismiss a child's choice by, for instance, deciding it is too hard or too easy for them. The reading-to-teacher session determines the child's place on the proficiency ladder. Free readers are aware of this, too. In an interview with two 'proficient' girls in a Year 5 class about what was in their book bags, one of them commented at some length about the three books she had, discriminating between the one she called her reading book which she would take to the teacher if asked to read aloud; the one she liked to read at home to herself, and was in the process of recommending to her friend, and another book which fitted more easily into those sporadic moments in class when children who had finished other work could read to themselves. These books had all been chosen by her, but to fit particular contexts. They were not interchangeable. She had two main reasons for not taking the book she liked to read at home to the teacher. Partly she did not like reading it in class as there was too much noise, and it was hard to get the kind of quiet absorption she liked at home; but partly she knew there were words in the book which she was not sure how to say aloud, or even quite what they meant. When reading to herself she would skip over these, as they did not detract from her enjoyment of the story. In a read-aloud session this strategy would not be available to her. Such a failure to deal with every word would presumably count against her in the proficiency stakes.

The way reading aloud to the teacher happens in school frames the text (in this instance, the reading book) and its readers in terms of proficiency. The questions such moments serve to answer are does the reader have the requisite proficiency to deal with this text? Even when, with more confident readers, teachers no longer see this as an issue of text-decoding skills, they continue to monitor children's levels of understanding of what they have read by eliciting narrative retellings or other kinds of comments on the text, which simultaneously act as a check that reading really has gone on. Likewise they continue to record evaluative comments on the child's performance in their reading record books. No wonder children continue to understand the act of reading aloud as judging their proficiency. In this instance the context exerts an effect on how readers think about what it means to read and to be a reader.

Many of the texts in use in school also act to link reading to proficiency. They do so as physical objects, through their use of typeface and layout, through the ways in which they combine verbal text and pictures. This is particularly true of fiction books. In recent years, the publishing industry has made increasing efforts to differentiate their products by segmenting the children's book market. Using new categories of texts, such as 'Read Alone' books, the industry has produced a reading ladder, which distinguishes between texts according to the presumed level of competence of their readers as well as their interests. This is reflected in their style and layout. Children can recognise an 'easy' book from a 'hard' book because of the way it looks. The books they have chosen to read thus also spell out their place on the proficiency ladder to others. Whilst many of the girls in our case study sites were quite happy to go along with teacher judgements about their proficiency as readers, whether they were perceived as able or weak, many of the boys were not. This showed up both in terms of the kinds of books boys and girls chose for themselves during those times when they were not restricted to their 'reading book' and in how they commented upon them. During quiet reading time, a weak girl reader in a Year 3 class had chosen *Mrs Wobble the Waitress* from the class library. Asked why she had chosen that book she had no hesitation in saying 'Because it's easy, there are no hard words in it'. She had appropriated the kinds of definitions about her competence from the reading for proficiency slot and applied it to her reading elsewhere. One boy in the same class, and in the same group for English work, was meanwhile refusing to read his allotted reader on grounds it was too babyish, whilst his friends often complained that the reading books they could choose from were dull and boring: 'We get stuck with all the easy ones'. In quiet reading time they eschewed books which spelt out their proficiency level. The girls lived within the teacher definitions of their competence, the boys resisted.

The notion that children must 'choose wisely', i.e. according to their proficiency level, whilst more strongly marked in some schools than others, clearly plays a key part in the reading curriculum. Teachers see their ability to match the reader to a book at the right level for them as a key skill in helping children become proficient readers. Yet being an independent reader, the horizon towards which all this careful induction is leading, clearly involves much more than this. In the National Curriculum documentation, concerns with proficiency dominate in the descriptions of reading at Key Stage 1. Move up through the level descriptors and proficiency-led definitions of what children should be able to do wither away to be replaced by definitions centred around notions of choice. The English National Curriculum for Reading at Key Stage 2 begins with the following statement: 'Pupils should be encouraged to develop as enthusiastic, independent and reflective readers. They should be introduced to a wide range of literature and have opportunities to read extensively for their own interest and pleasure, and for information.'

If 'reading for proficiency' is played out most strongly around the reading-aloud-to-teacher slot, 'reading for choice' gets its fullest expression during quiet reading time. In each of the classrooms we observed, one corner of the class would contain at least one comfy chair, usually on a part of the floor which was carpeted and close to the class library or book corner. During quiet reading time children would generally get access to this furniture. In some classrooms it was possible to lounge on beanbags, spread out on the floor, or recline on the comfy chair. In this respect the disposition of the setting invoked the comfort of a well-furnished front room. Children could, as it were, take time out from the rigours of proper lesson time when they had to sit up straight and pay attention. The setting for quiet reading time invokes the possibilities of domestic leisure, even when, practically speaking it can only do so in a token way – there are never enough comfy chairs for everyone to have one. Once again, what reading for choice might mean is partly suggested by the social setting in which the activity of quiet reading takes place. A greater range of texts is normally available during this slot than at other times, and in general there is less close monitoring of the use children make of the resources. (Indeed, in the most closely monitored setting we observed, quiet reading time nevertheless enabled children to smuggle in the largest number of unofficial materials.) For at least some of the time, children are expected to choose for themselves what they want to read; they may have a certain amount of freedom about how they read too: sharing with a friend; talking as well as reading; using the texts to play games; solving puzzles; taking turns; reading in a group; listening to story tapes. In these respects, they are at least partially encouraged to direct the activity for themselves. Not all children make the same use of the degree of freedom they have.

The school's view of reading is built around the mobilisation of resources in different settings. The resources themselves are not neutral but already partially inscribe what it might mean to be a reader. But they do so in contradictory ways. So far in the account above, we have outlined in general terms some of the key distinctions in ways of doing reading which run across sites. In each of the four case study schools, the general distinction between procedural reading, reading for proficiency and reading for choice could be found. Differences lay in the relative weightings given to each one. So, for instance, two of our case study schools, one middle class and one working class, made the proficiency ladder highly visible, through their organisation of activities and resources in the classroom, if in different ways. The other two did not. Reading for choice was the main way of framing reading in only one of the classrooms we observed. Whilst reading for choice remains a strong frame at the rhetorical level, both in teacher talk about their practice, and in official documentation, on the ground it is harder to find.

## MASCULINITY, FEMININITY AND THE READING CURRICULUM: THE PUPILS' PERSPECTIVE

So far we may seem to have said comparatively little about gender. The competing frames for the reading curriculum of proficiency and choice seem at first sight to be established on gender neutral terrain. And yet, it is precisely around these terms that gender gets played out most strongly by the children themselves. Our data show that the reading curriculum is always in part imbued with notions of proficiency, through the organisation of routine activities in the class, and through the nature of the texts which form its basis. It is precisely where proficiency and choice definitions of reading collide or intersect that a gender politics of reading gets done. Choice and proficiency have everything to do with gender.

In a variety of different ways the proficiency curriculum makes public children's standing as readers. The fact that 'free readers' are accorded privileges which others do not have, and have different opportunities to read texts which others are forbidden, serves to underline this. Any classroom text which a child reads will signal in a number of different ways their place on the proficiency ladder: scheme books are colour coded into stages; while non-scheme books' length, print size, layout, line length, density of pictures to text, use of chapters, all spell out a proficiency ranking. (Public libraries and bookshops shelve their books separately according to these criteria, too.)

Proficiency rankings matter – to teachers, to parents, to children. But they also matter differently to boys. Low proficiency rankings seem to conflict more with their own self-esteem and classroom activities which highlight their low ranking seem to cause them more problems. For instance, in one of the classrooms we observed, a routine activity during the week was to get children to read in pairs, when a more able reader would work with a less able reader. In almost all cases in this classroom the weakest boys were paired with more able girls. More able girls in this role adopted the voice of the teacher. They would comment on the boys' performance as they took turns to read: 'Good boy, Jack, well done'. Weak girls on the receiving end of this kind of praise and advice didn't seem to mind, and simply enjoyed the attention and joint activity. Weak boys bridled at being patronised. By contrast more able boys working with their peers seemed largely to ignore their partners and read as if to themselves. Their sense of how to manage the encounter was quite different. Where proficiency rankings are made most visible, weaker boys spend an inordinate amount of time trying to get off the proficiency ladder. Boys are in flight from negative proficiency judgements in ways which girls are not.

Proficiency orientations to the reading curriculum impact on choice. In those settings when children have most freedom to choose – the greatest range of texts, and opportunities to make use of them in different ways – boys are much more inclined to choose non-fiction. But boys' choice of non-fiction books is often highly motivated, not only by interest in a particular topic, or its specific mode of address, but because non-fiction books offer escape from the fine-grading of a proficiency ladder. They also offer opportunities for different kinds of reading. Dorling Kindersley, for instance, whose style has been much imitated, is not part of the educational publishing organisations. Unlike publishers who are, they deliberately eschew using large print size as a way of indicating the intended proficiency level of many of their non-fiction books. With popular series like 'Eyewitness', which we saw in use in Year 3 classrooms, to all intents and purposes the style of the text as physical object signals 'adults' as the intended readership. Children who choose such books to read during quiet reading time escape signalling their actual proficiency as child/beginning readers, whilst leaving themselves with plenty to do with the texts, precisely because it is possible to steer around these kinds of non-fiction texts using visual images rather than the writing. Flick through the pages and find an image that interests you, then comment to a friend about it. This may well involve drawing on information from other sources rather than the text itself. Many of the weaker boy readers, given the opportunity, would make a beeline for these kinds of texts in a free-choice context. One boy reader, the weakest in his Year 5 class, having been instructed by the teacher that pupils were to choose only fiction books for their class library this term, obstinately opted for a Dorling Kindersley book on Weapons and Armour, and got it into the class library, too. He was the only member of the class to break the injunction, and for whom it presumably mattered that much. These kinds of non-fiction texts never get into proficiency slots, and indeed, teachers often expressed some unease to us over their general readability. Should they really be in free-choice slots at all if children couldn't adequately deal with the written text?

Paradoxically, the kinds of texts which encourage readers to steer round them by means other than the written word also provide one of the few arenas where more and less able boys can meet on a level, as it were, without regard to who might be more proficient at what. Indeed weaker boys can muster their expertise in response to such a text, using the pictures as prompts, without having to fight their way through the print to identify what is going on. This is an advantage in relation to boys' status politics. The disadvantage is that in relation to schooling, many of the strategies weaker boys employ to save face with their peers effectively militate against them making much progress on the school's terms. The combination of strategies they use result in weaker boys simply spending less time reading.

In this chapter we have been discussing boys' preferences and avoidance strategies in the context of the official school curriculum, and the ways in which reading is organised, resourced and regulated by it. To grasp the whole picture of boys' development as readers we would need to go further than there is space to do here, and examine more closely the other varied contexts which bring texts and readers together. We know that social networks in and out of the classroom influence what and how boys' read. These social networks seem to operate on different principles from the girls'. Boys' social networks can ensure that some books become status objects or the focus around which they do status politics. Boys trade off their knowledge of texts with each other. In some circumstances this allows able boy readers to provide camouflage for less able readers in the classroom, offering short cuts to the work of reading in class. We know that boys use these networks to re-define school work as play (see also Solsken, 1993).

We know that texts matter. That texts construct child readers: girls easily buy into this, but boys are more diffident about being construed as children rather than adults. That whilst educational publishers and teachers often make strenuous efforts to achieve gender neutrality and balance in their stock, out of school texts for this age group are often highly gendered and deliberately marketed as such. In the cross media entertainment market, texts are designed to appeal to boys as boys or girls as girls in a traditional and straightforwardly commercial way. We also know that fewer overtly 'girly' texts get into school except as girls' private property – and that in public arenas they meet with overwhelming disapproval, embarrassment or outright rejection from both boys and women teachers. Yet it is not unusual to find magazines and books in classrooms which address boys' out-of school interests, put there in an attempt to lure them into reading. Non-fiction books remain solidly geared towards boys' perceived interests, and are seen that way by pupils. From this perspective alone, concerns about an overly feminised reading curriculum seem profoundly misplaced.

Boys and girls react to the culture of the school reading curriculum and the contradictions embedded within it in different ways. The messages schools provide about what reading is and how it is done, about the texts which form its basis, are clearly significant in shaping boys' and girls' sense of themselves as readers or non-readers. At a time when proficiency is the watchword at all levels of curriculum activity, it actually seems important to keep alive the notion of choice, but make the possibilities of choice in the classroom much richer and more meaningful for both boys and girls. As a first step towards this objective, we would suggest schools pay more attention to the reading curriculum they already operate so that they can identify the opportunities it provides for children to develop as less constrained readers, as well as any problems it puts in their way. Concentrating on the balance between proficiency and choice, whilst not the whole story, helps us understand how the conditions for both underachievement and fiction/non-fiction preferences or avoidance are partly created through the official reading curriculum. It is a first step towards re-working what the school puts on the deck.

## NOTE

1. The Fact and Fiction Research Project, 1996–98, based at Southampton University, and funded by the Economic and Social Research Council (ESRC). The project team are Gemma Moss and Dena Attar.

# 11

## Teacher Identity in Popular Culture[1]

### SANDRA WEBER AND CLAUDIA MITCHELL

Real-life setting I: A large family reunion where many distant cousins who have travelled from afar are meeting for the first time.

Male Cousin #1:   So, what do you do for a living?
Male Cousin #2:   I'm a grade school teacher.
Male Cousin #1 (eyes glazing over): Oh, that's nice. So . . . have you heard the news about Aunt Laura, isn't it outrageous?

Real-life setting II: A high school staff room during lunch hour.
Female teacher to another: I simply hate it when my husband or children say 'you're talking just like a teacher!' I mean I know I am a teacher, but it feels like such a put-down when people tell me I look or act or sound like one.

The above excerpts from field-notes we have been keeping for almost a decade give voice to the underlying unease, ambivalence, or confusion teachers may sometimes feel about their professional identity and work, especially when confronted with some of the negative images of Teacher held by people outside the profession. The staff room quote poses the further question or problem of whether teachers themselves internalise certain aspects of prevalent social images of Teacher (for example, teachers have low status and are uninteresting) and integrate them into their evolving views about themselves and their work in schools. Are mental and visual images really of any importance to teacher identity and the culture of schools? The next section briefly outlines the stances taken by researchers and scholars on this question.

### THE SIGNIFICANCE OF TEACHER IMAGES TO TEACHERS' WORK AND IDENTITY

Everybody and anybody seems to have an image or idea or opinion about who teachers are and how they are supposed to look, act, and talk. This, of course, is not surprising, given the thousands of hours most people spend as observers of teachers from the student's side of the desk during their compulsory schooling. As scholars such as Britzman (1992) and Polan (1993) assert, this familiarity poses problems for real life teachers:

(Teacher identity) . . . is an identity that is at once familiar and strange for we have all played a role opposite a teacher for a significant part of our lives . . . The identity of teacher, however, does not seem so transparent once one steps into teacher's role; once there, role and identity are not synonymous . . . The two are in dialogic relation and it is this tension that makes for a 'lived experience' of teacher.

(Britzman, 1992, p. 29)

For both teachers and students, expectations of what a teacher is like may be based on deeply ingrained stereotypical images:

For many students, the teacher is not a conduit to knowledge that exists elsewhere: the teacher is an image, a cliché in the sense both of stereotype but also photographic imprinting that freezes knowledge in the seeming evidence of a look, where the image predetermines what the person means to us . . . The medium is the message, and the image of the professor often matters more than the ideas of the lesson.

(Polan, 1993, p. 32)

Much earlier, Mead (1951; 1962) pointed out that the stereotypes that are prevalent in the popular culture and experience of childhood play a formative role in the evolution of a teacher's identity and are part of the enculturation of teachers into their profession. Her observations and theory went largely unheeded for decades. Referring to Lortie's (1975) work on stereotypical images of teaching, Britzman (1991) too, raises the connection between professional identity and stereotypes, saying that

the persistency of stereotypes does more than caricature the opinions and hopes of a community. Such images tend to subvert a critical discourse about the lived contradictions of teaching and the actual struggles of teachers and students. Stereotypes engender a static and hence repressed notion of identity as something already out there, a stability that can be assumed . . . trapped within these images, teachers come to resemble things or conditions; their identity assumes an essentialist quality and, as such, socially constructed meanings become known as innate and natural. (p. 5)

Cole and Knowles (1998) and Zeichner and Tabachnick (1981), among other researchers, have demonstrated through longitudinal studies that even before taking up teaching as a career, people have already formed many preconceived notions of what teachers do and who they are. As Bullough *et al.* (1991) contend, these initial conceptions or images of teaching are tacit, implicit, and seldom articulated, which makes them all the more important to consider if teachers do not want to be left more or less to the mercy of the silent shaping these images exert on professional self-image and actions.

How do images exert their influence? Bullough *et al.* (1991) suggest that, through their metaphorical power, images are both the building blocks of teachers' thinking schemata, and the filters through which teachers unconsciously assess their pedagogical knowledge. Elbaz (1991) similarly observes that images

speak particularly to the integrated nature of teachers' knowledge in its simultaneously emotional, evaluative and cognitive nature, and also convey the personal meanings which permeate this knowledge. One teacher's sense of her classroom as 'home', another's view of her subject matter sometimes as a 'barrier to hide behind', at other times a 'window on what students are thinking', both allow us to share in the teacher's experience precisely as she sees fit to express it. (p. 13)

Eraut (1985) uses the term image to refer to the many visual memories or snapshots of children and situations that enter teachers' minds in the course of everyday teaching – what Bandman (1967, p. 112) earlier termed picture preferences. In referring to what they call teachers' personal practical knowledge, Connelly and Clandinin (1985) say that images are expressed in the everyday language and actions of teaching, a view also taken up by Johnston (1992) who reports that images provide a language that can help teachers make explicit the subconscious assumptions on which their practice is based. Calderhead and Robson (1991) note that an image can help to synthesise knowledge about teachers, children, and teaching methods.

A variety of teacher images may be involved in shaping teacher identity and actions (Weber and Mitchell, 1995). De Castell (1988), for example, reports on the image of teaching as warfare, especially predominate among some high school teachers. Bullough's (1991) findings on primary and secondary teachers indicate that many beginning teachers see teaching as a form of mothering or nurturing. He also uncovered images as diverse as teacher-as-butterfly, teacher-as-policewoman, teacher-as-chameleon, and of course, teacher-as-bitch. Joseph and Burnaford (1994) noted with some astonishment the recurrence of the image of teacher-as-witch not only in fictional accounts but also in narratives written by teachers themselves.

Most of the school-based imagery discussed thus far is a product of people's numerous real-life encounters with teachers and with the stories other people tell about their teachers. But there is an influential source of imagery acquired outside of school that may be even more powerful in shaping the culture of teaching – the popular culture in which teachers and their students are raised.

## TEACHER IDENTITY AND THE IMAGERY OF POPULAR CULTURE

This chapter focuses on how cultural images outside of school can infiltrate and affect the culture inside of school, particularly in relationship to teacher identity and to both teachers' and student's expectations of how teachers should look and act. Using a Cultural Studies methodology based on the work of Fiske (1989) and McRobbie (1994), we have been investigating how teachers are portrayed in popular culture, interviewing children and teachers, taping discussions about popular teachers in movies and books, and conducting critical close analyses of more than thirty popular teacher novels, films, and television programmes. How are teachers portrayed in popular culture, and how do they react to popular images?

As the work of Giroux and Simon (1989) and Joseph and Burnaford (1994) illustrate, teachers as a group are widely talked about, caricatured, and portrayed in popular culture. Leave school? It would be hard to leave it totally behind, even if we wanted to. Although it may be easy enough (sometimes) to physically leave the school building that we work or learn in, once outside, school seems to be ever present, whether or not we notice. Look around and listen: schoolyard chants mock teachers, back-to-school fliers and advertisements strewn with school images come unbidden in the mail. Scores of popular television programmes for children and adults are set in school environments or involve teachers. These include animated shows like 'The Simpsons' or 'The Magic School Bus', the highly popular teen-age 'Beverly Hills 90210', 'Hearts and Minds', 'The Baby Sitters Club', and 'Grange Hill', just to name a few.

In a shop selling newspapers, books, or magazines, Archie comics featuring Miss Grundy stare out from the racks, or school novel series such as Sweet Valley High or the Enid Blyton books line the shelves of the children's section. And as for cinema – If it isn't *The Prime of Miss Jean Brodie* or *To Sir With Love*, then it's *The Substitute, Sarifina, Matilda, Clueless, Dangerous Minds, Kindergarten Cop, Mr. Holland's Opus, Waterland, Romy and Michelle's High School Reunion, In & Out*, and so on. A never ending parade of celluloid teachers keeps them omnipresent in the public eye. Reading the newspaper, it's hard to escape editorials, cartoons, and letters about education. It seems everyone has an opinion. Want to buy a toy for a child? There's Teacher Barbie, or chalkboards or magnetic letters, or Play School toys or the Little Professor calculator or Arthur's Terrible Teacher Troubles CD Rom amongst which to choose, for starters.

By the time we graduate from high school, most of us, including future teachers, will have spent over thirteen thousand hours observing teachers in schools from the student's side of the desk. Its very familiarity makes school a natural background or setting for popular narratives that focus on the many significant personal and social events of everyday life– growing up, making friends and enemies, getting hurt, learning the social codes, falling in love, experiencing boredom, excitement, triumph, and failure, playing, trying to survive, trying to figure out just who we are, trying to figure other people out. Yet despite the prevalence of popular images of teachers, the relative silence of the research literature on the topic evokes the unwarranted assumption that these popular images don't enter the classroom with the students and teachers.

We are not entirely alone in suggesting that how people think about teaching may be shaped in many ways by the images of teacher in popular culture that they encounter in their daily lives. Margaret Mead (1951; 1962) was one of the first to recognise the power of image in the media, literature, and other forms of popular culture to create a personal sense of what is possible, normal, usual. This sense becomes part of our identity, a view supported by Giddens (1991). The research of Lipsitz (1990) suggests that images in popular culture can even displace personal memories, making cultural images even more influential on teacher actions at times then their own prior personal experience of schooling.

What does popular imagery say about teachers? Joseph and Burnaford (1994) contend that memory often perpetuates the horrible images rather than the positive ones, thereby affecting the teaching profession in a negative way. The continued popularity of such images as teacher-as-tyrant, teacher-as-buffoon, and teacher-as-bitch, and the preponderance of negative rhymes and chants about teachers suggest that there could be some truth to Joseph and

Burnaford's assertion. But they also acknowledge a current of progressive, positive images – 'empowered teachers . . . who celebrate their influence and creativity' (p. 18) – that counter the negative images of teaching in popular culture. As Giroux and Simon (1989) suggest, teachers are not merely victims of society's cultural imagery. Although they are born into powerful socialising metaphors, some teachers manage to break and recreate images while making sense of their roles and forging their self-identities.

Joseph and Burnaford (1994) assert that contemporary understanding of teachers and teaching would be greatly informed by searching for the heterogeneity that images offer. Decades ago, for example, Waller (1932) proposed that favourable stereotypes represent the community ideal of what a teacher ought to be, and unfavourable ones represent the common opinion of what a teacher actually is.

Mead (1951; 1962) described the image of teacher that dominated America in the first half of this century as one of white, middle-class respectability, femininity, docility, and order. In reviewing twentieth-century images of teaching in North American popular culture, Joseph and Burnaford (1994) found many similar images.

Are today's stereotypes different from yesterdays? An analysis of over 500 drawings of teachers done by children and teachers reveals the persistent and pervasive presence of traditional images of teaching as transmission of knowledge from all-knowing teacher into empty vessel student (Weber and Mitchell, 1995; Weber, 1990). Reminiscent of Goodlad's (1984) study of over 1,000 American schools, the typical teacher portrayed in the pictures drawn by both teachers and children was a white woman pointing or expounding, standing in front of a blackboard or desk. We were led to conclude (as Lortie noted in the 1970s), that the traditional stereotypes described by Mead in the 1950s remain firmly entrenched in today's children (some of whom will be tomorrow's teachers) and in today's teachers (all of whom were among yesterday's children), despite the common perception that teaching methods nowadays are radically different. In reflecting and commenting on the pictures they drew for us, many prospective teachers became aware of the power that past experience and stereotypes seem to have on them. They expressed, often with consternation, their ambivalence in relation to the dominant transmission images of teaching culturally embedded in the teaching profession.

Rumelhart's (1980) schema theory offers the explanation that beginning teachers inevitably pick and choose what they will respond to in teacher education. Drawing on their past experience, they seek first and foremost confirmation of what they assume to be true about themselves as teachers and about teaching. When these views prove faulty, as they often do during student teaching, beginning teachers must find a way to adjust to the situation, to make what Lacey (1977) labelled an 'internalised adjustment' by using various coping strategies aimed either at self-preservation (Rosenholtz, 1989), or at reframing the situation. In so doing, they may develop in directions quite different from those predicted by the widely discussed progressive-traditional shift (Zeichner and Grant, 1981), and in ways quite at odds with those often sought by teacher educators (Bullough, 1991). As Anderson (1977) suggests:

> the more fully developed a schema, the less likely it will be to change . . . individuals will go to great lengths in order to maintain a strongly developed schema – and related conception of self as teacher – such that apparent inconsistencies and counterexamples may be easily assimilated . . . People whose important beliefs are threatened will attempt to defend their positions, dismiss objections, ignore counter examples, keep segregated logically incompatible schemata. (pp. 425–9)

There is a tendency, however, to oversimplify the socialising nature of cultural imagery, reducing it to a one-dimensional bogeyman to be disdained, fought, or most often, simply ignored. As the remainder of this chapter will illustrate, a nuanced and systematic close reading of popular imagery can make teachers more aware of their own school culture and enable them to use it for their own professional development through self-study.

## USING POPULAR TEACHERS TO STUDY OURSELVES

I was only two years out of high school myself when I first saw *To Sir With Love* . . . I marvelled at the heady freedom Sir seemed to be offering: rather than continuing to plod through the boring exercises of the prescribed high school curriculum, Sir suggested that they use class time to talk seriously about Life. In a dramatic act of rebellion, he flung the school textbooks into the wastebasket, saying 'Those are out. They are useless to you.' Oh, how I wished I had a teacher like Mark Thackeray when I was in high school, someone who recognised the dull, lifeless nature of the official curriculum that was uncaringly and unrelentingly force-fed to us hour after hour, day after day . . . For me, at that time, the movie offered a seductive glimpse of possibilities: schooling as meaningful, as connected with life, work aspirations, even love and romance subjects much on the mind of adolescent girls . . . I remember identifying with Sir as he battled with cynical teachers, prejudice and ignorance, ultimately rejecting a much more prestigious career as an engineer for the love of teaching, for the love of children. Romantic!? Heady stuff?! Prior to seeing the movie, I had never even considered a career in teaching, but I did not forget that film. It lingered somewhere in the sedimentary collage of images that form the inchoate, primary material for thinking and feeling. (Weber and Mitchell, 1995, pp. 137–8)

The above excerpt was written by a teacher reflecting on her reactions decades earlier to the movie *To Sir With Love*, a film that was based on the autobiographical book written by engineer/teacher E.R. Braithwaite in 1959 about his teaching experience in an inner city high school in London, England. Almost thirty years later, we meet an American, Lou Anne Johnson, a beginning English teacher in a special Academy programme for underachieving teenagers in an inner city high school. Like Braithwaite, in her efforts to reach and help her students, she has some very gripping and powerful teaching experiences to relate in a readable and moving book, *My Posse Don't Do Homework* (1992). The book sells enough copies to be widely available in paperback, read not only by teachers, but also by the general public. The writing is clear and effective, featuring lots of dialogue that makes you 'see' and 'hear' the characters, most of who are purportedly dramatised and romanticised composites of her real-life experience.

Depicting her students and herself as fallible, uncertain, but highly appealing and worthwhile heroes and heroines, Ms. Johnson reveals at least some of the foibles and *faux pas* in her attempts to get involved with her students' lives outside as well as inside of school. These includes buying things for her students out of her own pocket, bailing them out of sticky situations with the police, ignoring school rules when she finds them inappropriate, capitalising on her marine training and close-combat skills, taking her class on unusual field trips, finding out the hard way that she is ignorant of the 'street code' that guides her students' actions, and giving them all an A to start the semester, an A that is theirs 'to lose' or to keep.

Some teachers might shake their heads in disapproval at certain of Ms. Johnson's actions. But many readers, especially prospective teachers, cannot help identifying with the character 'Miss Johnson,' empathising with her frustrations and cheering each triumph in her efforts to help students. She is a flawed but tough and well-meaning heroine for the 1990s, one who seemingly bucks the system for the sake of her students and struggles to survive in a tumultuous and sometimes overwhelming personal and professional world.

Ms. Johnson's written account sinks deeper into contemporary popular culture when the book is re-scripted, embellished, and dramatised in a slick, hip Hollywood movie, *Dangerous Minds*, featuring superstar Michel Pfeiffer as 'Miss Johnson'. To the beat of its 'hot' rap sound track, the film demonises school administrators as uncaring, mean, and cowardly bureaucrats and bullies. The movie version of Ms Johnson is a neophyte – a vulnerable, yet strong and determined saviour of her stereotyped Black and Hispanic students. The film increases and heightens the book's violence and eliminates some of its nuances, imposing a classic 'teacher story' narrative on the snapshot vignette format of the original *My Posse Don't Do Homework. Dangerous Minds* is widely discussed and reviewed in both 'high' and 'low brow' publications. It has arrived.

The movie is such a commercial (popular) success that the book is re-released with the movie title, *Dangerous Minds*, replacing the original title. The motion picture sound track sells well too. American television executives, always on the look-out for potential hit programmes, buy a one-hour weekly television drama series, *Dangerous Minds*, as a vehicle for television star, Annie Potts. The show is given a prime time evening slot and does well enough to last a year in the highly competitive (some might say vicious) rating wars that shelve or cancel most new shows after only a few weeks. Meanwhile, the movie version is released on videotape for both rental and purchase.

Thus, to summarise: a teacher's real experience is filtered through her memory and narrative art into a book that shares her views and feelings about her teaching with a wide audience. The book is eventually adapted into several 'reel texts' (movie, TV series episodes) that are consumed by legions of moviegoers, television audiences, record album buyers, and video renters.

Consumption ('reading') of the reel texts becomes the 'real experience' of perspective teachers, moviegoers, teenagers, film critics, and the like. The evolution, mutation, and transposition of one teacher's experience from the text of her life to the lives of many continues. A few years after the release of the movie, many people who saw it graduate from teachers' college, and years from now, could use the movie as a prompt for remembering, seeing it again and perhaps realising how their viewing of the movie has changed, or how certain of its images have silently coloured their views of teaching. This chapter investigates several uses of popular teacher texts as memory prompts, cases for professional development, and conduits to self-study.


## THE CUMULATIVE CULTURAL TEXT CALLED 'TEACHER'

The different yet connected versions of *Dangerous Minds* demonstrate how a strand of what we call 'the cumulative cultural text of teacher' evolves (see Mitchell and Weber, 1998). A series of varying Miss Johnson's blends into the multi-layered repository of popular teacher images that is peopled by the generations of real and fictitious teachers embodied in books, films, TV programs, comics, songs, even Teacher Barbie dolls. Composite representations of Miss Johnson take their place amongst previous generations of film and book teachers – Miss Dove (*Good Morning Miss Dove*), Miss Brodie (*The Prime of Miss Jean Brodie*), Mr. Thackeray (*To Sir With Love*), *Our Miss Brooks*, Sylvia Ashton Warner (*Teacher*), Mr. Keating (*Dead Poets' Society*), Mr. Escalante (*Stand and Deliver*), Miss Masembuko (*Sarifina*) to mention only a few, and is soon joined by Mr. Holland of *Mr. Holland's Opus*. At least three other teacher films follow in the span of just one academic year. The next academic year begins with the release of yet another blockbuster, *In & Out*, about a fictitious gay high school English teacher who is 'outed' to both himself and the entire television viewing world by one of his former students during an Academy Awards acceptance speech. And so it continues . . . A multitude of teacher images feeds the wellspring of the popular culture into which we are born and raised, some of us to become teachers. These images overlap, contradict, amplify, and address each other as they compete for our attention in an intertextual clamour.

Like the character Miss Johnson, many of these fictionalised teachers are based on the experiences of real-life teachers or former students turned authors. But popular images take on a face and life of their own that often overshadows the originals. When people picture 'Sir' in their minds, it is actor Sidney Poitier, not teacher/author Braithwaite they see. Similarly, Maggie Smith will forever be associated in some people's minds with the teacher Jean Brodie. Is it Michelle Pfeiffer or an image conjured from the book that people see as Miss Johnson?

The movie images may not be truly representative of the real Ms. Johnson's original experience, or of the racial discrimination that Braithwaite experienced and expressed in his book. But as Lipsitz (1990) contends, once seen, some visual images are hard to erase – they are what sticks to those who see the movies. The fictional re-writes and re-presents the real, becoming a different kind of reality for the reader/audience who experiences popular images. And they keep on coming – the high viewing ratings for the British made television movie, *Hearts and Minds* is just one of many examples that could be cited to demonstrate the continuing popularity of school on the telly and in the cinema.

The extended life enjoyed by many popular images of teachers is made possible through the same kind of intertextual and generative types of variation and serialisation that transformed and advertised the image of Miss Johnson, giving it presence, longevity, and power. Both implicitly and explicitly, individual episodes and versions contextualise, influence, build on, and refer to each other, collaboratively constituting the cumulative text which is casually passed on from one generation to the next. A book inspires a movie which generates both a sound track album and a new edition of the book as well as a television drama series. But as Fiske (1989) points out, this serialisation into multiple texts only happens if there is something commercially viable in the initial representation – something that captures people's interest, draws them in, or addresses them in a meaningful way that sells. In other words, popular texts wouldn't be popular unless they managed to tap into the particular desires of many readers. In that sense, they serve as a kind of mirror for society, and have something very important to reveal to us about ourselves.

## USING POPULAR TEACHER IMAGES FOR PROFESSIONAL DEVELOPMENT

What do popular teacher images have to do with teacher education or professional development? The success of books and movies such as *Dangerous Minds* sets Miss Johnson up as a possible model or case, displaying, inserting, and enshrining her image as a popular text to be consumed by teens and adults, including practising and future teachers. Some teachers recommend the book to each other, pass it around, and discuss it in the staff room over lunch. When the movie is available, many teachers see it, although some have told us that they are embarrassed to be seen consuming popular teacher movies which they liken to being caught red-handed reading a tabloid magazine or paper. Some identify with certain scenes, or question their own reality in light of the book and movie 'fictions.' Others dismiss it cavalierly as Hollywood trash having nothing whatsoever to do with their teaching reality. But you cannot condemn what you have not noticed.

Movies and books about teachers have much potential to address school practice. 'As a perspective teacher, I found inspiration for my practice by reading the popular teaching narratives of the time, books such as Sylvia Ashton-Warner's (1963) *Teacher*, Clark Moustakas' (1963) *The Authentic Teacher*, or Virginia Axline's (1964) *Dibs*, as well as the classics, especially Plato's Socratic dialogues and some of Dickens' novels. These books were suggested but not required reading, an afterthought tacked onto course bibliographies but seldom discussed in class.

Like so many of my fellow education students, I found that some of these narratives spoke far more directly to my own pedagogical concerns as a future teacher than did the dry and often inept lectures and texts of my formal university courses. Not only did those stories inspire and engage me, they made me think. They made me ponder my own actions in a different light. They helped me understand the spirit, intent, and philosophical orientation that underlay the models and jargon of the time' (Weber, 1993, p. 73).

To some extent, teacher movies, books, and TV programmes serve as a kind of informal or alternative curriculum for adults who wish to become teachers. In the countless classrooms of fiction and film in which they all spend time, teachers are exposed to both right and left wing romanticised images of teaching, image-texts that can be agents of change and subversion, or conversely, unnoticed but powerful agents of reproduction and conservatism. The implausibility of some images and the juxtaposition of contradictory messages within the same image problematise everyday conceptions of Teacher. The cumulative and inter-generational cultural text of teacher forms the unnoticed backdrop against which teachers may struggle to clarify their professional identities.

Jane Isenberg (1994) points out that popular texts can be useful to teachers in discussing their work with non-teachers. Because so many people have read the books or seen the movies, teachers can talk or write about their work in a way that is more accessible or intelligible to others by framing it in terms of popular images. Isenberg even goes so far as to suggest that popular images sometimes validate or legitimise what teachers do in the eyes of their families and the general public. Some of the public sympathy for fictive teacher narratives might rub off on the profession!

How to read this cumulative text? Our previous work (Weber and Mitchell, 1995) suggests that there is no one simple interpretation for particular images and metaphors, but there are ways to harness the popular to professional ends. Echoing the growing call by those who study popular culture or images in relation to teaching (e.g. Butler, 1997; Brunner, 1991; Provenzo *et al.*, 1989; Giroux and Simon, 1989; McRobbie, 1992; Moss, 1989; Hamilton, Barton and Ivanic, 1994; Prosser, 1998; Joseph and Burnaford, 1994), our suggestion is to unmask and use the collage of contradictory images, clichés, and stereotypes of teaching to advance professional development. But how might one do this?

## WAYS TO USE POPULAR TEACHER IMAGES FOR PROFESSIONAL GROWTH

In a series of studies we conducted on our own work with experienced and future teachers, (see Mitchell and Weber, 1999) we found promise in the following techniques:

1.  Do Close Readings of Popular Texts
Studying and comparing popular texts carefully can make us more critically aware of popular stereotypes of teachers' work and roles, and expose the political and social agendas and tacit messages that these popular texts support, critique, or reproduce.

2.  Use Popular Texts as Cases
By deliberately considering popular texts as cases of other people's experiences or possible experiences, we can more easily critique certain teaching practices (because it is someone else's) and articulate our own ideals and beliefs against the text, as a first step towards self-examination and self-expression.

3.  Use Popular Texts as Conduits to Self-Study
The goal here is to conduct specific interrogations of our own identity, practice, and beliefs by using popular stories to provoke or jolt us into authentic self-study. This involves carefully monitoring and honestly examining our own emotional reactions to the texts.

4.  Use Popular Texts to Re-Visit the Past and Re-Imagine the Future
By re-visiting films or books that influenced us in the past, we can get in touch with early motivations and images, evaluate them from the distance granted by the passage of time, trace the influence they might have had or still have on us, and re-situate ourselves through our current reactions and critique to a deeper commitment to professional growth.

5.  Use Popular Texts to Develop an Empowering Sense of Community
Popular texts provide a ready-made shared pool of images that we can use to compare and share our visions, fears, and personal experiences, even with our students. Watching or reading or discussing these texts with colleagues has the potential to create a sense of community, spark critique of the status quo, and perhaps even motivate collective action in the face of shared concerns or problems.

6.  Create Popular Texts to Express Professional Visions
Teachers can be authors or film-makers or scriptwriters. One way to influence the popular is to participate in it by actively putting one's own vision 'out there'.

Studying popular teachers closely exposes the hidden messages that all stereotypes contain. There may even be something entertaining about their blatant exaggeration. Therein lies the danger. Because stereotypes are so often caricatures, it can be tempting to regard them as humorous images that have nothing to do with the reality of teaching. It may be too easy to overlook the kernel or possibility of truth that may lie hidden within.

When people's teaching fantasies or fears or hatreds or yearnings are suddenly projected full force onto a movie or television screen, catching them off guard, they might laugh at with embarrassment or dismiss them as outrageous caricaturisations or libellous distortions and misrepresentations. Teachers might understandably prefer to keep them well hidden, even from themselves if possible. However, by ignoring or repressing them, we give them free reign to influence our rationalisations and decisions without detection. In other words, we must be careful to take images seriously even when they seem innocuous. Close readings can be helpful in that regard.

Close readings are critical analyses of popular 'texts'. Like Fiske (1989) we consider films, television, toys and other artefacts as texts that can be read, interpreted, and critically analysed. Close readings are sometimes easier to do in sets of two or three because comparison and contrast help throw each text into relief, highlighting details that may otherwise escape attention. Comparing new teacher texts with ones remembered from childhood contextualises and traces emerging identity. For example, in *Reinventing Ourselves as Teachers: Beyond Nostalgia*, Mitchell and Weber (1999) offer a close comparative reading of two films: *Dangerous Minds* and *To Sir with Love*. They warn that critiquing a teacher movie or book is not necessarily critiquing oneself. It is easier, after all, to see the flaws and strengths of other teachers, especially larger than life fictitious ones. People are not always eager to remember painful events. Suppressing them from consciousness often seems both easier and wiser to do. It may be easier initially, for example, to find the courage to condemn a mean or cruel act done by a fictional administrator than to remember one's rage at a feared or despised real-life one. It may be easier at first, to recognise a film teacher like Miss Brodie's obsessive need to live her life through her students than to confront one's own neediness or to notice that Marc Thackeray ('Sir') addressed his female students as sluts before recognising one's own sexist language or actions. In other words, the vicarious, emotional, and sometimes cathartic experience of popular texts can provide a safe starting point for exploring one's professional identity. Moreover, words, labels, acts and images from fiction can be useful in re-telling our own stories and even in transforming our view of ourselves and others. It is only when close readings are applied honestly to our own lives that we are in a position to reinvent (or camouflage) ourselves. This point is demonstrated by Butler (1997) who used teacher movies to provoke reflection amongst preservice teachers on the potential of the teacher role as advocate for social change, school reform, or justice.

## CODES AND CONVENTIONS OF ROMANCE IN POPULAR TEXTS OF TEACHING

Many popular representations of teachers are what might be described as hero images, but culture is also replete with images of teachers as villains, including mean, unfair, sexless, lifeless, boring drones who are the anti-heroes of teaching and schooling. Both sets of images are 'romantic' because of their inherent hero/anti-hero quality.

Writers and producers draw upon particular codes, conventions, and recurring themes to structure and shape their popular teacher texts. Of course, not all fictionalised teacher texts use all of these conventions, but our analysis of a representative sample of twenty popular novels and films documents the consistent re-occurrence of the ones listed below. By describing these conventions, we make it easier to recognise and use them for critical close readings of other texts.

1. Teacher heroes are usually outsiders who are teaching through circumstance rather than choice.
2. Teaching is natural, you do not need training if you've got the right stuff.
3. Teacher heroes are rare and stand out in contrast to anti-hero teachers.
4. Teacher heroes liberate students by defying the official school rules and curriculum.
5. Real learning occurs outside of school.
6. Teachers become heroic through a turning point of sudden enlightenment, divine intervention, or the 'aha' experience.
7. Teaching is a heroic and solitary act. Teachers do not work collectively for reform.
8. Teacher heroes are devoted to their students and are rewarded with their undying love and gratitude in a dramatic scene

The structure of most teacher texts is highlighted by those few image-texts that showcase the 'dark side of teaching', even for the hero. For example, such films as the *The Children's Hour*, *An Angel at my Table*, and *Waterland* present dramatic images of teachers who are destroyed while teaching with little or no hope held out for their joyful return to teaching. Indeed, together, they present unrelentingly black but romantic images of teachers as isolated and doomed people, of teaching as the surest path to personal undoing, a total nervous breakdown, or even suicide. These books and films serve as counter-texts that highlight the more prevalent images of teachers as heroes devotedly working and winning against the odds.

How do popular romantic texts affect teachers and students? Do they create unrealistic and potentially harmful expectations by encouraging teacher fantasy at the expense of reality as Robertson (1997) suggests? Do popular teacher images set beginning teachers up for disappointment, encouraging them to go into teaching to fulfil a deep desire to love and be loved, or a need to be needed or to save people, not necessarily the best motivations to take up the vocation? Do would-be teachers forget that for every hero-image, there are countless anti-hero images that create student expectations of teachers as mean and crabby, or inept and uninteresting?

In their fantasies, at least, people like to think of themselves as the exception, the hero who is not like the others. Hence the potential for these romantic texts to feed self-delusion. As de Lauretis (1994) contends, popular texts offer spectators places in which to replay fantasies that are both in the text and in the viewer.

Since we cannot make these texts disappear, our suggestion is to use the very things that make these texts 'dangerous' to mitigate their power. The hope, as Robertson (1997) writes, is that:

> The curriculum of teacher education can develop ways to assist beginning teachers in disrupting fantasy's confines. Popular culture may by used within pedagogy to explore what fantasy hopes for and ignores when it imagines teaching. Screenplay pedagogy can work to disrupt those moments of feeling trapped in a history produced but unchangeable. Part of the lesson involves imagining how to teach in the absence of miracles. (p. 139)

Through critical self-study, stereotypes are unmasked, at least partially, fantasy and desire are more honestly acknowledged, and critical questions are asked, making possible a re-invention of self as a teacher who is a more savvy consumer or producer of popular culture.

## PAST IMAGES, FUTURE DEVELOPMENT: REVISITING INFLUENTIAL POPULAR TEXTS

As the following quotation suggests, some popular texts are more engaging than others, potentially playing a significant role in teacher development and practice by evoking or symbolising some of our deepest professional aspirations.

> It was Sylvia Ashton-Warner, Bel Kaufman, E. R. Braithwaite, John Holt, and Herbert Kohl who taught me how to survive and teach in the urban classroom . . . When, during the course of my recent musings, these teacher-authors reappeared in my consciousness, I recalled how they had validated my affection for many of my students, as well as my horror at the biases and misanthropy of some of my colleagues; how they had shared their mistakes and triumphs in the classroom with me, thus helping me to recognise and acknowledge my own; how they had made me cry over the implacability of 'the system,' while at the same time showing me how to manipulate its constraints; and how they had taken me with them on their forays across cultural boundaries . . .
>
> By sharing how I experienced *Teacher, Up the Down Staircase, To Sir with Love, How Children Fail*, and *36 Children* in the early years of my career, I demonstrate the enormous importance of popular teaching narratives such as these in the professional development of educators. (Isenberg, 1994, pp. xiv–vi)

The original teacher-authored books on which so many movies are based might prove even more helpful than the movies, since the reader of a book must conjure up his or her own images to embody the written text, injecting or projecting a personal vision into/onto the teacher text. This leads to the following suggestion: What books have influenced you? Re-read them. Which scenes provoke the strongest emotional reaction? Why? Discuss with others.

## RE-EVALUATING THE POPULAR

Popular culture is not only unreflective or superficial. Popular culture contains avant garde elements, provocative ideas, even models for self-critique. There are even occasions when popular teacher texts demonstrate how to ask critical questions. For example, Isenberg describes the inspiration for self-reflection that she found in the popular text, *Up the Down Staircase*, by Bel Kaufman. She begins by quoting the main character, Sylvia Barrett:

> I had set out to tell you exactly what happened. But since I am the one writing this, how do I know what in my telling I am selecting, omitting, emphasising; what unconscious editing I am doing? Why was I more interested in the one black sheep (I use Ferone's own cliché) than in all the white lambs in my care? Why did I (in my red suit) call him a child? (p. 316)

Isenberg uses the above quote to make a parallel with her own quest for self-knowledge:

> Here Barrett models the kind of reflection in which I needed to engage; her questions about her own motives and behaviour as a teacher, a woman, and a writer were reassuring to me since I constantly asked myself similar ones. And I had no doubt that her responses to Ferone are indeed influenced to some extent by the fact that she finds him attractive and has unconsciously flirted with him. (Isenberg, 1994, p. 43)

Why do some teachers (especially women) find themselves feeling uncomfortable admitting that they liked or were really moved by a popular teacher text? Robertson (1997) suggests it is because the texts really do contain elements of our secret fantasies and desires, elements that are not socially acceptable in professional discourse. But there are professionally legitimate reasons to honestly admit to elements we like in popular culture: not all teacher texts are unidimensional or superficial. There is often a degree of meaningful complexity or depth or an element of truth that makes some of these texts engaging in the first place. They convey a counter-text that can be heard, if one listens. For example, Isenberg seems to be onto something when she writes:

> Like that of Sylvia Barrett, Braithwaite's pedagogy is not especially revolutionary, but his personal involvement and investment in the teaching process make it more meaningful than it would have been otherwise. By spending time and energy preparing relevant material, taking students on field trips, and openly explaining his own perspective, Braithwaite imbues his teaching with the caring that Nel Noddings (1984) advocates – caring that makes all the difference. In a sense, he himself becomes part of the curriculum, as his students study him for clues on how to live and learn in a difficult world. (p. 67)

Buried in the sentimental, dangerous and isolating romanticisation of many popular texts are some useful messages. Perhaps the most important one is that we teach who we are through how we live. At the very least, the popular could stir up controversy and debate in the teaching profession. For those who find popular texts dangerously misleading or reactionary, the most appropriate course of action might be to start putting alternative popular images out there. After all, as we discuss below, many of these popular culture teachers have emerged from the lives of angry teachers.

## WHAT IF TEACHERS WERE IN CONTROL OF POPULAR CULTURE?

By evaluating popular texts in the context of the lives of the teacher/authors who produce them, Isenberg (1994) finds that:

> Teaching narratives are plainly told by angry authors who describe the suffering of a disempowered constituency in the hope of ending that suffering. They are structured around crises of literacy, identity, and control and operate within constraints and conventions that are politically determined . . . teacher-narrators are usually politically motivated; teacher authors use their own experience to bear witness to terrible, ludicrous, or simply counterproductive things that happen within schools. (p. 105)

Although Isenberg's close readings of the texts she discusses are overly nostalgic and not as critical as we would wish, there may be something to her claim that many teacher-writers try to represent 'an inarticulate constituency, children and teenagers, who suffer as a result of the failures of our educational system and the people who prescribe and implement its policies in a society which routinely devalues children' (p. 110). Like children, the voices of teachers have been muted, even stifled, in the debates about schooling. One way to remedy that is to speak out, write, produce, and create. There is no medium more influential than the popular. Is that where teachers should continue to reinvent themselves, out in a broad public forum?

## Suggestion

Alone or as a group, write an outline for a movie scenario or a novel about teachers, one that you think might put an important image out there, one inspired perhaps, by your reaction to a popular text you have seen or read, one that represents your own teaching fantasy or reality or critique.

In the face of the unrealistic or negative teacher images that bombard us from all sides, it is easy to be discouraged. But the sheer volume makes for a certain richness and complexity that may be more liberating than first glance readings indicate. Close readings of popular culture bring into focus the shadowy, contradictory, and overlapping images that filter our vision, offering metaphoric stories that speak to our collective and individual experience.

It is understandable that the teaching profession would want to distance itself from many of the stereotypes and images of teachers and teaching with which it is saturated. But it is necessary to first uncover and face the pervasive images that might be curtailing our ability to truly integrate new views of teaching into personal philosophies and practice. An insistence on reaching a single and definitive interpretation of the stereotypes and metaphors of teaching, as either exclusively conservative or emancipatory, oversimplifies lived experience, leading to a poor, or very partial reading of the cumulative cultural texts of teacher and teaching. Contradictory stories and images can help create a deeper and more complete understanding or 'reading' of teaching.

## NOTE

1. Part of the research on which this chapter is based was funded by the Social Sciences and Humanities Research Council of Canada and the 'Fonds pour la Formation de Chercheurs et l'Aide à la Recherche (FCAR)'. We are most grateful for their continued support.

# References

Abercrombie, N., Hill, S. and Turner, B. (1994) *Dictionary of Sociology*, Harmondsworth: Penguin.

Abercrombie, M.L.J. (1984) *Changing higher education by the application of some group analytic ideas*, paper at the 8th International Conference of Group Psychotherapy, Mexico City.

Abu Lughod, J. (1991) Going beyond global babble, in King, A.D. (ed.) *Culture, Globalization and the World-System*, London: Macmillan.

Acker, S. (1990) Teachers' culture in an English primary school: continuity and change, *British Journal of Sociology of Education*, Vol. 11, No. 3, pp. 257–273.

Acker, S. (1994) *Gendered Education: Sociological reflections on women, teaching and feminism*, Milton Keynes: Open University Press.

Acker S. (1995) Carry on caring: the work of women teachers, *British Journal of Sociology of Education*, Vol. 16, No. 1, pp. 21–36.

Adelman, C. (1998) Photocontext, in Prosser, J. (ed.) *Image Based Research: A Sourcebook for Qualitative Researchers*, London: Falmer Press.

Ainscow, M., Hargreaves, D.H., Hopkins, D.M. and Black-Hawkins, K. (1994) *Mapping Change in Schools: the Cambridge Manual of Research Techniques*, obtainable from Barbara Shannon, School of Education, University of Cambridge, Shaftesbury Road, Cambridge CB2 2BX.

Ainscow, M., Hargreaves, D.H. and Hopkins, D. (1995) Mapping the process of change in schools, *Evaluation Research in Education*, Vol. 9, No. 2, pp. 75–90.

Alexander, R. (1984) *Primary Teaching*, London: Cassell.

Alexander, R. (1992) *Policy and Practice in Primary Education*, London: Routledge.

Alexander R. (1995) *Versions of Primary Education*, London: Routledge.

Allan, J., Brown, S. and Munn, P. (1991) *Off the Record: Mainstream Provision for Pupils with Non-Recorded Learning Difficulties in Primary and Secondary Schools*, Edinburgh: Scottish Council for Research in Education.

Allen, J. (1992) Post-Industrialism and post-Fordism, in Hall, S., Held, D. and McGrew, T. (eds) *Modernity and its Futures*, Cambridge: Polity Press.

Alvesson, M. (1993) *Cultural Perspectives on Organizations*, Cambridge University Press.

Anderson, C.S. (1982) The search for school climate: a review of the Research, *Review of Education Research*, Fall, Vol. 52, No. 3, pp. 368–420.

Anderson, R.C. (1977) The notion of schemata and the educational enterprise: general discussion of conference, in Anderson, R.D., Spiro, R.J. and Montague, W.E. (eds) *Schooling and the Acquisition of Knowledge*, Hillsdale, NJ: Lawrence Erlbaum Associates.

Angus, L. (1996) Cultural dynamics and organizational analysis: leadership, administration and the management of meaning in schools, in Leithwood, K., Chapman, J., Carson, P., Hallinger, P. and Hart, A. (eds) *International Handbook of Educational Leadership and Administration*, Part 2, Dordrecht: Kluwer.

Angus, M. (1995) Devolution of school governance in an Australian state school system: third time lucky?, in Carter, D.S.G. and O'Neill, M.H. (eds) *Case Studies in Educational Change: An International Perspective*, London: Falmer Press.

Anthony, P. (1994) *Managing Culture*, Buckingham: Open University Press.

Apple, M.W. (1986) *Teachers and Texts: A Political Economy of Class and Gender Relations in Education*, New York: Routledge and Kegan Paul.

Apple, M.W. (1996) *Cultural Politics and Education*, New York: Teachers College, Columbia University.

Apple, M.W. and Beane, J. (1999) *Democratic Schools*, Buckingham: Open University Press.

Argyris, C. (1958) *Personality and Organisation: The Conflict between the System and the Individual*, New York: Harper and Row.

Arnove, R. (1996) Partnerships and emancipatory educational movements: issues and prospects, *Alberta Journal of Educational Research*, Vol. XLII, No. 2, pp. 170–77.

Ashton-Warner, S. (1963) *Teacher*, New York: Simon and Schuster.

Averch, H. (1971) *How Effective is Schooling?* Santa Monica: Rand Corporation.

Avis, J., Bloomer, M., Esland, G., Gleeson, D. and Hodkinson, P. (1996) *Knowledge and Nationhood: Education, Politics and Work*, London: Cassell.

Axline, V.M. (1964) *Dibs: In Search of Self*, London: Houghton Mifflen Co.

Back, L. (1996) New ethnicities and urban culture: racisms and multiculture, in *Young Lives*, London: UCL Press.

Bailey, L. (1995) The correspondence principle and the 1988 Education Reform Act, *British Journal of Sociology of Education*, Vol. 16, No. 4, pp. 479–494.

Balibar, E. and Wallerstein, I. (1991) *Race, Nation, Class: Ambiguous Identities*, London: Verso.

Ball, S.J. (1987) *The Micro-Politics of the School: Towards a Theory of School Organisation*, London: Methuen.

Ball, S.J. (1990) *Politics and Policy-Making in Education: Explorations in Policy Sociology*, London: Routledge.

Ball, S.J. (1994) *Education Reform: A Critical and Post-Structural Approach*, Buckingham: Open University Press.

Bandman, B. (1967) *The Place of Reason in Education*, Columbus, OH: The Ohio State University Press.

Barber, M. (1997) A reading revolution: how we can teach every child to read well, in Barber, M. (ed.) *Perspectives on School Effectiveness and School Improvement*, London: Institute of Education University of London.

Barker, M. (1997) Why simply tackling poverty is not enough, *Times Educational Supplement*, 12 September, p. 17.

Barr, I. (1997) *Values and the Hidden Curriculum*, a paper given at the Gordon Cook Foundation Conference, Edinburgh 1997.

Barrs, M and Pidgeon, S. (1993) *Reading the Difference*, London: Centre for Language in Primary Education.

Barth, R. (1990) *Improving Schools From Within: Teachers, Parents and Principals Can Make the Difference*, San Francisco: Jossey-Bass.

Barthes, R. (1972) *Mythologies*, London: Jonathon Cape.

Barthes, R. (1984) *Camera Lucida: Reflections on photography*, London: Fontana.

Barton, L. (1997) Inclusive education: romantic, subversive or realistic?, *International Journal of Inclusive Education*, Vol. 1, No. 3., pp. 231–242.

Bate, P. (1994) *Strategies for Cultural Change*, Butterworth-Heinemann.

Bates, R. (1987) Corporate culture, schooling and educational administration, *Educational Administration Quarterly*, Vol. 23, No. 4, pp. 79–155.

Baudrillard, J. (1988) *America*, London: Verso.

Beare, H., Caldwell, B.J. and Millikan, R.H. (1989) *Creating an Excellent School: Some New Management Techniques*, London: Routledge.

Beck, U. (1992) *Risk Society: Towards a New Modernity*, London: Sage.

Belenky M., Clinchy, B., Goldberger, N. and Tarak, J. (1986) *Women's Ways of Knowing*, New York: Basic Books.

Bell, L. (1989) Ambiguity models and secondary schools: a case study, in Bush, T. (ed.) *Managing Education; Theory and Practice*, Milton Keynes: Open University Press.

Bennett, S.M., Desforges, C., Cockburn, A. and Wilkinson, B. (1984), *The Quality of Pupil Learning Experience*, London: Lawrence Erlbaum.

Berger, J. (1989) *Another Way of Telling*, Cambridge: Granta Books.

Berger, P. (1963) *An Invitation to Sociology: A Humanistic Perspective*, Harmondsworth: Penguin Books.

Bernstein, B. (1970) Class and pedagogies: visible and invisible in *Class, Codes and Control, Vol. 3, Towards a Theory of Educational Transmission*, London: Routledge and Kegan Paul.

Bernstein, B. (1977) *Class, Codes and Control, Vol. 3*, second edition, London: Routledge and Kegan Paul.

Bernstein, B. (1990) *The Structuring of Pedagogic Discourse: Class Codes and Control*, Vol. 4, London: Routledge.

Bernstein, B. (1997) 'Official Knowledge and Pedagogic Identities: The Politics of Recontextualising'. In I. Nilsson and L. Lundahl (eds) *Teachers, Curriculum and Policy: Critical Perspectives in Educational Research*. Umea, Sweden, Department of Education, Umea University, 165–180.

Billig, M. (1978) *Fascists: A Social Psychological View of the National Front*, London: Harcourt Brace Jovanovich.

Birmingham City Council Education Department (1996) *Improving on Previous Best: An Overview of School Improvement Strategies in Birmingham*, Birmingham: Birmingham City Council Education Department.

Blackmore, J. (1995) Breaking out from a Masculinist Politics of Education, in Limerick, B. and Lingard, B. (eds) *Gender and Changing Education Management*, Rydalmere, NSW: Hodder Education.

Blase, J. (1991) The micropolitical perspective, in Blase, J. (ed.) *The Politics of Life in Schools: Power, Conflict, and Cooperation*, London: Sage.

Bottery, M. (1990) *The Morality of the School: The Theory and Practice of Values in Education*, London: Cassell.

Bowles, S. and Gintis, H. (1976) *Schooling in Capitalist America*, London: Routledge and Kegan Paul.

Boyd, B. and Reeves, J. (1996) *Listening to Children's Voices*, paper presented at the British Educational Research Association Conference, Lancaster University.

Brah, A. (1997) *Cartologies of Diaspora: Contesting Identities*, London: Routledge.

Braithwaite, E.R. (1959) *To Sir, with Love*, London: Bodley.

Brecht, B. (1965) *On Everyday Theatre: The Development of an Aesthetic*, London: Methuen.

Britzman, D.P. (1991) *Practice Makes Practice: A Critical Study of Learning to Teach*, Albany: State University Press.

Britzman, D.P. (1992) The terrible problem of knowing thyself: toward a poststructural account of teacher identity, *Journal of Curriculum Theorizing*, Vol. 9, No. 3, pp. 23–46.

Broadfoot, P. and Osborn, M. (1993) *Perceptions of Teaching: Primary School Teachers in England and France*, London: Cassell.

Broadfoot, P. and Osborn, M. (1995) *Primary Schooling and Policy Change in England and France*, London: School Curriculum and Assessment Authority.

Brookover, W.B., Beady, C. and Flood, P. (1978), Elementary School Social Climate and School Achievement, *American Educational Research Journal*, Vol. 15, pp. 301–318.

Brown, A. (1997) *Organisational Culture*, London: Pitman.

Brunner, D. (1991) *Stories of Schooling in Films and Television: A Cultural Studies Approach to Teacher Education*, paper presented at the American Educational Research Association Annual Conference, Chicago, IL.

Burnage Report (1989) *Murder in the Playground*, London: Longsight Press.

Bullough, R.V. (1991) Exploring personal teaching metaphors in preservice teacher education, *Journal of Teacher Education*, Vol. 42, No. 1, pp. 43–51.

Bullough, R.V. Jr., Knowles, J.G. and Crow, N.A. (1991) *Emerging as a teacher*, New York: Routledge.

Butler, J. (1993) *Bodies that Matter, On the Discursive Limits of 'Sex'*, London: Routledge.

Butler, F. (1997) *From reel to real: film narrative in a Bahamian teacher education program*, paper presented at the American Educational Research Association Annual Conference, Chicago, IL.

Button, L. (1982) *Developmental Groupwork with Adolescents*, London: Hodder and Stoughton.

Calderhead, J. and Robson, M. (1991) Images of teaching: student teachers' early conceptions of classroom practice, *Teaching and Teacher Education*, Vol. 7, No. 1, pp. 1–8.

*Cambridge Journal of Education* (1996) Special edition: *The Emotions in Teaching*, Vol. 23, No. 3, pp. 293–306.

Campbell, R.J., Neill, S., and Evans, L. (1991) *Workloads, Achievement and Stress: a study of teacher time at Key Stage 1*, University of Warwick/ATL.

Campbell, R.J., and Neill, S. (1994) *Primary Teachers at Work*, London: Routledge.

Canaan, J. (1996) One thing leads to another: drinking, fighting and working-class masculinities, in Mac an Ghaill, M. (ed.) *Understanding Masculinities: Social Relations and Cultural Arenas*, Buckingham: Open University Press.

Cartier-Bresson, H. (1952) *The Decisive Moment*, New York: Simon and Schuster.

Chandler, D. (1997) *Semiotics for Beginners*, London: Cobley and Jansz.

Children's Literature Research Centre (1996) *Young People's Reading at the end of the Century*, London: Roehampton Institute.

Chin, R. and Benne, K.D. (1970) General strategies of effecting change in human systems, in Bennis, W.G., Benne, K.D. and Chin, R. (eds) *The Planning of Change* (second edition), London: Holt, Rinehart and Winston.

Chisholm, B., Kearney, D., Knight, H., Little, H., Morris, S. and Tweedle, D. (1986) *Preventative Approaches to Disruption*, Basingstoke: Macmillan.

Chitty, C. (1997) The School Effectiveness Movement Origins, Shortcomings and Future Possibilities, *The Curriculum Journal*, Vol. 8, No. 1, pp. 45–62.

Chubb, J. and Moe, T. (1990) *Politics, Markets and America's Schools*, Washington: Brookings Institution.

Clark, D.L. and Guba, E. (1965) *An Examination of Potential Change Roles in Education*, paper presented on Innovation in Planning School Curriculum, University of London.

Cockburn, C.K. (1987) *Two-Track Training: Sex Inequalities and the YTS*, London: Macmillan.

Cohen, P. (1986) *Rethinking the Youth Question*, working paper No. 3 Post-16 Education Centre, London: Institute of Education.

Cohen, P. (1988) The perversion of inheritance: studies in the making of multi-racist Britain, in Cohen, P, and Bains, H. (eds) *Multi-racist Britain*, London: Macmillan.

Cohen, P. (1989) *The Cultural Geography of Adolescent Racism*, London: University of London.

Cohen, P. (1993) *Home Rules: Some Reflections on Racism and Nationalism in Everyday Life*, London: University of East London.

Cohen, R. and Hughes, M. with Ashworth, L. and Blair, M. (1994) *School's Out: The Family Perspective on School Exclusion*, London: Barnardos and Family Service Unit.

Cohen, S. (1972) *Folk Devils and Moral Panics*, Paladin.

Cole, A. and Knowles, J.G. (1998) *Researching teaching: exploring teacher development through reflexive inquiry*, Boston: Allyn & Bacon.

Coleman, J.S., Cambell, E., Hobson, C., McPartland, J., Mood, A., Weinfeld, F. and York, R. (1966), *Equality of Educational Opportunity*, Washington: National Centre for Educational Statistics.

Collier, J. (1986) *Visual Anthropology: Photography as a Research Method*, New York: Holt, Rinehart and Winston.

Collier, J. and Collier, J. Jnr (1986) *Visual Anthropology: Photography as a Research Method*, New York: Holt, Rinehart and Winston.

Commission for Racial Equality (1996) *Exclusion From School: The Public Cost*, London.

Connell, R.W. (1989) Cool guys, swots and wimps: the inter-play of masculinity and education, *Oxford Review of Education*, Vol. 15, No. 3, pp. 291–303.

Connell, R.W. (1995) *Masculinities*, Cambridge: Polity Press.

Connell, R.W., Ashenden, D.J., Kessler, S. and Dowsett, G.W. (1982) *Making the Difference: School, Families and Social Divisions*, London: George Allen and Unwin.

Connelly, F.M. and Clandinin, D.J. (1985) Personal practical knowledge and the modes of knowing: Relevance for teaching and learning, in Eisner, E. (ed.) *Learning and Teaching the Ways of Knowing*, 84th Yearbook of the National Society for the Study of Education, Chicago: University of Chicago Press.

Cooper, M. (1988) Whose culture is it, anyway?, in Lieberman, A. (ed.) *Building a Professional Culture in Schools*, New York: Teachers College Press.

Cornell, F.G. (1955) Socially Perceptive Administration, *Phi Delta Kappan*, Vol. 36, March, pp. 222–231.

Corrigan, P. (1979) *Schooling the Smash Street Kids*, London: Macmillan.

Cowie, H., Boulton, M. and Smith, P.K. (1992) Bullying: Pupil Relationship, in Jones, N. and Jones, E. (eds) *Learning to Behave*, London: Kogan Page.

Cray, D. and Mallory, G.R. (1998) *Making Sense of Managing Culture*, International Thomson Business Press.

Croll, P. (1996) (ed.) *Teachers, Pupils and Primary Schooling: Continuity and change*, London: Cassell.

Cuban, L. (1990) A fundamental puzzle of school reform, in Lieberman, A. (ed.) *Schools as Collaborative Cultures: Creating the Future Now*, New York and London: Cassell.

Cullen, M.A., Johnstone, M., Lloyd, G. and Munn, P. (1997) *Exclusions from School and Alternatives: The Case Studies*, a report to SOEID Edinburgh: Moray House Institute of Education.

Cullingford, C. and Morrison, J. (1995) Bullying as a formative influence: the relationship between the experience of school and criminality, *British Educational Research Journal*, Vol. 21, No. 5, pp. 547–560.

Dale, R. (1989) *The State and Education Policy*, Milton Keynes, Open University Press.

Dale, R. (1994) *Constructing a new education settlement: neo-liberal and neo-Schumpeterian Tendencies*, paper presented to the NZARE Conference, University of Auckland.

Dalin, P. and Rolff, H. (1993) *Changing the School Culture*, London: Cassell.

David, M., West, A. and Ribbens, J. (1994) *Mothers' Intuition: Choosing Secondary Schools*, London: Falmer Press.

Davies, B. (1979) Education for sexism: moving beyond sex role socialisation and reproduction theories, *Educational Philosophy and Theory*, Vol. 21, No. 1, pp. 1–19.

Davies, B. (1989) *Frogs and Snails and Feminist Tales: Pre-school Children and Gender*, Sydney: Allen and Unwin.

Davies, L. (1997) The rise of the school effectiveness movement, in White, J. and de Lauretis, T. (1994) *The Practice of Love: Lesbian Sexuality and Perverse Desire*, Bloomington: Indiana University Press.

de Castell, S. (1988) Metaphors into models: the teacher as strategist, in Holborn, P., Wideen, M. and Andrews, I. (eds) *Becoming a teacher*, Toronto: Kagan and Woo Ltd.

de Lauretis, T. (1994) *The Practice of Love: Lesbian Sexuality and Perverse Desire*, Bloomington: Indiana University Press.

Deal, T.E. and Kennedy, A. (1983) Culture and school performance, *Educational Leadership*, Vol. 40, No. 5, pp. 140–141.

Deem, R., Brehony, K. and Heath, S. (1994) Governors, schools and the miasma of the market, *British Education Research Journal*, Vol. 20, No. 4, pp. 535–550.

Delamont, S. (1980) *Sex Roles and the School*. London: Routledge.

Delfattore, J. (1992) *What Johnny Shouldn't Read*, New Haven: Yale University Press.

Department for Education and Employment (1997a) *Excellence for all children: meeting special educational needs (the Green Paper)*, London: The Stationery Office Limited.

Department for Education and Employment (1997b) *Excellence in Schools, an Education White Paper*, London: The Stationery Office Limited.

DES (1989) *Discipline in Schools*, Report of the Committee of Enquiry chaired by Lord Elton, London: HMSO.

Dey, I. (1993) *Qualitative Data Analysis*, London: Routledge.

DfEE (1997) *The Implementation of the National Literacy Strategy – Literacy Task Force*, London: HMSO.

Dollimore, J. (1991) *Sexual Dissidence: Augustine to Wilde, Freud to Foucault*, Oxford: Clarendon Press.

Drummond, M.J. (1993) *Assessing Children's Learning*, London: David Fulton.

Drummond, M.J. (1995) The concept of competence in primary teaching, in McKenzie, P., Mitchell, P. and Oliver, P. (eds) *Competence and Accountability in Education*, Aldershot: Arena.

Edmonds, R.R. (1979) Some Schools Work and More Can, *Social Policy*, Vol. 9.

Eichenbaum, L. and Orbach, S. (1983) *What do Women Want?* London: Michael Joseph.

Elbaz, F. (1991) Research on teacher's knowledge: the evolution of a discourse, *Journal of Curriculum Studies*, Vol. 23, No. 1, pp. 1–19.

Elliott, J., Bridges, D., Ebbutt, D., Gibson, R. and Nias, J. (1981) *School Accountability*, Oxford: Blackwell.

Eraut, M. (1985) Knowledge creation and knowledge use in professional contexts, *Studies in Higher Education*, Vol. 10, pp. 117–133.

Esland, G. (1996) Knowledge and nationhood: the new right, education and the global market, in Avis, J., Bloomer, M., Esland, G., Gleeson, D. and Hodkinson, P. (eds) *Knowledge and Nationhood: Education, Politics and Work*, London: Cassell.

Evans, K. (1974) The Head and His Territory, *New Society*, 24 October.

Evans, L., Packwood, A., Neill, S., and Campbell, R.J. (1994) *The Meaning of Infant Teachers' Work*, London: Routledge.

Evetts, J. (1990) *Women Teachers in Primary Education*, London: Routledge.

Fanon, F. (1967) *Black Skins, White Masks*, London: Paladin.

Featherstone, M. (1995) *Undoing Culture: Globalization, Postmodernism and Identity*, London: Sage.

Fielding, M. (1996) Beyond Collaboration: on the importance of community, in D. Bridges and C. Husbands (eds) *Consorting and Collaborating in the Education Market Place*. London: Falmer Press.

Fink, D. (1997) *The Attrition of Change*, unpublished doctoral thesis, Milton Keynes: Open University.

Fink, D. and Stoll, L. (1998) Educational change: easier said than done, in Hargreaves, A., Fullan, M., Lieberman, A. and Hopkins, D. (eds) *International Handbook of Educational Change*, Leuven: Kluwer.

Finlayson, D.S. (1970) *School Climate Index*, Slough: NFER.

Finlayson, D.S. (1973) Measuring school climate, *Trends in Education*, No. 30.

Finlayson, D.S. (1975) Organisational climate, *Research Intelligence*, Vol. 1, pp. 22–36.

Finlayson, D.S. (1987) School climate: an outmoded metaphor?, *Journal of Curriculum Studies*, Vol. 19, No. 2, pp. 163–173.

Fiske, J. (1989) *Understanding popular culture*, Boston: Unwin Hyman.

Fiske, J., Hodge, B. and Turner, G. (eds) (1987) *Myths of Oz*, Sydney: Allen and Unwin.

Fullan, M. (1982) *The Meaning of Educational Change*, New York: OISE/Teachers' Press.

Fullan, M. (1991) *The New Meaning of Educational Change*, New York: Teachers College Press.

Fullan, M. (1993) *Change Forces: Probing the Depths of Educational Reform*, London: Falmer Press.

Fullan, M.G. (1996) Turning systematic thinking on its head, *Phi Delta Kappan*, Vol. 77, No. 6, pp. 420–423.

Fullan, M.G. (1997) Emotion and hope: constructive concepts for complex times, in Hargreaves, A. (ed.) *Rethinking Educational Change with Heart and Mind*, ASCD Yearbook Alexandria: VA.

Fullan, M., Bennett, B. and Rolheiser Bennett, C. (1990) Linking classroom and school improvement, *Educational Leadership*, Vol. 47, No. 8, pp. 13–19.

Fullan, M.G. and Hargreaves, A. (1991) *What's Worth Fighting For? Working Together For Your School*, Toronto: Ontario Public School Teachers' Federation. Published as *What's Worth Fighting For in Your School* (1992), Buckingham: Open University Press.

Fuller, F. (1969) Concerns of teachers: a developmental approach, *American Educational Journal*, Vol. 6, pp. 207–26.

Furlong, A. and Cartmel, C. (1997) *Young People and Social Change: Individualization and Risk in Late Modernity*, Buckingham: Open University Press.

Gardiner, J. (1997) Inclusion on the way in, *Times Educational Supplement*, 24 October, p. 8.

Garrett V. (1997) Managing change, in Davies, B. and Ellison, L. (eds) *School Leadership for the 21st Century: A competency and knowledge approach*, London: Routledge.

George, D. (1959) *English Political Caricature*, Oxford: Oxford University Press.

Gerrard, N. (1997) Kelly is no longer invisible, and we care for her and want to help. Pity it's too late, *The Observer*, 5 October, p. 18.

Gerth, H.H. and Mills, C.W. (1948) *From Max Weber: Essays in Sociology*, Routledge & Kegan Paul.

Gewirtz, S., Ball, S.J. and Bowe, R. (1995) *Markets, Choice and Equity*, Milton Keynes: Open University Press.

Ghouri, N. (1997) Exclusions 'spiral out of control', *Times Educational Supplement*, 26 September, p. 12.

Giddens, A. (1991) *Modernity and Self-Identity: Self and Society in the Late Modern Age*, Stanford, CA: Stanford University Press.

Giddens, A. (1994) Living in a post-traditional society, in Beck, U., Giddens, A. and Lash, S. (eds) *Reflexive Modernization: Politics, Tradition and Aesthetics in the Modern Social Order*, Cambridge: Polity Press.

Gillborn, D. (1990) *'Race', Ethnicity and Education: Teaching and Learning in Multi-Ethnic Schools*, London: Unwin Hyman.

Gillborn, D. (1995) *Racism and Anti-Racism in Real Schools*, Buckingham: Open University Press.

Gilligan C., (1982) *In a Different Voice*, Cambridge, Mass: Harvard University Press.

Gilroy, P. (1987) *There Ain't No Black in the Union Jack*, London: Hutchinson.

Giroux, H.A. and Simon, R. (1989) *Popular Culture, Schooling, and Everyday Life*, Toronto: OISE Press.

Goffman, E. (1956) *Preservation of Self in Everyday Life*, Harmondsworth: Penguin.

Goleman, D. (1996) *Emotional Intelligence*, London: Bloomsbury.

Goodlad, J. (1984) *A place called school*, New York: McGraw-Hill.

Gorman, T., White, J., Brooks, G., Maclure, M. and Kispal, A. (1988) *Language performance in schools: a review of APU language monitoring 1979–83*, London: HMSO.

Grady, J. (1996) The scope of visual sociology, *Visual Sociology*, Vol. 11, No. 2, pp. 10–24.

Gramsci, A. (1971) *Selections from the Prison Notebooks*, London: Lawrence and Wishart.

Green, A. (1996) Education, Globalization and the Nation State, paper presented at the symposium Education, Globalization and the Nation-State: Comparative Perspectives at the World Congress of Comparative Education Societies, University of Sydney.

Grumet, M.,(1988) *Bitter Milk: Women and Teaching*, Amherst: University of Massachusetts Press.

Hall, S. (1991) The local and the global: globalization and ethnicity', in King, A.D. (ed.) *Culture, Globalization and the World-System*, London: Macmillan.

Hall, S. (1992) New ethnicities, in Donald, J. and Rattansi, A. (eds) *'Race', Culture and Difference*, London: Sage/The Open University.

Hall, S. (1997) The work of representation, in Hall, S. (ed.) *Representation: Cultural Representations and signifying Practices*, Milton Keynes: The Open University.

Halpin, A.W. and Croft, D.B. (1963) *The Organisational Climate of Schools*, Chicago: University of Chicago.

Halpin, D., Power, S. and Fritz, J. (1997) Opting into the Past? Grant Maintained Schools and the Reinvention of Tradition, in Glatter, R., Woods, P.A. and Bagley, C. (eds) *Choice and Diversity in Schooling: Perspectives and Prospects*, London: Routledge.

Hamilton, D. (1997) Peddling feel-good fictions, in White, J. and Barber, M. (eds) *Perspectives on School Effectiveness and School Improvement*, London: Institute of Education, University of London.

Hamilton, M., Barton, D. and Ivanic, R. (eds) (1994) *Worlds of Literacy*, Clevedon; Philadelphia; Adelaide: Multilingual Matters Ltd.

Hammersley, M. (1997) Educational research and teaching: a response to David Hargreaves' TTA Lecture, *British Educational Research Journal*, Vol. 23, No. 2, pp. 141–162.

Hammersley, M. and Woods, P. (1984) *Life in School; The Sociology of Pupil Culture*, Milton Keynes: Open University Press.

Handy, C. (1985) *Understanding Organisations*, London: Penguin.

Handy, C. and Aitken, R. (1986) *Understanding Schools as Organizations*, Penguin Books.

Hargreaves, A. (1992) Cultures of teaching: a focus for change, in Hargreaves, A. and Fullan, M.G. (eds) *Understanding Teacher Development*, Cassell/Teachers' College Press.

Hargreaves, A. (1994) *Changing Teachers, Changing Times: Teachers' Work and Culture in the Postmodern Age*, London: Cassell.

Hargreaves, A. (1997a) From reform to renewal: a new deal for a new age, in Hargreaves, A. and Evans, R. (eds) *Beyond Educational Reform: Bringing Teachers Back In*, Buckingham: Open University Press.

Hargreaves, A. (1997b) Rethinking educational change: going deeper and wider in the quest for success, in Hargreaves, A. (ed.) *Rethinking Educational Change with Heart and Mind*, ASCD 1997 Yearbook: Alexandria, VA: Association for Supervision and Curriculum Development.

Hargreaves, A. and Woods, P. (1984) *Classrooms and Staffrooms*, Milton Keynes: Open University Press.

Hargreaves, A., Earl, L. and Ryan, J. (1996) *Schooling For Change: Reinventing Education for Early Adolescents*. London: Falmer Press.

Hargreaves, D.H. (1982) *The Challenge for the Comprehensive School*, London: Routledge.

Hargreaves, D.H. (1994) *The Mosaic of Learning: Schools and Teachers for the Next Century*, London: Demos.

Hargreaves, D.H. (1995) School culture, school effectiveness and school improvement, *School Effectiveness and School Improvement*, Vol. 6, No. 1, pp. 23–46.

Hargreaves, D.H. (1996) *Teaching as a Research-Based Profession*, London: Teacher Training Agency.

Hargreaves, D.H., Hester, J.K., and Mellor. F.J. (1975) *Deviance in Classrooms*, London: Routledge and Kegan Paul.

Hargreaves, D.H. and Hopkins, D. (1991) *The Empowered School*, Cassell.

Harper, D. (1987) *Working Knowledge: Skill and Community in a Small Shop*, Chicago: University of Chicago Press.

Harris, K. (1996) The corporate invasion of schooling: some implications for pupils, teachers and education, AARE SET: Research Information for Teachers, 2.

Harty, S. (1994) Pied Piper revisited, in Bridges, D. and McLaughlin, T.H. (eds) *Education and the Market Place*, London: Falmer Press.

Harvey Jones, J. (1988) *Making It Happen: Reflections on Leadership*, Fontana/Collins.

Held, D. (1989) The decline of the nation state, in Hall, S. and Jacques, M. (eds) *New Times: The Changing Face of Politics in the 1990s*, London: Lawrence and Wishart.

Henig, J.R. (1994) *Rethinking School Choice: Limits of the Market Metaphor*, Princeton, Princeton University Press.

Hewitt, R. (1986) *White Talk, Black Talk: Inter-Racial Friendship and Communication Amongst Adolescents*, Cambridge: Cambridge University Press.

Hickman. M. (1995) *Religion, Class and Identity: The State, the Catholic Church and the Education of the Irish in Britain*, Hants: Avebury.

Hickox, M. and Moore, R. (1992) Education and post-Fordism a new correspondence, in Brown, P. and Lauder, H. (eds) *Education for Economic Survival: from Fordism to post-Fordism*, London: Routledge.

Hillgate Group (1987) *The Reform of British Education*, London: Claridge Press.

Hirst, P., and Thompson, G. (1996) *Globalization in Question: The International Government and the Possibilities of Governance*, Cambridge: Polity Press.

Hochschild, A. (1983) *The Managed Heart: Commercialization of Human Feeling*, Berkeley: University of California Press.

Hofstede, G. (1991) *Cultures and Organizations*, HarperCollins.

Hollands, R.G. (1990) *The Long Transition: Class, Culture and Youth Training*, London: Macmillan.

Hopkins, D., Ainscow, M. and West, M. (1994) *School Improvement in an Era of Change*, London: Cassell.

House, E.R. (1974) *The Politics of Educational Innovation*, Berkeley, CA: McCutchan.

House, E.R. (1979) Technology versus craft: a ten year perspective on innovation, *Journal of Curriculum Studies*, Vol. 11, No. 1, pp. 1–15.

House, E.R., Kerins, T. and Steele, J.M. (1972) A test of the research and development model of change, *Educational Administration Quarterly*, Vol. 8, No. 1, pp. 1–14.

Hoy, W.K. (1990) Organisational climate and culture: a conceptual analysis of the school workplace, *Journal of Educational and Psychological Consultation*, Vol. 1, No. 2.

Hoyle, E. (1982) Micropolitics of educational organisations, *Educational Management and Administration*, Vol. 10, No. 2, pp. 97–98.

Hoyle, E. (1986) *The Politics of School Management*, London: Hodder and Stoughton.

Huberman, M. (1992) Critical introduction, in Fullan, M.G. *Successful School Improvement*, Buckingham: Open University Press and Toronto: OISE Press.

Huberman, M. (1993) The model of the independent artisan in teachers' professional relations, in Little, J.W. and McLaughlin, M.W. (eds) *Teachers' Work: Individuals, Colleagues and Contexts*, Teachers' College Press.

Huberman, M. and Miles, M.B. (1984) *Innovation Up Close*, New York: Plenum.

Isenberg, J. (1994) *Going by the Book: The Role of Popular Classroom Chronicles in the Professional Development of Teachers*, Westport, CN: Bergin & Garvey.

Jackson, P. (1968) *Life in Classrooms*, New York: Holt Rinehart.

Jameson, F. (1991) *Postmodernism or the Cultural Logic of Late Capitalism*, London: Verso.

Janis, I. (1972) *Victims of Groupthink*, Boston, MA: Houghton Mifflin.

Jeffcutt, P. (1993) From interpretation to representation, in Hassard, J. and Parker, M. (eds) *Postmodernism and Organizations*, London: Sage.

Jeffrey, B. Woods, P. (1996) Feeling de-professionalized: the social construction of emotions during an OFSTED inspection, *Cambridge Journal of Education*, Vol. 26, pp. 325–43.

Jencks, C. (1972), *Inequality: A Reassessment of the Effect of Family and Schooling in America*, New York: Basic Books.

Johnson, D.W. and Johnson, R.T. (1984) *Structuring Cooperative Learning: Lesson Plans for Teachers*, Minnesota: Interaction Book Company.

Johnson, D.W., Maruyama, G., Johnson, R. and Nelson, D. (1981) Effects of competitive and individualistic goal structures on achievement: a meta-analysis, *Psychological Bulletin*, Vol. 89, No. 1, pp. 47–62.

Johnson, L. (1992) *My Posse Don't Do Homework*, New York: St. Martin's Press.

Johnston, S. (1992) Images: A way of understanding the practical knowledge of student teachers, *Teaching & Teacher Education*, Vol. 8, No. 2, pp. 123–36.

Johnstone, M. and Munn, P. (1992) *Discipline in Scottish Schools*, Edinburgh: Scottish Council for Research in Education.

Johnstone, M. and Munn, P. (1992) Truancy and attendance in Scottish secondary schools, SCRE *Spotlight* No. 38, Edinburgh: Scottish Council for Research in Education.

Johnstone, M. and Munn, P. (1997) *Primary and secondary teachers' perceptions of indiscipline*, Confidential Research Report to the Educational Institute of Scotland Edinburgh: Moray House Institute of Education.

Jones, S. (1988) *Black Youth, White Culture: The Reggae Tradition from JA to UK*, London: Macmillan.

Joseph, P.B. and Burnaford, G.E. (eds) (1994) *Images of Schoolteachers in Twentieth-Century America: Paragons, Polarities, Complexities*, New York: St. Martin's Press.

Judd, J. (1998) Tough words to test our children, *The Independent*, 21 Mar.

Kanter, R.M. (1984) *The Change Makers*, Unwin.

Kaufman, B. (1964) *Up the Down Staircase*, New York: Hearst.

Kelchtermans G. (1996) Teacher vulnerability: understanding its moral and political roots, *Cambridge Journal of Education*, Vol. 26, No. 3, pp. 307–24.

Kenway, J. with Bigum, C., Fitzclarence, L. and Collier, J. (1996) Pulp fictions? Education, markets and the information superhighway, in Carlson, D. and Apple, M. (eds), *Critical Educational Theory in Unsettling Times*, University of Minnesota Press.

King, R. (1978) *All Things Bright and Beautiful: A Sociological Study of Infant Schools*, Chichester: Wiley.

Kress, G. and Van Leewen, T. (1996) *Reading Images: The Grammar of Visual Design*, London: Routledge.

Lacey, C. (1977) *The Socialization of Teachers*, London, Methuen.

Lane, J. (1994) Supporting effective responses to challenging behaviour: from theory to practice, in Gray, P., Miller, A. and Noakes, J. (eds) *Challenging Behaviour in Schools: Teacher support, practical techniques and policy development*, London: Routledge.

Lash, S. and Urry, J. (1987) *The End of Organized Capitalism*, Cambridge: Polity Press.

Lawn, M. and Grace, G. (eds) (1987) *Teachers: the Culture and Politics of Work*, London: Falmer.

Lawrence, B. and Hayden, C. (1997) primary School Exclusions, *Educational Research and Evaluation*, Vol. 3, No. 1, pp. 54–77.

Lees, S. (1987) The structure of sexual relations in school, in Arnot, M. and Weiner, G. (eds) *Gender and the Politics of Schooling*, Milton Keynes: Open University Press.

Lewin, K.R., Lippitt, R. and White, R.K. (1939) Patterns of aggressive behaviour in three 'social climates', *Journal of Social Psychology*, Vol. 10, pp. 271–99.

Lindsay, G. (1997) Are we ready for inclusion?, in Lindsay, G. and Thompson, D. (eds) *Values into Practice in Special Education*, London: David Fulton.

Lipsitz, G. (1990) *Time Passages: Collective Memory and American Popular Culture*, Minneapolis: University of Minnesota Press.

Little, J. W. (1990) The persistence of privacy: autonomy and initiative in teachers' professional relations, *Teachers College Record*, Vol. 91, No. 4, pp. 509–36.

Lloyd, G. and Munn, P. (forthcoming) Services for children with social, emotional and behavioural difficulties in school, in Hill, M. (ed.) *Effective Ways of Working with Children and Families*, London: Jessica Kingsley.

Lortie, D. (1975) *Schoolteacher, A Sociological Study*, Chicago: University of Chicago Press.

Louis, K.S., Kruse, S.D. and Associates (1995) *Professionalism and Community: Perspectives on Reforming Urban Schools*, New York: Corwin Press.

Louis, K.S. and Miles, M.B. (1990) *Improving the Urban High School: What Works and Why*, New York: Teachers College Press.

Low, C. (1997) Is inclusivism possible?, *European Journal of Special Needs Education*, Vol. 12, No. 1, pp. 71–79.

Lyotard, J.F. (1984) *The Postmodern Condition: A Report on Knowledge*, Manchester: Manchester University Press.

Mac an Ghaill, M. (1994a) *The Making of Men: Masculinities, Sexualities and Schooling*, Buckingham: Open University Press.

Mac an Ghaill, M. (1994b) (In)visibility:sexuality, masculinity and 'race' in the school context, in Epstein, D. (ed.) *Challenging Lesbian and Gay Inequalities in Education*, Buckingham: Open University Press.

Mac an Ghaill, M. (1996) (ed.) *Understanding Masculinities*, Buckingham: Open University Press.

MacBeath, J. (1998) The coming of age of school effectiveness, keynote address, International Congress of School Effectiveness and Improvement, Manchester.

MacBeath, J. and Mortimore, P. (1993) Improving School Effectiveness, Proposal for a Research Project for the Scottish Office Education Department, Edinburgh, December 1993.

MacGilchrist, B., Mortimore, P., Savage, J. and Beresford, C. (1995) *Planning Matters: The Impact of Development Planning in Primary Schools*, London: Paul Chapman.

Mackenzie, G. (1997), The caring doctor is an oxymoron, *British Medical Journal*, Vol. 315, pp. 687.

Marshall, C. (1991) The chasm between administrator and teacher cultures: a micropolitical puzzle, in Blase, J. (ed.) *The Politics of Life in Schools: Power, Conflict, and Co-operation*, London: Sage.

Martin, J. (1985) Can organisational culture be managed?, in Frost, P., Moore, L., Louis, M., Lundberg, C. and Martin, J. (eds) *Organisational Culture*, Beverly Hills: Sage.

Martin, J. (1992) *Cultures in Organizations*, Oxford University Press.

McIntyre, D. (1997) The profession of educational research, *British Educational Research Journal*, Vol. 23, No. 2, pp. 127–140.

McKenzie, J. (1993) Education as a Private Problem or a Public Issue? The Process of Excluding 'Education' from the 'Public Sphere', paper presented to the International Conference on the Public Sphere, Manchester, 8–10 January.

McLaughlin, M.W. (1990) The Rand change agent study: macro perspectives and micro realities, *Educational Researcher*, Vol. 19, No. 9, pp. 11–15.

McLaughlin, M.W., Talbert, J.E. and Bascia, N. (1990) *The Contexts of Teaching in Secondary Schools: Teachers' Realities*, New York: Teachers College Press.

McLaughlin, M.W. and Talbert, J.E. (1993) *Contexts That Matter for Teaching and Learning*, Palo Alto: Center for Research on the Context of Secondary School Teaching.

McLean, M. (1992) *The Promise and Perils of Educational Comparison*, London: Tufnell Press.

McMurray, J. (1958) quoted in Fielding, M. (1996) Beyond Collaboration: On the Importance of Community, in Bridges, D. and Husbands, C. (eds) *Consorting and Collaborating in the Education Market Place*, London: Falmer.

McRobbie, A. (1992) Post-Marxism and cultural studies: a post-script, in Grossberg, L., Nelson, C. and Treichler, P. (eds) *Cultural Studies*, New York: Routledge.

McRobbie, A. (1994) *Postmodernism and popular culture*, London: Routledge.

Mead, M. (1962) *The School in American Culture*, Cambridge, MA: Harvard University Press. (Original work published in 1951.)

Meek, V.L. (1988) Organizational culture: origins and weaknesses. *Organization Studies*, Vol. 9, No. 4, pp. 453–73.

Meighan, R. (1981) *A Sociology of Learning*, Eastbourne: Holt, Reinhart and Winston.

Mellor, A. (1993) *Bullying and How to Fight It: A Guide for Families*, Edinburgh: Scottish Council for Research in Education.

Mellor, A. (1995) *Which Way Now? A Progress Report on Action Against Bullying in Scottish Schools*, Edinburgh: Scottish Council for Research in Education.

Mercer, K. and Julien, I. (1988) Race, sexual politics and black masculinity: a dossier, in Chapman, R. and Rutherford, J. (eds) *Male Order: Unwrapping Masculinities*, London: Lawrence and Wishart.

Metz, M.H. (1991) Real school: a universal drama amid disparate experience, in Mitchell, D.E. and Metz, M.E. (eds) *Education Politics for the New Century: The Twentieth Anniversary Yearbook of the Politics of Education Association*, London: Falmer Press.

Miles, M.B. (1987) Practical guidelines for administrators: how to get there, paper presented at the Annual Meeting of the American Educational Research Association.

Mitchell, C. and Weber, S. (1999) *Reinventing Ourselves as Teachers: Beyond Nostalgia*, London: Falmer Press.

Molnar, A. (1996) *Giving Kids the Business: The Commercialization of America's Schools*, Boulder, Colorado: Westview/Harper Collins.

Morgan, G. (1993) Strengths and limitations of the culture metaphor, in Preedy, M. (ed.) *Managing the Effective School*, Milton Keynes: Open University Press.

Morgan, G. (1997) *Images of Organization*, Thousand Oaks: Sage.

Morris, E. (1997) Equality and the sum of its parts, *Times Educational Supplement*, 26 September.

Mortimore, P. (1980) The study of secondary schools: a researcher's Reply, in *The Rutter Research*, Perspectives 1, School of Education, University of Exeter.

Mortimore, P., Sammons, P., Stoll, L., Lewis, D. and Ecob, R. (1988) *School Matters: The Junior School Years*, Wells: Open Books.

Mosely, J. (1995) *Turn Your School Around*, Cambridge: LDA.

Moss, G. (1989) *Un/popular Fictions*, London: University of London Press.

Moss, G. and Rumbold, E. (1992) The right to teach, *Special Children*, June/July.

Moustakas, C. (1963) *The Authentic Teacher*, New York: Ballantine.

Mumby, D. and Stohl, C. (1991) Power and discourse in organization studies: absence and the dialiectic of control, *Discourse and Society*, Vol. 28, No. 2, pp. 313–32.

Murdoch, I. (1985) *The Sovereignty of Good*, London: Arts Paperback.

Murray, R. (1989) 'Fordism and post-Fordism', in Hall, S. and Jacques, M. (eds) *New Times: The Changing Face of Politics in the 1990s*, London: Lawrence and Wishart.

National Commission on Education (1995) *Success Against the Odds: Effective Schools in Disadvantaged Areas*, London: Routledge.

National Consumer Council (1996) *Sponsorship in Schools*, London: National Consumer Council.

Newmann, F. (1993) Beyond common sense in educational restructuring: the issues of content and leadership, *Educational Researcher*, Vol. 22, No. 2, pp. 4–13.

Nias, J. (1989) Redefining the 'cultural perspective', *Cambridge Journal of Education*, Vol. 19, No. 2, pp. 143–146.

Nias, J. (1989) *Primary Teachers Talking: A Study of Teaching as Work*, London: Routledge.

Nias, J. (1998) Teachers' moral purposes: stress, vulnerability and strength, in Huberman, M. and Vandenberghe, R. (eds), *Teacher Burnout*, Cambridge: Cambridge University Press.

Nias, J., Southworth, G. and Campbell, P. (1992) *Whole School Curriculum Development in Primary Schools*, London: Falmer.

Nias, J., Southworth, G. and Yeomans, R. (1989) *Staff Relationships in the Primary School: A Study of Organizational Cultures*, London: Cassell.

Noddings, N. (1984) *Caring: A Feminine Approach to Ethics and Moral Education*, Berkeley: University of California Press.

Noddings, N. (1992) *The Challenge to Care in Schools*, New York: Teachers' College Press.

Noddings, N. (1994) An ethic of caring and its implications for instructional arrangements, in Stone, L. (ed.) *The Education Feminism Reader*, New York: Routledge.

Ofsted (1994) *Improving Schools*, HMSO.

Ogbonna, E. (1993) Managing organisational culture: fantasy or reality?, *Human Resource Management Journal*, Vol. 3, No. 2, pp. 42–54.

Osborn, M., Broadfoot, P., Planel, C. and Pollard, A. (1997a) Social class, educational opportunity and equal entitlement: Dilemmas of schooling in England and France, *Comparative Education*, Vol. 33, No. 3, pp. 375–93.

Osborn, M., with Croll, P., Abbott, D., Broadfoot, P. and Pollard, A. (1997b) Policy into practice and practice into policy: Creative mediation in primary classrooms, in Helsby, G. and McCulloch, G. (eds) *Teachers and the National Curriculum*, London: Cassell.

Parker, A., Russo, M., Sommer, D. and Yaeger, P. (1992) *Nationalisms and Sexualities*, London: Routledge.

Parsons, C. (1996) Permanent exclusions from school in England: trends, causes and responses, *Children and Society*, Vol. 10, pp. 177–186.

Patterson, J.L., Purkey, S.C. and Parker, J.V. (1986) *Productive School Systems for a Nonrational World*, Alexandria, VA: Association for Supervision and Curriculum Development.

Perrow, C. (1974) Zoo story or life in the organisational sandpit, in *Perspectives on Organisations*, DT 352 Units 15 and 16, Milton Keynes: Open University Press.

Peter, M. (1997) The keys to understanding (interview with Baroness Warnock), *Special!*, Spring, pp. 11–13.

Peters, T. and Waterman, R. (1982) *In Search of Excellence: Lessons from America's Best-Run Companies*, New York: Harper & Row.

Plant, R. (1987) *Managing Change and Making It Stick*, London: Fontana.

Plowden Committee (1967) *Children and Their Primary Schools*, London: HMSO.

Polan, D. (1993) Professors' Discourse, *A Journal of Theoretical Studies in Media and Culture*, Vol. 16, No. 1, pp. 28–49.

Pollard, A. (1985) *The Social World of the Primary School*, London: Holt, Reinhart and Winston.

Pollard, A., Broadfoot, P., Croll, P., Osborn, M. and Abbott, D. (1994) *Changing English Primary Schools? The Impact of the Education Reform Act at Key Stage One*, London: Cassell.

Pring, R. (1997) Educating persons, in Pring, R. and Walford, G. (eds) *Affirming the Comprehensive Ideal*, London: Falmer.

Prosser, J. (1992) Personal reflections on the use of photography in an ethnographic case study, *British Educational Research Journal*, Vol. 18, No. 4, pp. 397–411.

Prosser, J. (1998) The status of image based research, in Prosser, J. (ed.) *Image Based Research: A Sourcebook for Qualitative Researchers*, London: Falmer Press.

Prosser, J. (ed.) (1998) *Image-Based Research: A Sourcebook for Qualitative Researchers*, London: Falmer.

Prosser, J. (ed.) (1998) *Images in Educational Research*, London: Francis and Taylor.

Prosser, J. and Schwartz, D. (1997) Photographs within the sociological research process, in Prosser, J. (ed.) *Image Based Research: A Sourcebook for Qualitative Researchers*, London: Falmer.

Provenzo, E.F. Jr., McCloskey, G.N., Kottkamp, R.B. and Cohn, M.M. (1989) Metaphor and meaning in the language of teachers, *Teachers College Record*, Vol. 90, No. 4, pp. 551–573.

Putnam, R.D. (1993) *Making Democracy Work*, New Jersey: Princeton University Press.

Pyke, N. (1997) Ruling for dyslexic makes legal history, *Times Educational Supplement*, 26 September.

Quinn, J.B. (1980) *Strategies for Change: logical incrementalism*, R.D. Irwin, cited in Kanter, *op. cit.*

Rattansi, A. (1992) Changing the subject? Racism, culture and education, in Donald, J. and Rattansi, A. (eds) *'Race', Culture and Difference*, London: Sage/The Open University.

Rees, T. (1992) *Women and the Labour Market*, London: Routledge.

Reich, R. (1991) *The Work of Nations: Preparing Ourselves for 21st Century Capitalism*, London: Simon and Schuster.

Reid, K. (1988) Bullying and Persistent Absenteeism, in Tattum, T. and Lane, D. (eds) *Bullying in Schools*, Stoke-on Trent: Trentham Books.

Reynolds, D. (1997) Good ideas can wither in another culture, *Times Educational Supplement*, 12 September.

Reynolds, D., Hopkins, D. and Stoll, L. (1993) Linking school effectiveness knowledge and school improvement practice: towards a synergy, *School Effectiveness and School Improvement*, Vol. 4, No. 1, pp. 37–58.

Rich, R. (1972) *The Training of Teachers in England and Wales during the Nineteenth Century*, Bath: Cedric Chivers.

Rieger, J.H. (1996) Photographing social change, *Visual Sociology*, Vol. 11, No. 2, pp. 5–49.

Roberts, P. (1994) Business Sponsorship in Schools: A Changing Climate, in Bridges, D. McLaughlin, T.H. (eds) *Education and the Market Place*, London: Falmer.

Robertson, J.P. (1997) Fantasy's confines: popular culture and the education of the female primary school teacher, *Canadian Journal of Education*, Vol. 22, No. 2, pp. 123–143.

Robertson, R. (1991) Social theory, cultural relativity and the problem of globality, in King, A.D. (ed.) *Culture, Globalization and the World-System*, London: Macmillan.

Robertson, S.L. (1993) The Politics of devolution, self-management and post-Fordism in schools, in Smyth, J. (ed.) *A Socially Critical View of the Self-Managing School*, London: Falmer Press.

Roland, E. (1988) Bullying: The Scandinavian Research Tradition, in Tattum, D. and Lane, D. (eds) *Bullying in Schools*, Stoke-on Trent: Trentham Books.

Roland, E. (1989) A system oriented strategy against bullying, in Roland, E. and Munthe, E. (eds) *Bullying: An International Perspective*, London: David Fulton.

Rosenholtz, S.J. (1989) *Teachers' Workplace: The Social Organization of Schools*, New York: Longman.

Rosenholtz, S.J. (1989) Workplace conditions that affect teacher quality and commitment: Implications for teacher induction programs, *The Elementary School Journal*, Vol. 89, No. 4, pp. 421–39.

Rossman, G.B., Corbett, H.D. and Firestone, W.A. (1988) *Change and Effectiveness in Schools: A Cultural Perspective*, New York: SUNY Press.

Rozmovits, L. (1995) The Wolf and the Lamb: An Image and its Afterlife, *Art History*, Vol. 18, No. 1.

Ruby, J. (1996) Visual Anthropology, in Levinson, D. and Ember, M. (eds) *Encyclopedia of Cultural Anthropology*, New York: Henry Holt and Co. Vol. 4, pp. 1345–1351.

Rudduck, J., Chaplain, R. and Wallace, G. (1996) *School Improvement: What Can Pupils Tell Us?*, London: David Fulton.

Rudduck, J. (1991) *Innovation and Change*, Milton Keynes: Open University Press.

Rumelhart, D.E. (1980) Schemata: The building blocks of cognition, in Spiro, R.J., Bruce, B.C. and Brewer, W.F. (eds) *Theoretical Issues in Reading Comprehension: Perspectives in Cognitive Psychology, Linguistics, and Education*, Hillsdale, NJ: Lawrence Erlbaum Associates.

Rutherford, J. (1990) A place called home: identity and the cultural politics of difference, in Rutherford, J. (ed.) *Identity: Community, Culture and Difference*, London: Lawrence and Wishart.

Rutter, M. Maughan, B. Mortimore, P. Ouston, J. (1979) *Fifteen Thousand Hours: Secondary Schools and Their Effects on Children*, London: Open Books.

Sammons, P., Hillman, J. and Mortimore, P. (1997) Key characteristics of effective schools: a review of school effectiveness research, in White, J. and Barber, M. (eds) *Perspectives on School Effectiveness and School Improvement*, London: Institute of Education, University of London.

Sander, A. (1986) *Citizens of the Twentieth Century*, Cambridge: The MIT Press.

Saphier, J. and King, M. (1985) Good seeds grow in strong cultures, *Educational Leadership*, Vol. 42, No. 6, pp. 67–74.

Sarason, S.B. (1971) (revised and re-printed 1985) *The Culture of School and the Problem of Change*, Massachusetts: Allyn and Bacon.

Sarason, S.B. (1993) *The Case for Change*, Jossey-Bass.

Sarason, S.B. (1996) *Revisiting 'The Culture of the School and the Problem of Change'*, New York: Teachers College Press.

Sartre, J.P. (1959) *Being and Nothingness – an essay on phenomenological ontology*, London: Methuen.

Scheerens, J. (1990) School effectiveness research and the development of process indicators of school functioning, *School Effectiveness and Improvement*, Vol. 1, No. 1, pp. 66–80.

Schein, E.H. (1985) *Organizational Culture and Leadership*, San Francisco: Jossey-Bass.

Schein, E.H (1992) Coming to a New Awareness of Organisational Culture, in Salalman, G. (ed.) *Human Resource Strategies*, London: Open University/Sage.

Schein, E.H. (1997) *Organizational Culture and Leadership* (2nd ed.) London: Jossey-Bass.

Schwartz, D. (1989) Legion Post 189: Continuity and change in a rural community, *Visual Anthropology*, Vol. 2, pp. 103–133.

Sebba, J. and Sachdev, D. (1997) *What Works in Inclusive Education?*, Barkingside: Barnardos.

Sedgwick, E.K. (1991) *Epistemology of the Closet*, London: Harvester, Wheatsheaf.

Seihl, C. (1985) After the founder: an opportunity to manage culture, in Frost, P., Moore, L., Louis, M., Lundberg, C. and Martin, J. (eds) *Organisational Culture*, Beverly Hills: Sage.

Simon, B. (1965) *Education and the Labour Movement, 1870–1920*, London: Lawrence Wishart.

Siskin, L.S. (1994) *Realms of Knowledge: Academic Departments in Secondary Schools*, Washington and London: Falmer.

Skeggs, B. (1991) Challenging masculinity and using sexuality, *British Journal of Sociology of Education*, Vol. 12, No. 1, pp. 127–140.

Skinner, J. (1996) Reflections . . . on experience, *Cambridge Journal of Education*, Vol. 26, No. 2, pp. 251–4.

Slattery, L. (1989) Goals set for nation's schools, *The Age*, 15 April.

Smith, D., Tomlinson, S. (1989) *The School Effect: A Study of Multi-Racial Comprehensives*, London: Policy Studies Institute.

Smith, R. and Curtin, P. (1997) Computers and life on-line: education in a cyber-world, in Snyder, I. (ed.) *Taking Literacy Into The Electronic Age*, Sydney: Allen and Unwin.

Smithers, R. (1997) Schools 'force out' disruptive pupils, *The Guardian*, 31 October, p. 7.

Smyth, J. (1991) International perspectives on teacher collegiality: a labour process discussion based on the concept of teachers' work, *British Journal of Sociology in Education*, Vol. 12, No. 3, pp. 323–346.

SOED (1992a) *Using Ethos Indicators in Primary School Self-Evaluation*, Edinburgh: HM Inspectors of Schools.

SOED (1992b) *Using Ethos Indicators in Secondary School Self-Evaluation*, Edinburgh: HM Inspectors of Schools.

SOEID (1997) Exclusion and In-School Alternatives, *Interchange 47*, Edinburgh: Scottish Office.

Solsken, J. (1993) *Literacy, Gender and Work in families and in school*, Norwood: Ablex.

Stern, G.G. (1963) *People in Context: Measuring person-environment congruence in education and industry*, New York: Riley.

Stevahn, L., Johnson, D.W. and Johnson, R.T. (1996) Integrating conflict resolution training into academic curriculum studies: results of recent studies, paper presented at the annual meeting of the American Educational Research Association, New York.

Stoll, L. and Fink, D. (1996) *Changing Our Schools: Linking School Effectiveness and School Improvement*, Buckingham: Open University Press.

Stoll, L. and Fink, D. (1998) The cruising school: the unidentified ineffective school, in Stoll, L. and Myers, K. (eds) *No Quick Fixes: Perspectives on Schools in Difficulty*, London: Falmer Press.

Stoll, L., Harrington, J. and Myers, K. (1995) Two British school effectiveness and improvement action projects, paper presented at the Eighth International Congress for School Effectiveness and Improvement, Leeuwarden, The Netherlands.

Stringfield, S., Ross, S. and Smith, L. (1996) *Bold Plans for Restructuring: The New American Schools Designs*, New Jersey: Lawrence Erlbaum Associates.

Striven, J. (1985) School climate: a review of a problematic concept, in Reynolds, D. (ed.), *Studying School Effectiveness*, London: Falmer Press.

Suchar, C.S. (1997) Grounding visual sociology research in shooting scripts, in *Qualitative Sociology*, Vol. 20, No. 1, pp. 33–55.

Tattum, D. and Tattum, E. (1992) Bullying: a whole-school response, in Jones, N. and Jones, E. (eds) *Learning to Behave*, London: Kogan Page.

Thomas, G. (1997) Inclusive schools for an inclusive society, *British Journal of Special Education*, Vol. 24, No. 3, pp. 103–107.

Thrupp, M. (1997) The school mix effect; how the social class composition of school intakes shapes school processes and student achievement, paper presented to the Annual Meeting of the American Educational Research Association, Chicago.

Tizard, B. and Hughes, M. (1984) *Young Children at School in the Inner City*, London: Lawrence Erlbaum.

Toffler, A. (1990) *Powershift*, New York: Bantam Books.

Tooley, J. (1995) *Dis-establishing The School*, Aldershot: Avebury.

Torrington, D., Weightman, J. and Johns, K. (1989) *Effective Management*, Hemel Hempstead: Prentice Hall.

Tropp, A. (1957) *The Schoolteachers*, London: Heinemann.

Usher, R. and Edwards, R. (1994) *Postmodernism and Education*, London: Routledge.

van Velzen, W., Miles, M., Eckholm, M., Hameyer, U. and Robin, D. (1985) *Making School Improvement Work*, Leuven: Belgium, ACCO.

Vlachou, A. (1997) *Struggles for Inclusive Education*, Buckingham: Open University Press.

Wallace, M. (1996) A crisis of identity, in *British Educational Research Journal*, Vol. 24, No. 2, pp. 195–216.

Waller, W. (1932) *The Sociology of Teaching*, Chichester: John Wiley.

Walters, M. (1994) *Building the Responsive Organisation: Using Employee Surveys to Manage Change*, Maidenhead: McGraw-Hill.

Warburton, T., and Saunders, M. (1996) Representing teachers' professional culture through cartoons, *British Journal of Educational Studies*, Vol. 44, No. 3, pp. 307–325.

Warburton, T. (1998) Cartoons and Teachers: Mediated Visual Images as Data, in Prosser, J. (ed.) *Image Based Research: A Sourcebook for Qualitative Researchers*, London: Falmer Press.

Webb, R. and Vulliamy, G. (1996) Impact of ERA on primary school management, *British Educational Research Journal*, Vol. 22, No. 4, pp. 441–458.

Weber, S.J. (1990) The teacher educator's experience: Generativity and duality of commitment, *Curriculum Inquiry*, Vol. 20, No. 2, pp. 141–159.

Weber, S.J. (1993) The Narrative Anecdote in Teacher Education, *Journal of Education for Teaching*, Vol. 19, No. 1, pp. 71–82.

Weber, S.J. and Mitchell, C. (1995) *That's Funny, You Don't Look Like a Teacher! Interrogating Images and Identity in Popular Culture*, London: Falmer Press.

Weick, K.E. (1988) Educational organisations as loosely coupled systems, in Westoby, A. (ed.) *Culture and Power in Educational Organisations*, Milton Keynes: Open University Press.

Weil, S. (1986), An essay on human personality, in Miles, S. (ed.) *Simone Weil: An anthology*, London: Virago.

Weiss, M. (1993) New guiding principles in educational policy: the case of Germany, *Journal of Education Policy*, Vol. 8, No. 4, pp. 307–320.

Westergaard, J. (1994) *Who Gets What: The Hardening of Class Inequality in Late Twentieth Century*, Cambridge: Polity Press.

Whatford, C. (1998) Rising from the ashes, in Stoll L. and Myers, K. (eds) *No Quick Fixes*, Falmer.

Wheldall, K. (1987) *The Behaviourist in the Classroom*, London: Allen & Unwin.

White, J. (1997) Philosophical perspectives on school effectiveness and school improvement, in White, J. and Barber, M. (eds) *Perspectives on School Effectiveness and School Improvement*, London: Institute of Education, University of London.

Whitehead, F. (1977) *Children and their Books*, London: Macmillan.

Whitty, G. (1985) *Sociology and School Knowledge*, London: Methuen

Whitty, G., Edwards, T., and Gewirtz, S. (1993) *Specialisation and Choice in Urban Education: The City Technology College Experiment*, London: Routledge.

Whitty, G., Power, S. and Halpin, D. (1998) *Devolution and Choice in Education: the School, the State and the Market*, Buckingham: Open University Press.

Wiener, M.J. (1981) *English Culture and the Decline of the Industrial Spirit 1850–1980*, Cambridge: Cambridge University Press.

Wieviorka, M. (1991) *L'espace du Racisme*, Paris: Seuil.

Wilkinson, H. (1995) Affirmative action, negative effect, *The Independent*, 28 July.

Willis, P. (1977) *Learning to Labour: How Working Class Kids Get Working Class Jobs*, Hampshire: Saxon House.

Winston, B. (1998) 'The camera never lies': the partiality of photographic evidence, in Prosser, J. (ed.) *Image Based Research: A Sourcebook for Qualitative Researchers*, London: Falmer Press.

Wolchover, J. (1997) Teachers at 'failing' school launch bid to block reform, *Evening Standard*, 25 September, p. 6.

Wolcott, H.F. (1973) *The Man In the Principal's Office*, New York: Holt, Rhinehart and Winston.

Wolpe, A.M. (1988) *Within School Walls: The Role of Discipline. Sexuality and the Curriculum*, London: Routledge.

Woods, P. (1992) Empowerment through choice? Towards and understanding of parental choice and school responsiveness, *Education Management and Administration*, No. 20, pp. 204–211.

Woods, P. (1993) Responding to the consumer: parental choice and school effectiveness, *School Effectiveness and Improvement*, Vol. 4, No. 3, pp. 205–211.

Woods, P. (1994) School Responses to the Quasi-Market, in Halstead, J.M. (ed.) *Parental Choice and Education*, London: Kogan Page.

Woods, P., Jeffrey, B., Troman, G. and Boyle, M. (1997) *Restructuring Schools, Reconstructing Teachers*, Buckingham: Open University Press.

Wright, E.O. (1994) *Interrogating Inequality: Essays on Class Analysis*, Socialism and Marxism. London: Verso.

Yeatman, A. (1994) *Postmodern Revisionings of the Political*, New York: Routledge.

Young, M.F.D. (ed.) (1971) *Knowledge and Control: New Directions for the Sociology of Education*, London: Collier-Macmillan.

Zeichner, K.M. and Grant, C. (1981) Biography and social structure in the socialization of student teachers: A re-examination of the pupil control ideologies of student teachers, *Journal of Education for Teaching*, Vol. 3, pp. 299–314.

Zeichner, K.M. and Tabachnik, R.B. (1981) Are the effects of university teacher education 'washed out' by school experience?, *Journal of Teacher Education*, Vol. 32, No. 3, pp. 7–11.

# Index